Richmond

"Richmond's Enterprises"
by Mark H. Dorfman
and William G. Moore

Featuring the photography of
Henley & Savage

Produced in cooperation with the
Metropolitan Richmond Chamber of Commerce

Windsor Publications, Inc.
Chatsworth, California

Richmond

A River City Reborn

A Contemporary Portrait by
James Schultz

For Margaret and Jimmy,
both of whom loved Richmond well

Windsor Publications, Inc.—Book Division
Managing Editor: KAREN STORY
Design Director: ALEXANDER D'ANCA
Photo Director: SUSAN L. WELLS
Executive Editor: PAMELA SCHROEDER

Staff for *Richmond: A River City Reborn*
Manuscript Editor: DOUGLAS P. LATHROP
Photo Editor: ROBIN STERLING
Senior Editor, Corporate Profiles: JUDITH L. HUNTER
Senior Production Editor, Corporate Profiles: UNA FITZSIMONS
Proofreader: MARY JO SCHARF
Customer Service Manager: PHYLLIS FELDMAN-SCHROEDER
Editorial Assistants: KIM KIEVMAN, MICHAEL NUGWYNNE, MICHELE OAKLEY,
KATHY B. PEYSER, THERESA J. SOLIS
Publisher's Representative, Corporate Profiles: WADE EMMETT
Layout Artist, Corporate Profiles: C.L. MURRAY
Background Artwork: BONNIE FELT
Designer: ELLEN IFRAH

Windsor Publications, Inc.
ELLIOT MARTIN, Chairman of the Board
JAMES L. FISH III, Chief Operating Officer
MAC BUHLER, Vice President/Acquisitions

Library of Congress Cataloging-in-Publication Data
Schultz, James, 1956-
   Richmond : a river city reborn : a contemporary portrait /by James Schultz. —
1st ed.
   p. 288 cm. 23 x 31
   Includes bibliographical references and index.
   ISBN 0-89781-338-3
   1. Richmond (Va.)—Civilization. Richmond (Va.)—Description—Views.
3. Richmond (Va.)—Industries. 4. Richmond (Va.)—Economic conditions.
I. Title.
F234.R55S38 1990
975.5'45'043—dc20   90-12532
                                                      CIP

This picturesque tree-lined entrance leads to the historic Shirley Plantation in nearby Charles City County.

CONTENTS

Chapter 7 NETWORKS *155*

Richmond's energy, communication, and transportation providers keep power, information, and products circulating inside and outside the area.

Chapter 8 MANUFACTURING *167*

Producing and distributing goods for individuals and industry, manufacturing firms provide employment for Richmond-area residents.

Chapter 9 BUSINESS AND FINANCE *183*

Richmond's solid financial base has provided a dynamic environment for economic growth and opportunity for both individuals and businesses in the community.

FOREWORD

The Metropolitan Richmond Chamber of Commerce is proud to sponsor this book. It chronicles changes in our metropolitan community over the past decade and provides a look into the future. Richmond's development from a small riverside settlement to a thriving center of commerce has not been smooth. Like any growing community, ours has had its false starts, its mistakes, its economic woes. But with the abiding confidence of its people, Richmond has been able to overcome many problems.

Richmonders believe in their community. Its amenities, educational quality, employment opportunities, recreation, location, cost of living, and other factors combine to make Richmond a great place to live and work. Richmonders are working hard to continue to improve their community. Thousands of volunteers working through hundreds of organizations are contributing their energy toward building Richmond's future.

Where will metropolitan Richmond be in the next decade, at the opening of a new century? If the past is an indication of the future, the metropolitan Richmond area will be at the center of a diversified economy. New technology will have created now un-dreamed-of jobs and businesses. The number of visitors, and the services and facilities needed to meet their demands, will continue to grow. There will be expanding opportunities for our young people in new technological and service areas. Local governments will continue to find cooperative ways to address community problems on a cooperative basis.

The Metropolitan Richmond Chamber of Commerce is proud to have played a role over the past 123 years in creating and maintaining an excellent environment for business. Through its educational programs, volunteer organizations, and lobbying efforts, the chamber intends to continue making a significant contribution to the business community and the future prosperity of metropolitan Richmond.

Gordon F. Rainey, Jr.
Chairman of the Board
Metropolitan Richmond Chamber of Commerce (1990-91)

The late afternoon sun highlights the majestic architecture of the Old City Hall, the Virginia Bell Tower, and the Medical College of Virginia in downtown Richmond.

ACKNOWLEDGMENTS

The Richmond of today is a far different place than the Richmond of my childhood recollections. For me, researching and writing this book has been a rediscovery of what Richmond is and can be, and for that I am grateful. But I couldn't have done it alone.

First, my thanks to Mike Sever at the Metro Richmond Chamber of Commerce, without whose initial recommendation and subsequent support my authorship of this book would never have been possible. I also owe a major debt of gratitude to Lisa Antonelli Bacon, who provided sustenance—both logistical and psychological—for my writings.

Thanks, too, to Windsor Publications acquisitions editor Pam Schroeder for her flexibility in accommodating what turned out to be a rather difficult schedule. Her continuing encouragement was most appreciated. I am also grateful to her colleague, manuscript editor Doug Lathrop, for his patience and good humor in confronting logistical and other challenges in guiding the final manuscript to completion.

The ever-affable Dave Clinger was a ready font of information throughout this project, always accommodating with a verification and quick to respond to my many inquiries. If there was a separate book credit for "research assistant emeritus," it would be Dave's for the asking. Jim Bacon and the staff of *Virginia Business* magazine should also be commended for putting up with my unannounced calls and visits, which they always handled with hospitable grace.

To the scores of men and women I interviewed: Many thanks for your time and honesty; I couldn't have written this book without you. To my family in Richmond, particularly Ann and Joe Lewis and Rosalie and Ed Phillips: You eased my mind many times and gave me a place to quite literally prop up my weary feet. Finally, my heartfelt gratitude to Mary Jane, Katy, and Jaike, who were invariably patient with that sometimes grumpy, gesticulating man who wandered often throughout their house.

Natural beauty and recreational opportunities abound in the greater Richmond area.

The ever-developing Richmond skyline, pictured here during the early stages of the Riverfront Plaza construction, teems with life and activity, reflecting a city that has endured throughout the years to become part of a leading metropolitan region buoyed by a vibrant economy.

1

PHOENIX BY THE RIVER

FIRE AND WATER ARE TWO of the primary agents that have benefited and bedeviled human beings for centuries. Too little or too much of either cause great harm; in abundance, and controlled, both bring great benefit. The history of many American cities has been dramatically affected by one or the other—none more so than Richmond, Virginia.

As eighteenth-century colonial capital, capital of the Confederacy during the Civil War, and present-day capital of the Commonwealth of Virginia, Richmond has seen its share of fire-induced catastrophe. In January 1781 British troops, under the command of the former American general Benedict Arnold, blew up a powder magazine and destroyed a foundry in Westham, outside of the city. Several houses and buildings in Richmond were also set ablaze. In the nineteenth century fire damaged Richmond flour mills; in addition, fire in the Midlothian coal mines in adjacent Chesterfield County eventually forced owners to cease operations there. But the fires that inflicted the most injury were those set by retreating Confederate troops to burn military stores and warehouses in the last days of the Civil War. In the aftermath, Richmond's entire downtown business district had been reduced to a smoldering ruin.

Nonetheless, as strong a physical impact as fire has had on Richmond's structures and inhabitants, it was water that captured the city's early commerce

---

A sweeping view of early Richmond is depicted in this 1833 aquatint entitled Richmond, From the Hill Above the Waterworks. *Engraved by W.J. Bennett from a G.G. Cooke painting, the James River is shown as it runs through the center with the Kanawha Canal visible in the foreground. Also seen on the hill from left to right are the state penitentiary, city hall, the state capitol building, and the Governor's Mansion. Courtesy, New York Public Library, Prints Division*

A typically busy day at the packet office during the Kanawha Canal's peak years is shown in this engraving by J.R. Hamilton before the advent of the railroad diminished the importance of the waterway. The great James River and the canal connected Richmond to outlying communities, transporting passengers, mail, and freight. From Harper's Weekly, *October 14, 1865*

and its civic imagination. And it is water that truly tells Richmond's tale—specifically that ribbon of water known as the James River.

Named by Jamestown founder Captain John Smith in honor of King James I of England, the James rises from the joining of the Jackson and Cowpasture rivers in the Virginia highlands. Zigzagging eastward through the Blue Ridge Mountains, the river descends through Richmond and enters Chesapeake Bay in sight of the cities of Hampton, Newport News, and Norfolk. The James runs some 340 miles in all; by the time it reaches the bay it has grown from a small mountain tributary to a flow fully five miles in width.

The fact that the James is navigable to the bay, and thence to the Atlantic Ocean, made for lively river commerce through the mid-nineteenth century. Passengers, freight, and mail were regularly ferried on the James and on the Kanawha Canal system that later paralleled the river. Tobacco, cotton, and coal were exported; itemized on import manifests were such things as English woolens and cutlery, French perfumes and wines, Brazilian coffee, and East Indian spices.

The development of railroads in the nineteenth century would eclipse the importance of the James, as would the advent of interstate trucking in the twentieth. But modern-day cargo transport on the river remains a robust commercial proposition. By the end of fiscal 1988, for example, the Port of Richmond had hosted 144 vessels carrying 459,350 tons of material, an increase of 40 percent over 1987 totals. Livestock, lumber, scrap iron, newsprint, tobacco, and even firebrick are among the items that today wend their way down the James, headed toward foreign ports of call.

Commerce aside, the James has often been the object of aesthetic comment by visitors and natives. The falls—that shallow portion of the river that bisects the modern Richmond metropolitan area and serves as the demarcation between the sandy, flat Tidewater and the clay and rock of Virginia's Piedmont—seems to attract a disproportionate share of the attention. William Byrd II, Richmond founder and eighteenth-century Williamsburg plantation owner, wrote that "the falls murmur loud enough to drown a scolding wife." In 1783 a German-born surgeon, David Schopf, passed through Richmond and commented:

A vast number of great and small fragments of rock fill the bed of the river as far as the eye can see . . . Through these the current, with foaming uproar, makes its way. What with the help of devious banks and the forests on both sides, the impression from a view of the whole is great and pleasing . . . The James River up from its mouth in the Bay, is one of the greatest and most beautiful of American streams.

For those with the time and money, traveling the James and the Kanawha Canal was an idyllic diversion. In the 1830s George William Bagby, a journalist and eventual editor of the *Southern Literary Messenger* in Richmond, journeyed on the Canal. Recalling the trip, Bagby wrote that as his packet boat approached Richmond, "however bold and picturesque the cliffs and bluffs near Lynchburg, and beyond, there was nothing from one end of the canal to the other to compare with the first sight of Richmond . . . it burst full upon the vision, its capitol, its spires, its happy homes, flushed with the red glow of evening."

Then, as now, the Richmond skyline impressed the eye of those seeing the city for the first time. An architectural world and a century-and-a-half removed from the Richmond skyline of the 1800s, today's cityscape would seem at first glance to have little in common with bygone skylines. Again, though, it is the James that links the present with the past. When Richmond's commercial core was reduced to rubble at the end of the Civil War, rebuilders did not abandon it, but instead concentrated efforts on a total reconstruction of the blocks closest to the James. The fruits of their labors still exist, in the form of late-nineteenth-century structures that are being redeveloped for modern use.

Modern buildings may tower over their diminutive ancestors, but they attest to the continued primacy of the near-river business core, the magnet to which financial and commercial interests are drawn. Many of Richmond's most impres-

Acknowledged as the founder of Richmond, William Byrd II actually opposed the establishment of a town on his James River property, probably out of concern that a town would mean competition for his prosperous store and tobacco warehouses. In 1737 Byrd finally yielded to pressure and had his friend Major William Mayo survey the townsite and divide it into lots. Byrd died just a few years later in 1744 at the age of 70. Courtesy, Virginia Historical Society

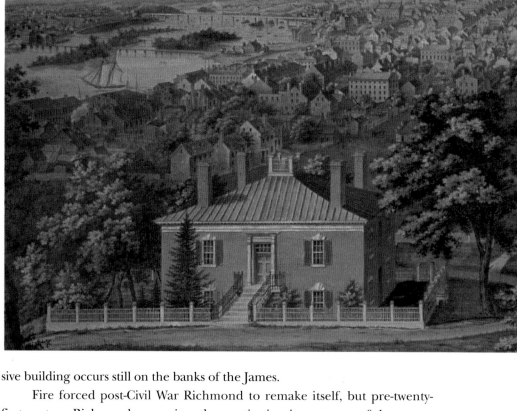

This colorful view of Richmond by Casimir Bohn was first published in 1851 and shows the vast growth of the developing James River community as seen from Church Hill. Courtesy, Valentine Museum

The grand state capitol building is pictured here in this wonderful postcard dated February 22, 1907. Courtesy, Valentine Museum

sive building occurs still on the banks of the James.

Fire forced post-Civil War Richmond to remake itself, but pre-twenty-first-century Richmond recognizes the continuing importance of downtown development and redevelopment. In recent years the pace of that development has escalated. Nationally, the days are long past when historic structures were routinely destroyed to make room for steel and glass spires. Richmonders, in part because of the city's history, have never been fond of large-scale destruction of historic buildings to accommodate expansive urban renewal. Most prefer to take building projects one at a time and integrate them into the existing environment, an approach labeled by Howard M. Jennings, Jr., assistant to the Richmond City Manager for downtown marketing and promotions, as "conservative incrementalism."

"One thing that [approach] has given us is a very nice physical environment," Jennings claims. "Richmond never 'blew' the way a lot of other cities blew in the '60s. Large-scale development in the metro area began in the 1970s, and since the early 1980s downtown's development trends have become much more broadly based. There's a deep confidence in the economy. We're beginning to get the full spectrum of development back downtown."

Architecturally speaking, Richmond-area developers appear to be keeping both conservatives and progressives happy. Some of Richmond's most innovative architectural design is occurring inside historic buildings, while late-twentieth-century architectural styles are agreeably ex-

pressed in imposing creations of stone, marble, and mirrored glass.

Richmond's present reinvigoration is not merely physical—it also flows for the joining of commercial, financial, political, and cultural interests. Unlike the Reconstruction era of more than a century ago, Richmond's black and white citizens are actively working together on making the region a better place to live. While the pace of change may seem too slow to some, it is fair to say that Richmond is no longer perceived as a straitlaced, sleepy Southern town.

Like the mythical phoenix, Richmond is rising once again, to regional prominence as a commercial center. Twenty-nine major corporations call the Richmond region home. The area today has as many *Fortune* 500 industrial corporate headquarters per capita as does New York City; on the *Forbes* 500 list, Richmond has outranked cities like Boston. More than 1,000 companies have moved to, relocated to, or expanded in the Richmond area in the past half-decade, and Richmond's stature as a major financial center and headquarters of the Federal Reserve Fifth District continues to grow.

Richmond's late-century rebirth transcends simple economic prosperity. Without an abundance of culture and other amenities, the Richmond region would not have the appeal it does for companies, the executives who run them, and the families of the men and women who work for them. As it moves toward the year 2000, Richmond has redesigned itself, creating a new identity even as it has created buildings and jobs.

The Civil War destruction of Richmond is apparent in this April 1865 view taken from the south side of the canal basin. The cannons and ammunition had been left behind by the fleeing Confederate Army. Courtesy, Library of Congress

REMAKING THE CITY   In time, the decade of the 1980s may come to be known as the Richmond Remaking. Certainly there was great physical change in the metropolitan region; commercial and residential construction exploded. But perhaps the biggest change was in perspective. Richmond-area leaders dispensed with a business-as-usual attitude in favor of a more assertive, proactive stance. The city on the James and its sister localities matured; regionalism replaced parochialism and cross-jurisdictional cooperation became a fact of life.

The word "Richmond" took on new meaning: not just as the name for a few square miles in the core city, but for many square miles in an entire region; not just a reference point for the downtown business district, but as a point of departure for Richmond's uptown, the East End, North- and South-side, and the West End. Even Richmond's "outtowns"—those emerging suburban downtowns in the surrounding counties—have come to benefit from their identification as parts of a greater whole. In the 1980s Richmond put itself on the map in unprecedented fashion.

This early 1900s kindergarten class was photographed at play in Monroe Park near the statue of Confederate General William Carter Wickham. Courtesy, Valentine Museum

The 1980s were witness to three major accomplishments: cooperation across political boundaries, a proactive approach to economic growth, and development of biracial cooperation. Formal and informal partnerships advancing the Richmond region were kindled. It was a time *for* and *of* change—no change bigger than the normally cautious, restrained relationship between Richmond's black and white citizens.

"For many years the city was not progressive in many areas. That was reflected in the relationship between whites and blacks," says Henry L. Marsh II, former Richmond mayor and now a partner in a Richmond legal firm that bears his name. "It goes without saying that we have a ways to go, but I must admit progress has been made. I do think Richmond is going to continue the remarkable expansion and development that has occurred over the past 15 years."

Marsh became mayor at a time when Richmond was recovering from an exhaustive and exhausting court case challenging the city's right to annex a portion of Chesterfield County. The case traveled all the way to the U.S. Supreme Court. The court ruled in favor of the annexation in 1977, but mandated a change in the elective practices of the Richmond City Council from an

at-large to a single-member-per-ward system. A black majority, the city's first, was subsequently elected to the nine-member City Council that same year. Marsh (who had served on the Council since 1966) was chosen Richmond's first black mayor. He would remain in that position until 1982, when Roy A. West, also black, would become mayor (West would be succeeded in 1988 by Geline B. Williams).

For the first time in city history, a majority of Richmond's black citizens found themselves—albeit indirectly—in the political driver's seat. The election of a black majority to the City Council was a slap in the face to the established political order and caused much consternation in certain circles. Some Richmonders were privately aghast that blacks could wield such political power, and in the former political citadel of the Confederacy at that. But others were glad that the winds of change had begun to blow, and were willing to give the new leaders a fair hearing.

In the aftermath of the political shakeup, black and white leaders set to work hammering out new coalitions and agendas. Rapprochement was their purpose as they began to work together on a more vigorous Richmond. As John V. Moeser, professor of urban studies and planning at Virginia Commonwealth University, put it in remarks before the Metropolitan Richmond Chamber of Commerce in 1986, "To have won at the polls and lost in the boardrooms would have been a hollow victory indeed. It would have led to the erosion of the tax base . . . Good race relations were important for business

Apothecary James Agnew "Polk" Miller established a well-appointed drugstore pictured here circa 1890 in all its Victorian elegance. An avid hunter, Miller created various concoctions to help cure his ailing hunting dogs, including his favorite setter, Sargeant. The present-day Sargeant's brand of pet care products, some of which have been derived directly from Miller's early remedies, are well known today. Courtesy, Valentine Museum

Richmond has successfully incorporated the new designs of contemporary architecture with the styles of the past, cherishing the city's many older structures, such as the magnificent Old City Hall pictured here.

and those in the corporate world knew [it] . . ."

The need for a positive relationship between black and white political and business leaders would lead, in 1982, to an alliance in the form of the nonprofit Richmond Renaissance. Composed of movers and shakers used to getting things done, Richmond Renaissance was one of the early catalysts in downtown revitalization. Their efforts continue into the 1990s.

"It was Richmond's time. The old guard reached out and shook hands with representatives of the new guard," says Clarence L. Townes, Jr., Richmond Renaissance deputy director. "The leadership had begun to talk with one another, saying, 'Let's reduce the rhetoric and find, through economic growth, common things that every part of the community, black and white, can take advantage of.' We have a less abrasive way to communicate frustrations, and the city is better for it."

Richmond was able to benefit from the activities of a group like Richmond Renaissance in large part because, to paraphrase Gertrude Stein, there was a lot of there there. As Howard Jennings observed, center-city Richmond was never abandoned and left to deteriorate, nor was it scarred by civil unrest.

The Richmond region enjoyed a balanced economy; in addition, downtown was home to the state capital. While many downtown businesses needed to see more money in the till, and retailers had left for the suburbs in the 1970s, the downtown infrastructure, while underutilized, remained intact.

It was relatively easy for developers, with the help of city government, to renovate and restore historic structures downtown while simultaneously embarking upon a number of large-scale building projects. By the early 1980s American cities had begun to remember their downtowns. Richmond had never forgotten hers; but in a process of rediscovery would nevertheless expand her horizons and redefine her boundaries.

A TWO-BILLION DOLLAR BOOM By the early 1990s, it is expected, approximately $1 billion will have been invested in a two-square-mile area of downtown

Downtown office workers enjoy a delicious lunch at one of Richmond's many fine dining establishments.

Richmond. This doesn't include another billion brick-and-mortar dollars in the surrounding counties of Chesterfield, Henrico, and Hanover. The surge in building activity, say the experts, is providing businesses with the kind of eye-grabbing space that is both practical and attractive.

"Prior to the mid-'70s there had been virtually no building in downtown Richmond of any significance," says Virginia Ritchie, president and executive director of the Central Richmond Association. "We had national-class business operating in less than national-class office space—and crowded at that. There was a pent-up demand for first-class office space."

Downtown Richmond also needed hotels. It got them in the 1980s. Construction of new properties or renovations of older structures increased room availability by 60 percent, adding some 3,000 rooms to area hotel inventory. Handsome new hotels, like the Richmond Marriott, the Omni Richmond, and the Radisson Hotel, vied with the spectacular restoration of the 1895-era Jefferson Sheraton and the charms of smaller properties like the Commonwealth Park Hotel, Berkeley Hotel, and Linden Row.

Several large projects were under way in downtown by the mid-1980s,

none more noticed than the $450-million James Center. Developed by Richmond-based CSX Corporation and Faison Associates of Charlotte, North Carolina, the project has been billed as the largest mixed-use, center-city development in the Southeast. Certainly it is one of the most visually striking; soaring white towers layered with reflective glass prominently announce the James Center on the Richmond skyline.

Visible to motorists crossing the James, the center is both symbol and edifice, its eight-acre, four-block expanse affirming the continuing importance of proximity to the river's edge. Thematically anchoring the center at street level is a metalline sculpture of three rough-hewn boatmen wrestling a sailboat to its moorings, an eloquent testimonial to the river traffic that once traveled the Kanawha Canal Great Turning Basin upon which the James Center now sits.

The modern appeal may be more aesthetic than commercial, but it is nonetheless powerful. Still, as much modern architectural excitement as the James Center has engendered in downtown, it is the juxtaposition of nineteenth-century buildings which adds further zest.

Cheek by jowl with the gleaming geometry of the center is the more idiosyncratic, renovated charm of Shockoe Slip, a former tobacco warehouse district. So named in the nineteenth century because cargo vessels could be moored nearby, Shockoe Slip has evolved into an area of art galleries, bookstores, specialty shops, restaurants, and nightclubs—some 90 enterprises in all. Streetcar rails are still embedded in its cobblestone streets, and historical markers tell the tale of commerce in earlier times. It takes but a small leap of imagination to picture the area as it once was: crowded with buyers and sellers, echoing with the curses of laborers loading fragrant hogsheads of tobacco.

Known to Richmonders as the "Slip," the neighborhood remains commercially vibrant as the region's preferred after-hours entertainment center. Residents and visitors alike flock to the Slip for a bite to eat or to share a favorite beverage with friends and coworkers.

"Shockoe Slip's revival made a big difference in business entertainment," says Robert P. Winthrop, Richmond resident and partner in the architectural firm Aquino & Winthrop. "Richmond now is much more cosmopolitan. It provides the only place in the metro area where you can barhop."

Richmond's near-river redevelopment continues to move east of the Slip to Shockoe Bottom and northeast to Tobacco Row, a former cigarette manufacturing area. Developers are creating new retail and residential uses for older buildings, without forgetting the role they played in Richmond's indus-

FACING PAGE: The Jefferson Davis Monument is silhouetted against the evening sky along historic Monument Avenue in the heart of Richmond.

ABOVE: Built on the site of an old Indian trading village, the 17th Street Farmers' Market is a lively downtown attraction and a great place to shop for fresh produce daily.

RIGHT: *This lighthearted couple takes advantage of a clear summer day by strolling through one of Richmond's scenic parks. The city boasts more than 90 recreational centers and park facilities.*

FACING PAGE: *Covering an area of four city blocks and eight acres near the river's edge, the striking James Center is considered to be the largest mixed-use center-city development in the Southeast.*

trial history. Taking the best of the old and the new, they are remaking Richmond in ways that will appeal to downtowners of the 1990s.

A 1987 Virginia Commonwealth University study predicted that the downtown Richmond work force will grow by between 15,000 and 20,000 by the turn of the century. Some of these workers will choose to live close to their places of employment. Others may commute to offices in the neighboring counties. Wherever they labor, these employees of the future will live in one of the most historically significant parts of Richmond. How and where they spend their money—analysts believe it will be close to home—will influence twenty-first-century patterns of redevelopment.

"These things move on the basis of demographics," Winthrop observes. "There are enough people and money to make [redevelopment] worthwhile. In the last few years a number of elements—restaurants and the like—have exploded. There's been a revival of corner groceries and corner bars. There are a whole new series of commercial concerns catering to these urban neighborhoods."

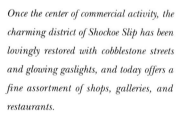

Once the center of commercial activity, the charming district of Shockoe Slip has been lovingly restored with cobblestone streets and glowing gaslights, and today offers a fine assortment of shops, galleries, and restaurants.

Robust new residential and commercial life is being breathed into Tobacco Row, a 20-acre stretch of 17 former tobacco factories and warehouses. The venture is the largest historic rehabilitation project in the nation. When complete in the mid-1990s, its 12 continuous blocks will have the look and feel of an urban village: 1,100 apartments, 2,000 parking spaces, swimming pools, tennis courts, and 300,000 square feet of commercial and retail space. Estimated construction costs are $123 million.

Meanwhile, commercial development of areas that front the James River proceeds unabated. The latest and largest project is Riverfront Plaza, a 950,000-square-foot "mid-rise" of two 20-story buildings under development by the Daniel Corporation. Scheduled for completion in the early 1990s, the $100-million-plus edifice is nicknamed the "Towers of Power" because of the size and influence of two of its future tenants: the law firm of Hutton and Williams (the state's largest) and regional brokerage house Wheat, First Securities, Inc. Observers say that projects such as Riverfront, highly visible in every sense of the word, attest to Richmond's refreshing vigor.

"As a newcomer, I see a positive synergism between the public and private sectors," says Kent J. Graeve, Daniel Corporation regional vice president. "I understand that such hasn't always been the case. But it is today. There's a healthy and encouraging momentum in this city."

OF STREETCARS, EXPRESSWAYS, AND OUTTOWNS　　Any account of Richmond revitalization must look beyond the city itself. The story of Richmond in the 1980s is as much a story of development in surrounding counties as it is of downtown renewal. But growth in suburban areas has not been limited to residential construction. In Richmond, as nationally, outlying localities have witnessed a dramatic increase in office building construction as the economy diversifies and turns from manufacturing to the service sector.

　　The two Richmond-area counties where commercial development has been most pronounced are Henrico and Chesterfield. In Henrico County, where the 1988 residential/commercial mix was 72 and 28 percent respectively, real estate values had ballooned to more than $8 billion by year's end—an increase of more than 13 percent over 1987 totals. In Chesterfield County, overall real estate value had risen by more than 12 percent by the end of 1988, to nearly $7 billion. Of that amount, 23.7 percent was the value of the county's commercial and industrial property, an increase of 3.2 percent over the figures of the prior two years.

　　Crystallizing around suburban commercial development are a variety of

Brookfield Office Park in Henrico County is an excellent example of the area's many pleasing commercial properties built within the past few years to house the rapidly developing service industry community.

Nearly half a billion dollars was invested into new road construction in the 1980s, helping to connect the greater Richmond community by way of an efficient and accessible highway system.

fledgling "downtowns," christened "outtowns" by *New York Times* architectural critic Paul Goldberger. Epicenters of the changing patterns in suburban living and working, outtowns have begun to equal their older brothers, central-city business districts, in commercial importance. Richmonders now talk of the "city" of Midlothian in Chesterfield County, of "downtown" Short Pump in Henrico County, or of the "town" of Brandermill, also in Chesterfield. All appear to be suburban cities-in-waiting.

"You start a city, and the downtown has it all, together," says Virginia Ritchie. "Gradually the residential-population part grows out, like a doughnut. What happens ultimately is that the edge gets so far from the center that it breaks off and forms a new center. At the same time the process begins again in the middle of the city."

In the case of Richmond, the advent of the electric streetcar in 1888 dramatically enlarged the size of the population "doughnut." Richmond was the first U.S. city served by this new mode of mass transit, an innovation that had spread to other American cities by the 1890s. Where the streetcars went, so went new neighborhoods. But the big revolution was yet to come. With the invention, mass production, and affordability of the automobile, previously rural areas were open to development. The country became a relatively short journey away from the factory.

FACING PAGE: From spacious custom-built homes to historic renovated town-houses, the greater Richmond area offers a vast selection of housing for gracious living.

Just as the James played a major role in Richmond's early history, the construction of a network of concrete tributaries would bring the city out and the counties in. On the highways, two-lane highways gave way to four, then to six- and eight-lane interstates. Like other cities, Richmond became laced with an extensive system of superhighways, a system that is being modified and improved as the region enters a new decade.

One of the most spirited debates in Richmond in the 1970s concerned the wisdom of constructing a downtown expressway. A range of groups and individuals vigorously opposed construction, believing that an expressway would destroy the character and physical history of downtown Richmond. A court case eventually settled the dispute; the Downtown Expressway was built, linking interstates 95 and 64 in the center of the city with the Powhite Parkway in Chesterfield County. Former Richmond City Planning Commission chairman and architect Marcellus Wright, Jr., says the decision giving the green light to Expressway construction has, in retrospect, benefited the entire region.

"The Expressway really gave the impetus to downtown rejuvenation," Wright remarks. "It was so meaningful to get the Expressway, not only to the center city, but to the whole metro area. It was a question of weighing the

ABOVE: Richmond's suburban communities have experienced an explosive period of population growth since the mid-1970s—an increase of more than 30 percent in Hanover, Henrico, and Chesterfield counties.

ABOVE: Designed by Thomas Jefferson in the neoclassical style in 1785, the Virginia State Capitol building houses one of the oldest functioning legislative groups in the Western hemisphere.

FACING PAGE: Lined with handsome homes and apartments, Monument Avenue is rich in history and natural beauty and features an exceptional collection of commemorative statues including those of Stonewall Jackson, Robert E. Lee, and Jefferson Davis.

advantages and the disadvantages. Transportation is the key word and time the key factor."

To echo Wright, time is the key—getting around Richmond is easier than ever before. To be sure, commuters still grumble during rush hour, and traffic in some places slows to a crawl around dinnertime. But compared to other cities, Richmond-area traffic congestion is moderate, particularly considering the enormous amount of recent growth.

A half-billion dollars' worth of new road construction begun in the mid-1980s has further connected the Richmond metropolitan area. I-295, Richmond's "beltway," which runs through Hanover and Henrico counties, is scheduled for final completion in the 1990s, as is Route 288, a roadway that will connect southern and eastern portions of Chesterfield County to I-95. A new $63-million highway and bridge system linking Henrico, South Richmond, and Chesterfield has recently been finished. In addition, approximately $15 million has been earmarked by Virginia's General Assembly for improvements to the region's urban and secondary roads.

Wright believes that the new road network has given downtown a much-needed boost, and in the process has also brought prosperity to the suburbs. "Good roads make for a viable area. The large centers in the suburbs are going to continue to prosper and flesh themselves out," he predicts. "There will be a continued vitality. At the same time, the central city will continue to flourish. They're going to be helping each other."

However well connected by roads the Richmond area may be, the fact remains that the suburbs have grown faster than the city they surround. In the 15-year period of 1975 to 1990, the Richmond city population has actually decreased, from 230,000 to 214,000. In that same period of time the counties of Hanover, Henrico, and Chesterfield have seen an aggregate increase of 31 percent, to an estimated 1990 population total of 466,000 over the three-county 1975 total of 325,000.

With the quickened tempo of suburban population growth and business relocation, there is inter-locality competition for industry and residents. Each jurisdiction has its own economic development office, and individual localities continue to pitch their specific appeal to interested parties. Increased competition would seem to imply less cooperation and provide more opportunity for messy infighting. Not so, officials assert emphatically. What is good for one is good for the whole.

"I don't think there's any element of unhealthy competition. Cooperation has grown and we've all prospered because of it," Hanover County Administrator Allan Williams maintains. "Our competition is not with one another. Our competition is with Baltimore, Norfolk, Greensboro, Atlanta, and Charlotte. We complement each other because we all offer something different."

"We all have to look at the region," says Lane B. Ramsey, Chesterfield County Administrator. "Richmond benefits from our growth and we benefit from Richmond's growth. I recently compiled a list of various projects on which we've collaborated. I have to classify regional cooperation as one of the accomplishments of the past 15 years."

A document for the Chesterfield County Management Team iterates more than 70 joint projects undertaken with neighboring counties and the City of Richmond. They run the gamut—from participation in the Capital Region Airport Commission, to financial support of Richmond's baseball stadium, the Diamond, to an extensive array of community development, public safety, human services, and leisure-oriented activities.

Regional cooperation was made official in 1978 with the formation of the Metropolitan Economic Development Council (MEDC). Composed of representatives from the counties of Hanover, Henrico, and Chesterfield, and the City of Richmond, MEDC markets the Richmond area to businesses thinking of relocating. The agency works closely with site selectors and company officials, providing them with relevant statistics and information on everything from local wage rates to per-square-foot office-space costs and cultural amenities. Once MEDC's job is done, it then is up to the individual localities to explain how and why prospects should move to their neighborhoods and business centers.

"A rising tide lifts all ships," says A.J. Christopher Wood, MEDC executive director. "Our organization offers a vehicle for separate parties to get together for a common cause. Richmond is looking beyond the comfort of its own environment; area leaders want to participate nationally and internationally. When we began to promote the region there really wasn't much knowledge of Richmond."

Promoting the region has paid dividends. Now, says Hanover's Williams, out-of-staters recognize the name Richmond, and they associate it with an

entire metropolitan area. "We've improved our visibility in the 1980s. We had to overcome some misconceptions; people used to see us as kind of stodgy and ingrown. That's changed profoundly—now people say 'hey, this town has a nice feel to it.'"

Some newcomers' first impressions of Richmond come at Richmond International Airport, which recently underwent an extensive expansion and face-lift. The renovation was overseen by the Capital Region Airport Commission, an organization composed of Chesterfield, Hanover, Henrico, and Richmond.

Arguably the largest of the inter-jurisdictional ventures to date, Richmond International (located 12 minutes from downtown Richmond in eastern Henrico) is proving to be a favorite for many of the metro area's frequent flyers. In a survey made public in early 1989, business travelers from the Richmond area praised Richmond International for its easy access, convenience of location, and cleanliness. Respondents also gave the airport above-average marks for its parking facilities, overall layout, luggage-handling services, boarding gates, ticket counters, and car-rental services.

Richmond has been recognized as one of the most livable urban areas in the nation and was ranked first by a 1988 Health *magazine article titled "The Ten Healthiest Cities in America."*

Area leaders believe that such large-scale cooperative efforts among the neighboring jurisdictions will intensify in years to come. Better to work together, they say, because cooperation helps everyone. "I see this metropolitan area as an apple," contends Henrico County Manager William F. LaVacchia. "Richmond [City] is the core. What happens to the core affects the counties. It's important that we continue these cooperative efforts, and I see that continuing. We've built a rapport we didn't have 10 years back."

LIVING THE RICHMOND LIFE   Richmond's renewal is occurring not only in suburban and downtown business districts, but in residential communities as well. Richmonders continue to migrate into downtown neighborhoods even as homes are built at a dizzying rate in neighboring counties. For those who call the Richmond area home, housing options and opportunities in the 1990s have never been more varied.

Former nineteenth-century suburbs have become the nucleus for the gentrified urban residential areas of the present. The stately homes lining Richmond's Monument Avenue, those found on the city's Northside, and those in Ginter Park are examples of Richmond's first significant postbellum suburban developments; today they are occupied by those preferring proximity to the faster tempos of city life. Farther out, the Victorian-era residences in Old Bon Air in Chesterfield County—once vacation getaway spots for the well-to-do coming to summer on or near the James River—have been the centers from which modern residential development has spread. They are reminders that many commuters still prefer to return to the "country" once the workday concludes.

Closer to center-city, some of Richmond's oldest neighborhoods have

Neighborhood children find adventure at this Church Hill playground in the shadow of Richmond's soaring office towers.

been or are being refurbished by new generations of Richmonders. Church Hill, Jackson Ward, and the Fan District (so called because of the appearance of its streets when seen from the air) are among the best known of these. Located as they are a scant few minutes from the downtown business district, their reincarnation as vibrant neighborhoods has helped boost downtown's image even as they provide handsome and convenient shelter.

"We have a statistically significant number of people—an unusually large number, actually—living in urban neighborhoods," says Robert Winthrop. "We're talking between 30,000 and 50,000 out of a total [city] population of 200,000. Compare that to Atlanta, Dallas, or Houston, where for all practical purposes there are zero. The reinforcing of the downtown neighborhoods by the middle class has played an important role in the health of downtown Richmond."

Richmond's twenty-first-century suburbs are already abuilding in Hanover, Henrico, and Chesterfield counties. Planned communities like Raintree in Henrico, Brandermill and Woodlake in Chesterfield, and Kings Charter in Hanover are but several of the multitude of suburban options encompassing literally hundreds of neighborhoods, big and small, traditional and contemporary.

In the 1980s the area gained national recognition for its ambience and quality of life. In 1986, in a case study by Partners for Livable Places (an organization partially funded by the National Endowment for the Arts), Richmond was selected as one of the 13 "most livable and innovative" metropolitan areas in the United States. And in 1988 Richmond was ranked first by *Health* Magazine in an article entitled "The Ten Healthiest Cities in America." The article cited Richmond's preeminence as a medical center, its lack of air pollution, and its abundant parks and recreation areas as major factors that put it on top.

Residents recognize that the area also has an embarrassment of cultural offerings and leisure-oriented activities, many sponsored or supported by some of Richmond's biggest corporations. These same businesses have turned their collective attention to the aesthetic improvement of the land bordering the James River, embarking on an ambitious series of physical improvements designed to revivify the waterfront as a park-like destination for workers, residents, and tourists.

James River Corporation, CSX Corporation, Ethyl Corporation, Virginia Power, and Reynolds Metals Company are collaborating with Richmond Renaissance, the City of Richmond, and the state government on $7 million worth of improvements to the downtown waterfront. An "urban walkway," Canal Walk, now connects Shockoe Slip and the James Center area with the riverfront. Pedestrians can stroll along the river's edge, past reconstructed canal locks and a former hydroelectric power station on their way to Brown's Island, which has been transformed into a public park. Current plans call for improvement to nearby Belle Isle, making it into an outdoor recreation center for white-water canoeists, rafters, kayakers, rockclimbers, and scuba divers.

Such proactive public-private activity led the authors of the Partners for Livable Places study to write:

Companies' support . . . and their role in the revival of the city core have enhanced the Richmond metropolitan area's growing reputation as a desirable place to live . . .

Throughout the first half of this century, change came reluctantly to the city, but in the past quarter-century or so, and especially in the past six years, the pace of change has accelerated to a remarkable degree. As a result, the Richmond area is shaping an image that is much more than a reflection of its Confederate-gray heritage; it is also a bright harbinger of a thoroughly modern metropolis that has preserved the best of its past and is carefully crafting the shape of its future.

But momentum is never guaranteed. Richmonders will have to continue to work to insure that the gains of the present don't become the forgotten goals of the future. VCU professor Moeser, writing in the March 1981 issue of *Richmond Lifestyle Magazine*, addressed himself to those concerns:

Slowly the word is spreading that Richmond no longer is simply the place to be from, but the place to be [emphases here and following are Moeser's]. *No longer is it the bathroom stop on the way to Washington, D.C., and points north, but it is a* destination, *and the charm which is associated with places like Savannah, Charleston, and New Orleans may soon be appropriately applied to this city . . .*

What's ahead . . . ? William Byrd II probably raised that question, not knowing, of course, that food riots and fire would befall Richmond over 100 years later during a civil war. And that same question was surely asked by those who witnessed those events, not knowing that the city would rise like a phoenix from the flames. And, in all likelihood, that question was raised by our grandparents, never predicting their grandchildren would witness, on one hand, racially based power struggles . . . and, on the other hand, a neighborhood renaissance, a preservationist trend, an economic awakening, and an emergent sense

of community . . . The kind of future we face will stem largely from choices we make now and our capacity to drop illusions, face reality and develop vision.

For those who might wonder "whither goest Richmond?" Hanover's Allan Williams makes a suggestion: consider the inherent integrity of the people—and consider the Richmond region. Doing so will provide a strong insight into what's in store for the future.

"One of the things we tend to do infrequently is give credit to the people who live here. We tout things like sewer, water, roads, and taxes that make the area such a good place to live," he points out. "But it's the people who set the tone more so than the physical structure. Whether they're the Brandermill type, Fan District folks, the residents of Jackson Ward, or the horse-country set in west Hanover, the people who live in the Richmond area are friendly, generous, lively, energetic, hardworking, and preservation-minded. The Richmond experience has to include the people."

Shaping the Richmond rebirth are newcomers and natives, working together to make a river city—this river city called Richmond—rise yet again to play a national role. It is a role that Richmond enjoys, and one that, as a new century dawns, the area seems more fit to play than ever before.

2
CHARTING
THE COURSE

ROBERT P. BLACK, PRESIDENT OF THE Fifth District Federal Reserve Bank, has a magnificent view of the James River from his 24th-floor office. On a clear day in early spring, floor-to-ceiling windows reveal the James frothing and glittering in the midmorning sun, wending its turbulent way past Richmond's central business district. In the near distance the Manchester and Lee bridges stretch forth, fingers of concrete reaching gracefully for the opposite banks of the river. A bit to the west, on the river's edge, the James River Corporation headquarters can be seen; closer, at the crest of a grassy ridge, the white buildings of Ethyl Corporation gleam, brilliant in the light of day. As one's eye roves east, the bustle of downtown Richmond can be seen, if not heard: cars and people scurrying between the man-made canyons of large buildings emblazoned with corporate logos. And to nearly every point of the compass, the far horizon is green, an oceanic swell of trees and forest.

This panorama is of the "new" Richmond—a city whose center is defined by the presence of financial interests and corporate headquarters, but also one to which the eye is inevitably drawn by man-made geometry and natural symmetry. What pleases Robert Black is that his view encompasses both beauty and commerce. "I came here in 1954 not wanting to be in a city this big. Now I plan to retire here," he says. "While Richmond has grown rapidly, it's certainly a very attractive place to live. When I travel, I always come back and breathe a sigh of relief that I live in Richmond where the living is so pleasant."

Richmond's choice in 1914 as the headquarters for the six-region Fifth District (including North and South Carolina, Virginia, West Virginia, Maryland, and the District of Columbia) was an undeniable coup for the area. But

The spectacular James Center development is an outstanding achievement of modern architecture and a tribute to the impressive growth of the city's business community.

The majestic James River flows by the ever-growing city skyline—the heartbeat of Richmond's dynamic economic center.

the arrival of the "Fed," as the bank is popularly known, was to prove more than a booster's dream come true.

When the Federal Reserve Act was passed by Congress in December 1913—no mean feat, given the deep-rooted turn-of-the-century mistrust of financial regulation—it provided for the creation of no more than 12 and no fewer than eight Reserve "districts." In the immediate aftermath of the signing of the act into law by President Wilson, competition among cities eager to play host to a "Fed" headquarters was fierce. As James Parthemos, author of *The Federal Reserve Act of 1913 in the Stream of U.S. Monetary History,* points out, some 37 cities across the nation vied for the honor. In the Southeast, the trio of Richmond, Baltimore, and Washington, D.C., scrambled to be selected, energetically promoting the merits of their respective locales in hearings before the Reserve Bank Organizing Committee.

FACING PAGE: The Richmond community actively and successfully campaigned to become the headquarters of the Fifth Federal Reserve District on April 2, 1914, just four months after the passage of the 1913 Federal Reserve Act.

On April 2, 1914, the committee announced the winner: Richmond. As the headquarters site for the Fifth District, Richmond would oversee financial transactions in North and South Carolina, Virginia, West Virginia, Maryland, and the District of Columbia. The business leaders who had lobbied long and hard for their city's selection were elated. The April 3 edition of the *Richmond Times-Dispatch* reported that Richmond officials abandoned their usual reserved demeanor by "joining hands and giving a loud cheer." The Fed's arrival in Richmond was not universally celebrated, however; on the contrary, it created not a little consternation in certain quarters.

ABOVE: Many new jobs and employment opportunities have been created in recent years as new businesses continue to locate in Richmond and continue to invest in the local economy.

In Baltimore and Washington, disbelief was the order of the day. The *Washington Post* sniffed that both cities "must do all reserve business through [a] comparatively small institution in the former capital of the Confederacy . . . [One must regard this] in the light of attaching a very large tail to a comparatively small dog."

Baltimore eventually appealed the decision to the Federal Reserve Board, which heard the case on January 7, 1915, and decided to postpone

action. Not until the U.S. Attorney General essentially denied the legal standing of the Baltimore plea on April 4, 1916, was the matter finally laid to rest. Richmond had finally and officially been annointed as the headquarters of the Fifth Federal Reserve District.

In the past eight or so decades, the Fed has provided a psychological anchor for the Richmond region in a rising commercial and financial tide. As in all human activity, perception is paramount—the perception of the Fed as a financial Gibraltar that even the most agitated of modern currents cannot overrun has played no small role in Richmond's recent resurgence.

CAREFUL BANKS STEER A PROGRESSIVE COURSE

Banking, long regarded as one of the most conservative of professions, changed profoundly in the decade of the 1980s. Competition from savings and loans, brokerage houses, and money-market funds led banks to press for changes in state and federal law. The new legislation provided for more depositor choice, and many more loan and investor options, than at any previous time in U.S. history. Also having a significant impact were the evolution and proliferation of powerful computers, changes which—when coupled with instantaneous global telecommunications—have in essence created a 24-hour-a-day world financial market. Even the most venturesome bankers of the early twentieth century would be hard pressed to imagine, much less navigate, the financial landscape of the near twenty-first century.

Notwithstanding their customary caution, Richmond banks in the 1980s continued a long-standing tradition of community activism. In addition to the usual loan and investment business, area bankers assumed a higher profile in community affairs—supporting local charities, underwriting cultural events, funding endowments at universities, and sponsoring sporting events. Providing such leadership is ultimately a matter of enlightened self-interest—as the Richmond area goes, so go Richmond banks. "Banking is a circular process. As the community prospers banks prosper," observes Lewis N. Miller, Jr., president of Central Fidelity Banks, Inc. "The best thing for our business is to see booming housing development, booming retail sales and an attractive quality of life. It makes no sense *not* to be supportive of the community."

The banks' presence is perhaps most visible in the downtown business district, site of four of the state's seven bank headquarters. In choosing the central business district as the primary site for their administrative operations,

FACING PAGE: A leading force in the region's banking community, statewide Central Fidelity Bank is ranked fourth among the commercial banking institutions of Richmond. Nearby Sovran Bank offers a complete line of services at its more than 350 offices throughout Virginia, Washington, D.C., and Maryland.

ABOVE: Richmond's downtown district experienced a surge of development in the 1970s when four of Virginia's state banks established their headquarters within the city's central business district.

The exciting and competitive financial community of Richmond boasts five member firms of the New York Stock Exchange, offices for all of the "Big Eight" accounting firms, and two of the largest law firms on the East Coast that handle the related legal issues of often complicated fiscal transactions.

Richmond banks got the downtown-development ball rolling in the 1970s. "There wasn't much around when we moved to this building in 1974," says C. Coleman McGehee, former chairman of the board of Sovran Bank, N.A. "It's been interesting to sit here for the last fifteen years and see the whole thing develop. Back in the '40s and '50s, Richmond was pretty much of a tobacco town. What it amounts to now is that the city has been discovered."

McGehee says that the pace of change is bound to escalate in coming years as interstate banking spreads. By 1992, banks in more than 30 states will be permitted to move monies across their neighbors' borders—in effect begetting the national banking system so dreaded by nineteenth-century financiers. As McGehee sees it, those unable to adapt and innovate to the new environment will "go the way of all good things."

Richmond-area banks have done well for themselves as they expanded well outside the boundaries of the metropolitan area: by 1989 the quartet headquartered in Richmond controlled close to $50 billion in total assets. Nevertheless, observers say, management hasn't forgotten its hometown. "Bankers have done a lot of things to improve economic development," says Fed president Black. "They've made it awfully attractive for business to locate here. They can take care of almost any conceivable need a company may have. The banks in Richmond are collectively very sound and strongly managed. They're also providing one whale of an amount of leadership."

But the story of Richmond's financial community in the 1980s is not just about banks. The area is home to five member firms of the New York Stock Exchange (only six cities have five or more) and a regional bond underwriter. Two law firms of 300 or more attorneys handle legal matters relating to complex financial transactions (only New York, Los Angeles, Houston, and Chicago have more megafirms). All Big Eight accounting firms have offices in Richmond. And Washburn Financial Press, a division of Richmond's Cadmus Communications Corporation, regularly beats out New York firms for large-scale printing projects.

Typical of the area's financial vitality has been the growth of Wheat, First

Securities. Founded in 1922, the firm has been guided by the founder's son, James C. Wheat, Jr., into the top ranks of the nation's regional brokerages. By the beginning of 1989 the firm was overseeing 92 offices as far-flung as South Carolina, Ohio, and Connecticut. In 1988 Wheat, First was the largest underwriter of initial public offerings of stock in the country. With the acquisition of the established Philadelphia firm of Butcher & Singer in late 1988, the brokerage further extended its reach—pumping its revenues up by some 66 percent in one fell swoop, to $200 million. Unlike many other brokerages damaged or crippled by the fallout from "Black Monday" (the 500-point tumble taken by the stock market in October 1987), Wheat, First actually strengthened its position by hiring scores of veteran brokers and aggressively pursuing expansion. The firm seems assured of continued good performance.

Such a formidable combination of financial smarts, market savvy, and logistical strength has put Richmond in an enviable position for a new century. An activist coalition of bankers and businessmen surprised Federal Reserve competitors at the beginning of the twentieth century; new generations of Richmond money managers promise to gratify investors and supporters at the beginning of the twenty-first. "The community has access to sophisticated financial and legal talent, which enables the area to support a number of large

The high technology of the flourishing computer industry maintains a strong presence in the Richmond business community.

corporations," maintains Richard G. Tilghman, chairman and chief executive officer of Crestar Bank. "On balance, the decade of the '80s has been superb. We've had some important in-migration of great corporations and we've had local corporations continue very strong growth profiles. In the '90s I see us keeping on keeping on. There's a lot of diversity here—we're not particularly vulnerable to any one thing going wrong."

GROWING UP AT HOME   Diversity is the word most often used when Richmonders are asked to reveal the area's economic strengths. Not surprisingly, that diversity has been bolstered in Richmond by the presence and growth of thousands of small businesses.

"If I was picking the one place in the United States to do business, that place would be the Richmond metro area," asserts Hugh Joyce, founder and president of the James River Air Conditioning Company. "The Richmond market has an advantage because it has a diversified business nucleus to draw on. It hasn't had and won't have the peaks and valleys seen in other parts of the nation. I've been here through several recessions and I've still been able to maintain growth and profits. Today in Richmond the opportunities for small business, although in certain ways more complex, are greater than ever."

Joyce began a one-man business from his home in 1968 with $6,000 in personal funds. The enterprise was far from effortless; the 16-hour-a-day, seven-day-a-week schedule he was forced to adopt didn't begin to pay off until the late 1970s. By 1985, 29 employees were working for the firm. By 1989 James River Air Conditioning was generating a cool $4.3 million in annual revenues through the efforts of a work force some 45 strong. Joyce was named Entrepreneur of the Year by the Metropolitan Richmond Chamber of Commerce and went on to win the Small Business Administration award as "Small Business Person of the Year" for Virginia.

Small businesses like Joyce's are, in Richmond as elsewhere, the backbone of the national economy. Nearly 90 percent of U.S. businesses are classified as "small" (having 500 or fewer employees), according to the Small Business Administration. The American love affair with business ownership shows no loss of intensity; from 1979 to 1983 alone, there was a 470-percent increase in employees' reporting of additional self-employment income. *Fortune* 500 corporations may attract a disproportionate share of publicity for deeds large and small (intended or otherwise), but it is the small businessperson who daily greases the wheels of commerce.

Downtown Richmond teems with activity during peak business hours.

Devotees in the Richmond area say there is no particular small-is-beautiful secret. Stick to the knitting, says Lee-Darden founder and vice president Mary D. Darden, but understand that your reputation will sooner or later precede you. "Richmond's economic health makes it a little easier to ride out the entrepreneurial tide," she contends. "But owning your own business makes it tough no matter what. A small business has to find a niche and fill it very well—you have to perform, keep your promises, and try to live up to expectations. Richmond is a word-of-mouth town. I like the fact that we get a lot of our business from personal referrals. If your work is good, people know about it. And people know when it's bad."

Knowing about small business and the funding problems it faces is vitally important for the economic future of Richmond, maintains S. Buford Scott,

chairman of the board of Scott & Stringfellow, Inc., a Richmond brokerage firm. Scott believes that while Richmond's financial community has done a fairly good job in supporting small business, there is always more to do. "Two things are required for the growth of business," he asserts. "One is the source of capital provided by investment banks. The other is a secondary market, the support of growing companies by investors willing to buy stock. All companies start small. A strong community, in order to remain strong, must encourage the birth, nurturing, and growth of small companies."

Entrepreneurs starting up in Richmond shouldn't expect the "damn the torpedoes, full speed ahead" philosophy prevalent in larger metropolitan areas with higher concentrations of fervid venture capitalists. But while fiscally conservative Richmond-area investors have never flocked to risky ventures, once they are persuaded that a company is sound, they prove to be loyal supporters. On the company end, there's a bit of a Catch-22: attracting investment to remain financially strong requires an enterprise to prove its current strength, a tough chore for many young up-and-comers. Underfunding itself may cause volatility, and volatility is the very thing that scares away cautious contributors.

Nonetheless, Scott says that, more so than most metro regions its size or larger, Richmond is a place where company management is accessible to would-be investors. Investors are therefore able to acquaint themselves with the people running the show, in effect establishing a psychological comfort zone that can prove invaluable as a firm evolves. "We have generally had good managers running Richmond companies," Scott remarks. "And they are more accessible and visible in Richmond than would be the case in Cleveland, Chicago, New York, or Boston. In particular, knowing the management of the

RIGHT: Serving the electricity needs of metropolitan Richmond is the Virginia Power Company, whose main offices are pictured here in this towering high-rise.

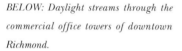

BELOW: Daylight streams through the commercial office towers of downtown Richmond.

smaller to medium-sized companies gives investors a sense of confidence."

Certainly, not all small firms are destined to evolve into corporate leviathans. No doubt only a few desire it. But for those companies planning to become the Richmond region's twenty-first-century leaders, several trailblazers offer instructive tales of their own.

One little-to-large homegrown success story is that of the James River Corporation. In 1969 former Ethyl Corporation employees Brenton S. Halsey and Robert C. Williams bought the Albemarle Paper Mill, then a one-machine, 100-employee specialty mill with $4 million in annual revenues.

Twenty years and a score of acquisitions later, their business is the world's second-largest manufacturer of paper pulp and paper products. By 1989, active in 30 U.S. states (as well as in Canada, Mexico, and five European countries), the firm operated 133 manufacturing facilities and employed in excess of 40,000 people. Sales had ballooned to a record $5.8 billion, a 15-percent increase over the 1988 fiscal year.

Few companies can match the astounding growth of James River. Nevertheless, the Richmond area in the 1980s seemed to have a healthy share of native companies that, through aggressive innovation and an eye to detail, managed the difficult transition from small to large. Many, like James River, keep buying and expanding, while managing debt and plowing what profits remain back into the company. One such is Circuit City Stores, Inc., the nation's largest retailer of consumer electronics and appliances. When the company's fiscal year ended in February 1989, revenues stood at $1.72 billion, a 27-percent rise that president and chief executive officer Richard L. Sharp described in a speech as "scratch[ing] the surface of this enormous opportunity . . . we have expansion opportunities remaining that represent $18 billion in market potential." Toward achieving the potential, Circuit City had opened 29 new stores by the end of 1989, bringing the company's grand total to 149. By March 1990 sales had increased by 22 percent, to $2.1 billion, and the company was projecting that by year's end 30 more stores would join its ranks.

Entrepreneurial activity and investment opportunities offer a broad and favorable range of future economic possibilities for the rapidly developing commercial sector of Richmond.

Circuit City founder Samuel S. Wurtzel fully intended that his small business would grow. Shortly after he began, at age 42 in 1949, to sell television sets out of the other half of a tire store, he began to run TV-program advertisements on the radio pages of local newspapers—at the time, a listing that was but 10 lines long. By the time his son Alan took over the chairmanship of the board, listings were considerably longer, signals were routinely bouncing off satellites, and nearly every American household owned at least one television. It was a new age, but Circuit City management decided to stay where Wurtzel's enterprise had matured.

"We stay here and grow here largely because it's such a great place to have a headquarters," says Edward J. Kopf, vice president of corporate planning for Circuit City Stores, Inc. "We have major offices in Los Angeles and Atlanta—in fact, we do more business in L.A. than anywhere else—but we're very happy where we are. Richmond has a culture that never lost a sense of service, the one thing

Now the world's second-largest manufacturer of paper pulp and paper products, the hometown James River Corporation has achieved phenomenal success since it was first established in 1969. Employing more than 40,000 people worldwide, James River operates 133 facilities throughout the United States, Canada, Mexico, and Europe.

that's helping us thrive."

Also thriving is Media General, a family business that began publishing newspapers in Richmond at the turn of the twentieth century, only to grow by near century's end into a communications conglomerate that owns television and radio stations, two cable networks, newsprint-paper operations, and trade and business publications. Over the past two decades the company has enjoyed steady profits, with revenues (charted for a 10-year period ending in 1988) increasing at an annual compound growth rate of 12 percent. Like Circuit City, Media General has expanded well beyond its home city and state, but chooses to keep its headquarters in Richmond.

"We could have our headquarters in Florida. We have two television stations and a newspaper there," says Media General vice chairman J. Stewart Bryan III. "But Richmond's central location makes it a very desirable place to headquarter a business. Anybody in the media business needs ready access to Washington, D.C., and New York—and we have from Richmond. It's an easy place to recruit top executives to. People come down here and like the life-style." Bryan, a Richmond native, adds with a smile that he's fond "of four equal seasons of three months each."

One of Richmond's oldest homegrowns was founded in 1887, a scant year after electricity had come to Richmond. Now known as the Ethyl Corporation, maker of specialty and petroleum chemicals, the firm is listed among the top 50 American exporters. Closer to home, the company has always been in the front ranks of the region's civic-minded corporations, active in a variety of projects to reinvigorate the downtown and riverfront areas. Recently, the company decided to fission off a part of itself. Ethyl's offspring will go by the name of Tredegar Industries, and will concentrate on the aluminum, plastics, and energy business. Net worth is set at $180 million, compared to its parent's $2-billion-plus worth of annual sales. Richmond will be corporate home for both.

"Ethyl has a unique position in the Richmond area. We're more than a hundred years old, and are a major international company," observes A. Prescott Rowe, Ethyl vice president of corporate communications:

We feel Richmond is a good place to do business—after all, we've given birth to another Richmond company. There's no reason to put our business somewhere else; it never

passed through our minds. We have an intense loyalty to this area. Everything is not roses, but everyone is trying to keep the wagons moving forward and we're trying to tackle problems from a public and private perspective. Richmond has a very involved and interested business community; not all communities have that luxury. Our history is here—and so is our future."

BLACK BUSINESS COMES OF AGE   One of the significant, if relatively unheralded, stories of the Richmond region in the 1980s concerns the steady evolution of black business. Although far fewer in number than so-called majority firms, area companies headed by blacks are looking ahead to the next century, aggressively reaching out to markets and clients in unprecedented fashion. For Richmond, where skin color historically determined social status and

One positive aspect of doing business in Richmond is the personal and accessible attitude on the part of local management in relation to potential investors, inspiring a strong sense of confidence and visibility in the economic marketplace.

degree of economic prosperity, this development is proof that more than just the downtown skyline is undergoing notable change.

While there were a number of thriving firms headed by free blacks in Richmond in the eighteenth and nineteenth centuries, it was only in the twentieth that black companies began to proliferate in earnest. But number alone does not long-term viability guarantee. Since, by any objective measure—size, total revenues, after-tax income, per-capita income—black business generally had a rougher go of it than white-owned firms, blacks who

wanted to stay in business for the duration had to carefully identify the products they sold and the customers they serviced. Shackled by repressive laws, hampered by white attitudes, and constrained by perceived cultural differences, blacks found it much easier to do business with members of their own race. Ironically, it was only in the aftermath of the 1954 Supreme Court decision outlawing segregation and a successful civil-rights movement that black business began to falter.

Richmond City Manager Robert C. Bobb, in remarks made before the Virginia Regional Minority Supplier Development Council in the spring of 1988, explained the incongruity:

Desegregation hurt some black enterprises. Since we no longer were forced to shop in separate stores and eat in separate restaurants, we decided to explore formerly forbidden territory. And we got hooked . . .

Black patronage, so vital to the established black business, dwindled as black consumers began spending money outside their communities. Black companies no longer were protected from competition for consumers. So, after having evolved outside of the mainstream economy, blacks suddenly were thrown into a fiercely competitive marketplace. Even today, many blacks would rather buy from a white instead of a black business, even if they're selling an identical product.

A number of Richmond's established black businesses were either sold or closed their doors in the 1970s and 1980s because they could no longer compete. In addition, the legality of a major affirmative-action initiative put into place by the City of Richmond in 1983 (requiring white contractors to subcontract at least 30 percent of their work to minority contractors) was successfully challenged before the U.S. Supreme Court. In essence, the court's January 1989 ruling sent Richmond-area advocates of affirmative action back to the drawing board.

Gladys Jackson-Weston, executive director and project director of the Metropolitan Business League (a local chapter of the National Business League, itself founded to support minority business) decries the Supreme Court decision. She points out that the City of Richmond program was practical and effective; participation by minority firms in the city's construction business had increased dramatically, from 1 to 40 percent. In addition, the program gave black businesses the chance to establish track records, improve credit ratings and establish relationships with local bankers. "It wasn't just about dollars. It was about opportunities, about getting a foot in the door," Jack-

With a history reaching back more than 100 years, the Ethyl Corporation is a prominent industrial force in Richmond and is listed as one of the top 50 exporters in the nation. Generating more than $2 billion in annual sales, Ethyl's picturesque headquarters are pictured here in the foreground of the city's skyline.

son-Weston maintains. "It allowed a business to grow and take on new employees. Either we provide the opportunity for honest work or we pay the economic and social consequences."

It is unclear how or if a new affirmative action plan can be reworked to confirm with the Supreme Court ruling. But however bleak the economic future may appear to some in the black community, others are persuaded that the 1990s will be the decade of the black entrepreneur. A new generation of black businesspeople in metro Richmond appear eager to profit in a variety of endeavors, some not traditionally associated with black enterprise.

One observer modestly optimistic about the future runs the oldest black-owned bank in the United States, Consolidated Bank & Trust Company. Founded by prominent Richmonder Maggie L. Walker in 1903, Consolidated began its banking life as the Saint Luke Penny Savings Bank. Today it manages assets in excess of $65 million. Bank chairman and chief executive officer Vernard W. Henley says that, while some black businesses have been hurt over the long term, the overall prospects look promising.

The growing need for office space and services to support Richmond's prominent banking industry, small business growth, and the area's healthy black business community, has resulted in a flurry of construction activity in the downtown district.

"We've gone through a shakeout period; you can just look at Richmond and the older black-owned businesses just aren't around. Now, though, we're going to see an increase in minority-owned firms of varying types, particularly ones working in computer-related fields. The firms that will emerge and become viable are going to be stronger and last. Their market will be the general market. And they're going to get better as they gain more experience."

For those black companies striving to carve out a market niche, the 1990s will likely be a time of strategic and targeted marketing. Some black entrepreneurs may succeed by aiming products or services solely at the black market, but the majority will seek customers of every race. "Business is not black or white. Business is green," Michael Clark, president of Clark Insurance Services Company, Inc. (CISCO), adamantly insists. "I believe it to the 10th power. Entrepreneurs, be they black or white, need to focus on marketing their products and services to the entire marketplace. While I'm black, I look at the marketplace as the marketplace: economic rules don't change on the basis of ethnicity."

In the 1990s more blacks in business may well forego the lengthy climb up the corporate ladder. Starting and staying self-employed has increasing appeal in the black community because of innate advantages that transcend simple financial reward. Black entrepreneurs are free to make their own way and their own decisions, constrained neither by corporate politics nor subtle on-the-job racism. Of course, getting a company going is a time-consuming, exhausting task, but as difficult as it is, there is much satisfaction ultimately to be had. "The corporate community is not the security blanket it was once thought to be," Clark says. "I try to encourage more and more blacks to become entrepreneurs. A black-owned business creates jobs and role models while increasing the nation's GNP; the more black-owned businesses prosper, the more the community prospers."

Clark, a former corporate recruiter and past president of the Metropolitan Business League, came to Richmond in 1973—he says that "Virginia was the most beautiful place and had the warmest people"—and by 1976 was in business for himself. What he's seen in the past two decades is encouraging, although he is by no means satisfied with the status quo. Clark would like to see more association and communication between blacks and whites, particularly of the sort pioneered and formalized by such groups as the Metropolitan Richmond Chamber of Commerce and Richmond Renaissance. Social interaction leads to familiarity, and familiarity often leads to mutually productive personal and business relationships. "Traditionally, Richmond has been void of social interaction between the races. From within both communities there are many who believe it should stay that way. The cure is exposure. Prejudice and racism are born out of ignorance; the best way to provide knowledge is face-to-face meeting."

Cleo J. Thornhill is also encouraged by the trend in Richmond toward biracial communication, cooperation, and conciliation. Although proud of the fact that his company is one of only a handful of black-owned mortgage companies in the United States, the founder, president, and chief executive officer of Eastern Mortgage Bankers, Inc., is quick to stress that business success comes from an emphasis on excellence, not from color or class. He concedes that, on average, a black may have to struggle more than a white counterpart to establish a business, but counsels persistence and pragmatism. "Some people do business with me because I'm a black mortgage banker. The majority do business with me because I'm a mortgage banker," he says. "A lot of people don't understand that you don't throw stones at the old boy network. You've got to penetrate that network—people do business with people they know. I try to make a concerted effort to approach and be approachable. In Richmond the reason for hope is that the wheels have been put into motion for people of all races to communicate."

On the surface, the statistical outlook for Richmond's black firms seems encouraging. Of the estimated 1,500 black-owned and -operated companies in the Richmond area (not including the self-employed or the majority of sole proprietorships), the 10 largest increased their revenues by 35 percent over a three-year period. From 1985 to 1987 total sales mushroomed to $93.4 million from $86.8 million. Still, that figure is a fraction of sales registered by comparable majority companies. Furthermore, there is a chronic funding problem; many blacks complain that it is difficult to obtain start-up and expansion loans from mainline Richmond banks.

Expansion of Richmond's black business community holds a promising future through the unflagging efforts of community leaders and organizations such as the Metropolitan Business League.

For their part, Richmond bankers recognize that they have to intensify their efforts in the black business community. One, Central Fidelity's Lewis Miller, says, "I don't think the banks do enough to help the minority community . . . Part of it is recruitment. Part of it's in the lending. We need to do more things, go out into the community, become more proactive." Another, Crestar's Richard Tilghman, claims that his bank is working hard to do away with any sort of racism, no matter how slight. In May 1989, for example, Crestar was recognized by the Virginia Regional Minority Supplier Development Council for a four-point program designed to encourage and actively support minority suppliers. "I'm sensitive to the simple [observation] that banks don't know how to lend money to the black community," Tilghman confesses. "Banks today are as color-blind as they can make themselves. Any resistance to the broad concepts [of evenhandedness] at the borrowing table has been reduced to the odd individual who hasn't gotten the message."

For Consolidated's Henley, better race relations in Richmond is heartening news, although he would prefer to see the pace of change quicken. "It's not happening very fast. But it *is* happening. I've been around long enough to see nothing happen," he says. "The more important part is that I don't see any pressure being placed on people to do it. That makes me believe it will have much more meaning because it's not forced. I would be the first to admit that not everything is totally open—but Richmond is changing all the time. There are plenty of opportunities here to grow and develop."

With more than 100 advertising agencies in the greater metropolitan area, Richmond has evolved into a nationally recognized advertising center. One of the organizations that played a pivotal role in this successful market is the award-winning Martin Agency. Chairman Harry Jacobs, is pictured here working with one of the agency's many innovative campaign concepts.

Because of historical and cultural factors, Richmond and her metropolitan citizens are perhaps more sensitive to, and therefore more effective in addressing, the public and private relationships between blacks and whites. Certainly, problems remain, but the fact that black business is expanding—with the help and encouragement of members of the majority business community—augurs well for Richmond's long-term economic health. In forging stronger, more productive personal and commercial ties, Richmond businesspeople—black and white—are crafting a valuable legacy for future generations.

FAR FROM THE MADISON (AVENUE) CROWD   It is not business per se that is the subject of David N. Martin's new book. Rather, *Romancing the Brand* is a volume written for businesspeople to explain the quirky, frustrating, fascinating, and necessary process of advertising in the modern age. Its tone is conversational, its perspective clear, its points persuasive. Founder of two agencies that bear his name, Martin is a tried and true veteran—and not coincidentally, one of advertising's most influential guiding lights. Crucially, his is a prominence achieved not in New York, Chicago, or Los Angeles, but in Richmond.

For Richmond's advertising agencies, the past decade has been a good one. The fortunes of local ad companies have generally increased alongside the region's robust economy. But Richmond's ad ventures have extended well beyond dollars and cents. Quietly, methodically, the area has become one of several regional advertising "hot spots" in the U.S., renowned for both results and originality.

Blazing the trail was Martin's professional progeny, The Martin Agency. A two-man shop when Martin and partner George Woltz opened their doors in 1965, by 1989 the enterprise had grown to 200 employees and billings of $115 million. Admired, envied and emulated by others in Richmond's ad community, the firm was largely responsible in the 1980s for making Richmond a nationally recognized advertising center. By the end of the decade, the influence was clearly apparent. Of the 10 members of *Adweek*'s 1989 Southeastern Creative All-Star Team, half were from Richmond agencies: three from The Martin Agency and two from the Richmond office of Norfolk-based Lawler Ballard. And *Adweek*'s choice for the nation's best copywriter was a former Martin employee turned free-lance writer living in Minneapolis.

Richmond's advertising rise is ultimately due to the seminal influence of advertising pioneers Cargill Wilson & Acree, founded in Richmond in 1950. Daring tradition, CW&A brought writers and graphic artists together in what came to be known as "creative teams." In an excerpt from his book, David Martin describes the process:

Because the writer was king in most advertising agencies through the 1950s, advertising grew up as a left-side [i.e. rational, logical] discipline. Advertisements were conceived in the mind of the writer, who then tapped them out on an old Underwood. The artist was called in after the fact to dress up the copy . . . This kind of advertising . . . was comfortable, safe, dull . . .

Sometimes, it takes an almost conscious effort to switch on the uninhibited right hemisphere with its imaginative flights of fancy. When the artist and writer became a team, this method of creating work changed and so did advertising . . . The writer/art director team method of working broke with the copywriter-dominated past. Although the Cargill agency had been structured this way since the mid-1950s, duality thinking came into most agencies in the early 1960s, when a creative revolution swept through advertising like Sherman burning his way through Georgia . . .

CW&A, bought out by New York firm Doyle Dane Bernbach, eventually shut down its Richmond operation in the mid-1970s and moved to Atlanta. Many of its ad graduates elected to emigrate south or west; several went to New York. A few, like Martin, founded or became key players in a number of innovative Richmond agencies. No matter the destination, all took with them an important lesson: With the proper attitude, organization, and creative mix, first-rate advertising could be done anywhere talented people were willing to congregate.

The 1980s trend toward advertising decentralization accelerated as sophisticated telecommunications and courier services became available and the real price of air travel declined. In an age of instantaneous communications and fast travel time, location became less relevant. Companies, too, were relocating and spinning off divisions in a variety of locations. Business was less interested in where a firm practiced advertising, as long as the agency generated results. Moreover, the relative handful of ad "creatives," disillusioned with the pace, cost, and quality of life in large metropolitan areas—as Martin puts it, "why live in poverty on $40,000 a year?"—began a gradual out-migration, a sort of ad brain drain that continues to the present time. Richmond, because of easy travel access, appeal as an attractive place to live, and an increasingly alluring reputation as an agency town, benefited enormously.

"What happened in the '80s was a national change in the point of view of a very small cadre of advertising writers and art directors," says Martin, pointing to figures that indicate about 17,000 creative types produce about $60-billion worth of advertising annually. "The best creative people want to go to a place where they can have their work produced well, are encouraged to take some risks, and have their work seen and judged by their peers. From a perceptual standpoint, Richmond ranks as one of the top four or five markets—and that's not talking money. From an advertising-volume/dollars standpoint, Richmond is much higher up in the rankings than the size of the metropolitan area would indicate. There's no shortage of [advertising] people who want to come to Richmond to work."

"It's hard to come to Richmond, drive down Monument Avenue, and not say, 'This is a beautiful city.'" John Siddall, former CW&A writer and cofounder of his own award-winning Richmond agency, Siddall Matus & Coughter, sides with Martin's assessment of the region's appeal. In addition to creative strength, Siddall says that regional agencies such as Richmond's offer more bang for the creative buck. Overhead and operating costs are generally less outside of large urban areas, thereby freeing more dollars to make and distribute effective print and TV ads. "Regional advertising is here to stay because the economies of scale make it work. [But] the regional agency's role is changing from the guru/mentor role to a partnership in which advertising

is only one of the many disciplines that have to be integrated with overall marketing efforts. I think that the area of greatest opportunity for regional agencies in the next 15 years is going to be business-to-business advertising. Because Richmond will continue to attract *Fortune* 1,000 regional headquarters, the future looks very bright."

What seems sure is that Richmond's ad outlook in the 1990s will differ from the previous decade's only in the details. Regardless of a spate of buyouts, mergers, acquisitions, and a bankruptcy or two, which collectively have shuffled key players into new slots, area agencies continue to proliferate—with small and medium agencies in particular plying a robust trade. A California agency has even opened a Richmond office. The Martin Agency continues to be the big boy on the block; by 1989 it was the 65th-biggest agency in the country (the fourth largest in the Southeast), had an impressive roster of national accounts, and received a grade of A from *Adweek* for creativity and management savvy.

As for David Martin, in 1988 he bowed out of the agency he sired to open a competing shop with brother Stephen H. Martin. Named in honor of the Martins' father, a former cowboy and advertising agency manager who died before he could strike out in the ad business on his own, Hawley Martin Partners started small, with $15 million in initial billings. But the Martins' aims are nothing if not ambitious. Their goal, David Martin says, is the same as it was when he was at the helm of the Martin Agency: to create an ad firm able to do justice to large regional and national accounts, in the process creating "advertising that makes a difference to the thinking process of the customer." And it'll be done close to home; Martin evinces no interest in leaving Richmond. Like Robert Black of the Federal Reserve, he apparently has found an agreeable place to craft a good life and practice an engaging craft.

Metropolitan Richmond's vital economy holds great promise for the future growth of this exceptional city.

3

THE NEW WAVE

SUSPENDED AS THEY ARE FROM the ceiling of the Virginia Aviation Muse-um, the brightly restored biplanes look as though they may yet again take to the air. Visitors are reminded of days when aviators flew in open cockpits, clad in leather headgear and oversized goggles, silk scarves billowing in a turbulent slipstream as their pioneering craft arced across the dome of the sky. On the museum's concrete floor, descendants of these earliest planes sit in patient array, propellers still, windshields unstained. Underneath their motor cowlings large rectangular trays filled with cat litter have been placed; staffers explain that the pans catch the oil that drips from still-flyable engines. Judging from the spit-and-polish appearance of these lovingly reworked aircraft—the 1916-era Spad VII, the 1932 Aeronca C-2N, the 1938 Stinson SR-10G Reliant, and the 1941 Monocoupe 110 Special—there is little doubt that flight would be but an experienced pilot and a full gas tank away.

Appropriately, these reminders of aviation's past are housed virtually cheek by jowl with Richmond's aviation present. The Virginia Aviation Museum is plainly visible from a new entrance road that leads to the recently renovated Richmond International Airport. A $38-million expansion of the terminal build-ing and a $4-million road upgrade have transformed the Richmond-area air-port—known formerly as Byrd Field—into a larger, more handsome, and operationally more efficient air-travel facility. Richmond International (alias RIC, the appellation known to air-flight pros) has traveled a far distance from its humble beginnings as a dirt road in a 1925-era cow pasture.

Charles Lindbergh, the first aviator to successfully complete a solo non-stop transatlantic flight, flew his famous plane, the *Spirit of St. Louis,* to Rich-mond on October 15, 1927, to dedicate Byrd Field. The city's fledgling airport was named in honor of Admiral Richard Evelyn Byrd, Virginia-born aviator, navigator, and one of the most famous Antarctic explorers of the early twenti-

The companies and residents that have moved into the area in recent years have discovered the well-kept secret that Richmond is a wonderful place to live. With a stable cost of living and solid growth potential, the region offers many amenities for both individual families and relocating corporations.

eth century. In honor of the occasion the primitive facility had been spruced up; a grandstand was erected and landing-field dirt was replaced by sod. A scant year later, the forerunner of Eastern Airlines, Pitcairn Aviation, was to begin airmail service from Byrd. By 1930 Pitcairn was providing passenger service between Richmond and New York City.

At the outbreak of the Second World War, the airport was leased to the Army Air Corps as a pilot training center. The U.S. Army Corps of Engineers designed and built three runways, a system which (although lengthened and strengthened) is still in use today. Passenger facilities were far from luxurious; the first terminal building was a modified Quonset hut. Two years after war's end, control of Byrd Field was once again returned to the City of Richmond, and by 1950 a new passenger terminal had been built.

The intervening quarter century would see its fair share of improvements and modifications, but the biggest change came in the mid-1970s, setting the stage for Richmond International's remake a decade later. The Capital Region Airport Commission (CRAC) was created by the Virginia General Assembly in 1975, and took official control of Byrd Field from the City of Richmond's Department of Public Works on January 1, 1976. From the beginning, the commission planned for the facility to become self-sufficient, independent of any and all subsidies. When CRAC assumed jurisdiction, it inherited all leases, fees, rates, and charges to airport tenants, as well as a substantial debt—including a now-eliminated $750,000 annual operating deficit. It would take some time to put the airport on firmer financial footing.

FACING PAGE: Established in 1925 with a single dirt landing strip in a rural pasture, Richmond International has come a long way from its simple beginnings when it was known as Byrd Field in honor of Admiral Richard Evelyn Byrd.

BELOW: An American Airlines jet discharges its passengers and unloads freight at the recently expanded Richmond International Airport.

"The commission pioneers really took on an awesome responsibility," says Gary Rice, RIC executive director. "Without the formation of a commission the growth of this facility that we've experienced since the early 1980s may not have come to pass, or may have been delayed. This airport was the first entity to fully benefit from strong regional cooperation."

At the time of its creation, commissioners representing the City of Richmond and Henrico County were appointed to sit on the CRAC board. Chesterfield County joined the commission in 1984, followed by Hanover County in 1985. The four localities are represented by 14 commissioners, each of whom is appointed to a four-year renewable term. Currently the commission is comprised of four commissioners apiece from the original two locales and three each from the jurisdictions of Chesterfield and Hanover.

The move to spruce up Richmond's airport was, in the opinion of many, long overdue. For some years the facility's shortcomings had been painfully apparent. The complaints centered around two primary insufficiencies: facilities were too small and there were too few services. Not a few shared the view of Paul Ellsworth, now president of the Metropolitan Richmond Chamber of Commerce, whose introduction to the Richmond area came in 1983 as he deplaned.

"When I got off the airplane, I saw three signs," he recollects. "One said Richmond International Airport, another said Byrd Airport and there was one that said something about a Capital Region airport. You literally had to walk

Nearly $42 million went into the modernization of Richmond International to help meet the growing air transportation needs of the community.

across the tarmac to get inside the terminal. And there was no taxi service to speak of. It was enough to stifle anybody's enthusiasm; I started to question my own sanity [in coming to Richmond]. Fortunately, all of that has been overcome in dramatic fashion."

In December 1984 CRAC was authorized to issue $28.6 million in revenue bonds to finance the majority of the airport's modernization. From a seven-bank consortium in Richmond came another $4.1 million, and federal contributions (primarily for airplane ramp renovations) totaled about $5 million. In constructing RIC's entrance road, the state of Virginia donated some $4 million, bringing to $42 million the total worth of all renovation.

Having finalized the financing, the commission then turned its attention to the specifics of needed improvements. On the list: second-level boarding bridges, a renovated lobby and a new central entrance, enlarged passenger waiting areas, and remodeled ticket counters. Remodeling work would also result in a larger and better-equipped baggage-claim area, extended curbside canopies for passenger shelter, expanded short- and long-term parking, and

Conveniently located near Richmond International on Eubank Road, the Airport Hilton offers 38 guest rooms and 122 suites for visiting travelers and tourists.

RIGHT: *Richmond International's air cargo facilities handled 66 million pounds of freight in 1988—an increase of 30 percent from the previous year. And with the recent construction of a 35,000-square-foot cargo building, the U.S. Postal Service joined the other air freight companies already in operation, which include among others, Federal Express, Beamon, and Burlington Air.*

FACING PAGE: *Located in the heart of downtown Richmond, the exciting Sixth Street Marketplace introduced a refreshing new wave of urban shopping in a charming turn-of-the-century environment. Now established as a major retail center, Sixth Street is the place to shop for merchandise and goods ranging from fine clothing to children's toys, and to sample a selection of international cafes and eateries.*

pedestrian walkways. In addition, exterior lighting was increased, graphic signage was created, and extensive landscaping of public access areas in and around the terminal was completed.

Before the renovation, says Rice, "You essentially had a 1950s-era terminal serving passengers in the 1980s. It was horrible. Any size airport in any city is a gateway to the community . . . [When visitors] arrive in a community, 99 percent of the time they do so through an airport and the first impression is of the airport. What the commission accomplished by developing an aesthetically pleasing environment is simply an investment for the future. [After renovation] I had some people tell me they thought they were in the wrong airport—it was that dramatic a change."

Rice, who describes his managerial approach as "lean and mean" and "fewer people, more results and more responsibility" emphasizes that now, when visitors come to Richmond by air for the first time, their impressions will

be favorable ones. "My attitude is when a passenger or customer arrives, they're going to know they've reached a professionally maintained facility. There's going to be a demarcation. They're going to know they've arrived at a place with pride, a place that's cared for."

RIC's facelift may be worthy of attention, but it is freight, and the airport's extensive air-cargo facilities, that also deserve scrutiny. Between 1981 and 1989 three air-cargo buildings were built, creating for RIC's air-freight operators a total of 77,000 square feet. The facility's air-freight business was certainly a brisk one; for a five-year period running through 1988, double-digit percentage increases in tonnage were posted annually. RIC moved 66 million pounds of freight through its air cargo terminals in 1988, a figure 30 percent higher than in 1987. By comparison, the national 1988 air-freight increase was about half that, 16.4 percent.

The most recent structure, a $3-million, 35,000-square-foot building, was dedicated in May 1989. As of the formal dedication, the building's primary

tenant was the U.S. Postal Service. The service joins fellow air-freighters Federal Express, Airborne Express, Burlington Air Express, Beamon, and Lassitor, and the air-cargo offices of American, USAir, and Delta airlines, all of which operate out of the airport.

Even though the total number of passengers using Richmond International in 1988 dropped a slight 1.4 percent (the first decrease since 1982), Gary Rice is upbeat about RIC's prospects for the 1990s. "First of all, the economy of the community drives the demand for an airport. While our terminal building is now a little ahead of demand, the forecasters say the area is going to significantly grow. Greater and greater demand will be placed on this airport. We'll see some expansion of the terminal facility, a significant expansion of the air-cargo facilities, and an unglamorous, unexciting, ongoing dealing with [the] infrastructure—something that only management gets gray hairs about. You'll see this airport become financially stronger."

RIC's expansion has not satisfied everyone. Critics have been heard to say that the remodeling was too little too late, noting that the airport is poised once again to outstrip its capacity. Richmond International's executive director impatiently dismisses such complaints. "Every single airport in the country has certain areas that are potential capital constraints—number or length of runways, size of aircraft parking ramps, curbside areas, parking lot sizes, access routes—you name it," Rice remonstrates. "What [CRAC] has done is develop a facility that is easily expandable with minimal disruption. Where demand is placed, we can respond to it. They've laid the groundwork to meet future demand."

ABOVE: From industrial quality control to the world of high finance, Richmond's work force provides a rich source of skilled professionals for the region's business community.

FACING PAGE: According to the Metropolitan Economic Development Council, the number of construction permits issued in Richmond in the early 1980s increased at a rate of 11 percent each year, and have doubled their actual value to more than $700 million.

THE NEW WAVE WASHES OVER RICHMOND   Air travel to Richmond has been made that much easier with bigger, better air facilities. Business relocation to Richmond has been made easier because of the region's bigger, better economy, which attracted a substantial influx of companies to the area in the 1980s.

In turn, this new wave of immigrants has created an economic momentum of its own, deepening the overall level of prosperity.

According to the first-ever comparison of state economies done by the Richmond Federal Reserve Bank, during the five-year period of 1982 through 1986 Virginia's gross state product (comparable to the U.S. GNP) grew an average of 5.8 percent a year, easily outpacing the national per-state average of 4.35 percent. And retail sales increased 7.8 percent annually, as opposed to 6 percent in the nation as a whole.

Richmond shared in the state bounty. According to figures compiled by the Metropolitan Economic Development Council (MEDC), for a six-year period from 1980 through 1986, area construction permits increased at a rate of 11 percent yearly, even as their value more than doubled from $350 million to $747 million. Retail sales also clipped along at double-digit rates—14 percent annually from 1975 through 1985. Effective buying income was up sharply, racing along at an impressive 16 percent annually throughout the same ten-year interval.

Even as the economic machine roared along, the cost of living was remaining stable. Comparing Richmond to other metropolitan regions within a radius of 1,500 miles, a 1987 MEDC study found that Richmond outperformed many. Based on an overall national cost average of 100, Richmond's final ranking was 102.1, compared to Boston's high of 153.0 and the low-cost winner, Akron, Ohio, which rated at 94.3. A specific category-by-category listing of Richmond-area costs compared to the national norm:

GROCERIES:	98.4
HOUSING:	100.8
UTILITIES:	98.8
TRANSPORTATION:	103.7
HEALTH:	102.7

The combination of robust growth and reasonable costs of living appears to have had a salubrious effect on the pocketbooks of Richmond-area residents. Commerce Department figures reveal that in 1987, Richmonders' per-capita income stood at $17,446—44th out of 318 metropolitan areas surveyed nationwide, and the highest of any metropolitan area in Virginia.

ABOVE: The per capita income in Richmond ranked 44th out of 318 metropolitan areas surveyed nationwide by the Commerce Department in 1987, and has continued to increase with each passing year.

FACING PAGE: CSX Transportation, Southern Railway System, and the Richmond, Fredericksburg, and Potomac Railroad all converge in Richmond, giving the region an important and essential distribution network.

Most of the newer companies that have relocated to the area have discovered that Richmond has a warm and welcoming community spirit, and this, combined with an affordable cost of living, has made the transition for their employees all the easier.

By all accounts, companies that moved into the area in the 1980s discovered what long-time inhabitants have known for quite some time: Compared to other metro areas in other states, Richmond is a bargain.

"As we got bigger and bigger it got to a point that it didn't make a lot of sense to be headquartered in a little town of 20,000, 60 miles from an airport." So says Arnold H. Dreyfuss, chairman and chief executive officer of Proctor-Silex, Inc., a division of NACCO Industries, Inc. "We had to move to a town that didn't kill our employees with cost. We knew we couldn't move to New York, Chicago, or Boston. Just to move to Richmond cost $2 million. We looked at five cities—Charlotte, Atlanta, Tampa, Nashville, and Richmond. Richmond seemed to give us the best answer; it became the center of our new world. In general we've been very satisfied with this community."

Dreyfuss says that another of his chief concerns was the availability of a

strong work force. What he has found in the Richmond area has eased his mind. "You can replace people in Richmond," Dreyfuss explains. "One of the reasons we wanted to move was because we weren't getting young people. They were moving to Columbus and Cincinnati."

Proctor-Silex arrived in Richmond in 1987. The company remains one of this country's leading manufacturers of small electric appliances, including toasters, toaster ovens, irons, popcorn poppers, and coffeemakers—all told, more than 100 different products. With manufacturing and distribution centers in Canada, Mexico, and three U.S. states, Dreyfuss needed easy access to transportation. Again, Richmond measured up. "I can get to our [Baltimore] distribution center in four hours," he points out, "and that's if I want to drive."

Transportation was also on the minds of officials of a *Fortune* 500 company that came to Richmond in 1981. In the aftermath of a merger between the Chessie System and Seaboard Coastline rail lines, CSX Corporation was looking for a headquarters city where its administrative operations could be effectively consolidated. Now an international leader in the rail, barge, and sea-cargo business, CSX was then concerned about remaining con-

nected to offices in Florida, Maryland, and Ohio.

"Richmond was halfway between Cleveland and Jacksonville, and close to Baltimore," observes Thomas E. Hoppin, CSX vice president of corporate communications. "Richmond emerged as the choice. It was not a surprise—people knew it was one of the four cities in the final running. It had to do with size and the stability of the political climate. It also had to do with the affordability of goods, services, and housing."

Beyond the economic appeal, Hoppin says that CSX was looking for less tangible qualities—ones that have no exact price tag, but ones that matter nonetheless. "There's a sense of community here that you don't find in most places," he remarks. "The life-style that people came to here was very, very comfortable. It was very easy to transition into neighborhood churches and social and humanitarian activities. Richmond turned out to be everything we expected it to be and more—wonderfully warm and livable.

"I also don't think we understood and fully appreciated the Richmond way of doing business. There's an awful lot of solicitation of business for its opinion. The business viewpoint is sought out and responded to. People disagree and then have lunch the next day. It's very different for those used to a more contentious environment. This is a very positive place to be living and working."

"Richmond is a pleasant surprise to the staff who moved from Chicago." John M. Fahey, president and chief executive officer of the Alexandria-based Time-Life Books, Inc., echoes the observations made by Hoppin of CSX. Time-Life moved its customer-service operations to Richmond in 1986. "The one thing [the staff] talk about is quality of life. They speak very highly of the area as a very interesting place—very diverse with lots of cultural opportunity."

From publishing and the retail market to high finance and international trade, metropolitan Richmond offers a wide selection of careers and professions for the area's skilled work force.

Time-Life Books knew from the outset that it would recruit the majority of its customer-service work force from the community to which its operations unit moved. A mere 35 of its management personnel were to be relocated, and plans called for 200 new workers to be hired right off the bat. Richmond was one of 10 cities nationwide the company considered.

"A whole lot of things made sense," Fahey says. "It's a growing city, has a good transportation network, and its costs—[building] occupancy, leasing, and labor—were competitive. In the Richmond marketplace, for instance, labor rates were about 20 percent lower than in Chicago. The work ethic is excellent. We have smart people; it's very fair to say that the staff talent level is at least as good as that in Chicago."

Although Fahey reports that, initially at least, management "was up to their eyeballs in crocodiles" mastering the logistics of a major move, things soon settled down. By 1989 the Richmond division had hired some 250 workers and had evolved into, in Fahey's words, "a first-rate operation."

The American headquarters of West Germany's Hohner AG has been in this country since the late nineteenth century. In 1982 Hohner, Inc., the division responsible for the U.S. and Canadian marketing of Hohner AG's musical instruments—today the well-known Hohner harmonica is but one among many products sold—moved to the region from its former administrative center near New York City. Marketing director Jack C. Kavoukian makes clear the reasoning behind his company's Richmond move.

"Long Island was getting very saturated traffic- and population-wise," Kavoukian says. "Cost-wise, taxes were among the highest in the country. Utilities were high too. There was no benefit for a national distributor like ourselves to be located in a major metropolitan area. Our wholesalers were all over the country.

"We had gone through some recession times. As we looked to the future [we realized that] if our cost of operation were lower it'd be a lot easier to make a profit in a down period. When we balanced everything out—property and utility costs, taxes—Richmond was the choice. It was almost dead center between the tip of Maine and the tip of Florida—and even a little closer to Chicago than New York. It seemed a great spot."

INTERNATIONAL FIRMS FLOOD INTO RICHMOND International trade, historically the exotic purview of inveterate travelers and adventurous merchants, became in the 1980s a daily fact of economic life. Although the heralded Age of the Global Economy appears to have arrived, many of its particulars have yet to appear in a mature form. There exists no true global free market, trade imbalances are all too common, and developing nations are struggling to compete on an equal footing with richer, industrialized countries. But one event due to occur by late 1992 does seem destined to have a truly global impact on trade: Member nations of the European Economic Community will eliminate virtually all trade barriers. The result will be the establishment of the world's largest consumer market, some 350 million strong.

As a state, Virginia is well positioned to capitalize on such an enticing opportunity. Aggressive marketing undertaken by the EEC's trade office in Brussels, Belgium, has resulted in expanded European investment throughout

the state and a number of joint ventures between Virginia business and firms based in Europe. In addition to Europe, state officials have also sought expanded trade with the so-called Pacific Rim nations, including China, Japan, Korea, and Taiwan.

Richmond itself is internationally recognized as a home to companies that are engaged in a multitude of worldwide ventures. Some of the region's largest firms—Reynolds Metals, James River Corporation, and Ethyl Corporation among them—have been working in Europe for a number of years and plan in the coming decade to actively expand the range of their operations to other continents.

Small companies also have been active. One, Marine Development Corporation (located in Hanover County), was chosen as the 1988 Virginia Exporter of the Year by the U.S. Small Business Administration. Marine Development assembles battery chargers and air conditioners for use on commer-

FACING PAGE: An invaluable player of Richmond's international trade is the Deepwater Terminal—a full-service port that accomodates oceangoing vessels of up to 559 feet in length.

cial, pleasure, and military boats, selling them domestically and to customers in South America, Australia, Europe, Taiwan, and Japan.

From 1985 through 1988 employment at Marine rose nearly 70 percent, from 60 to 100, even as overall revenues more than doubled to nearly $14 million from $6.5 million. For the fiscal year ending in 1988, the firm's exports brought in $1.5 million, about 11 percent of company revenues.

It's not just American companies that are looking beyond their home turf. Non-U.S. firms have also learned the lesson that international markets are becoming more profitable. Within the past decade scores of foreign concerns have reached out to U.S. shores, hoping to open new markets or to more effectively serve the ones already established. What was a relative trickle in the 1970s had, by the 1980s, become a virtual flood.

By 1989 the Richmond area had become home to more than 90 over-

ABOVE: The facilities at Richmond's Deepwater Terminal handle goods and cargo destined for Europe, South America, the West Indies, and even South Asia. Situated within a day's drive of about 50 percent of the nation's population and manufacturing facilities, the terminal will be a major center of international trade for years to come.

seas-based companies, many of which came to the region to establish their first-ever U.S. offices and plants. The Kent, England-based AGI Electronics, for instance, opened its first loudspeaker manufacturing operation in this country in Chesterfield County. By the end of calendar year 1989, the company was projecting the manufacture of 6,000 speakers and the doubling of its work force from 35 to 70 employees.

Fiorucci Foods Corporation, a maker of specialty Italian meat products, completed a $20-million manufacturing plant in Chesterfield County in 1987. It too was the company's first American venue. "The idea was to produce Italian-style specialties here in America," says executive vice president and chief operations officer James DiNicola. "The number-one reason for coming to Richmond was that it's a location close to the customer base—the ethnic communities from Boston to Miami. We're situated strategically on the East Coast and we're close to a good raw materials base. [The Fiorucci family] is very pleased with the area."

Richmond's strategic location is especially prized by firms who produce for, and must ship to, a global marketplace. In mid-1989 Italian specialty-equipment manufacturer Fresia SpA and subsidiary Fresia Engineering, Inc., came to Richmond, leasing 5,000 feet of warehouse and office space near Richmond International Airport. Officials of the company, which lists snow-removal equipment and aircraft towing tractors on its product list, said Fresia came to the area because of ready access to ports, rail travel, highway transportation, and the easy availability of a number of air-freight concerns.

A number of European countries were represented by companies that had ensconced themselves commercially in the Richmond area by 1989: Great Britain, France, Italy, West Germany, Switzerland, Austria, the Netherlands, Sweden, and Finland. There was even a furniture company from Yugoslavia. But not all the "immigrants" are European; Japanese companies and their subsidiaries also have found that the region is congenial to business.

"The Richmond area has been good in many respects. It's been a friendly climate in which to do business." So comments Stephen Zoller, vice president and general manager for San-J International, Inc., a wholly-owned subsidiary of San-Jirushi Corporation located in Kuwana, Japan. The company, founded in 1804, makes *tamari*, a soy sauce derived from fermented soybeans. "San-Jirushi wanted to begin sales in the U.S., to open a new chapter in company history by finding another market for their product. [The owners] made a number of trips to the States and ended up in Richmond for a number of reasons."

One of the reasons, Zoller says, its that the Richmond-area four-season climate is similar to that of Kuwana—important when considering the quality of the raw materials used in the complex *tamari* fermentation process. Also, high-quality soybeans are produced locally and are easy to obtain. San-J has a gargantuan appetite for the little bean; an estimated 900,000 pounds of soybeans and 500,000 pounds of soybean meal were used in 1988 by the company's $10-million processing facility in Henrico County to make about one million gallons of *tamari*.

Another Japanese venture concentrates on cars. In the spring of 1989 Mazda Motors of America, Inc., opened a state-of-the-art parts warehouse in eastern Henrico County. Automated and extensively computerized, the facility stocks parts from one-cent bolts to front-wheel-drive transmissions that cost several thousands of dollars. The facility opened with an inventory of 24,000 parts, and has room for 98,000. Mazda's warehouse serves 100 auto dealers in six states and the District of Columbia, and is expected to generate sales of $5 million per month by 1990.

Other Japanese firms working in the Richmond area by the later 1980s included Wako Chemicals USA, Inc.; Safetex, Inc.; Maruchan, Inc.; and Naito America Corporation, a company that manufactures and sells aluminum photo drums for use in laser printers and copy machines.

Geography, once the bane of international trade, has been rendered irrelevant by the realities of a shrinking globe. What will matter in the 1990s is finding a proper place from which one's products and services can proliferate profitably. For scores of international companies, the choice has been—and no doubt will continue to be—Richmond.

Temperate climate, a central location, a solid labor force, and access to extensive transportation networks were important factors in Fiorucci Foods Corporation's decision to locate its first American plant in Richmond. Pictured here at the Chesterfield County facility is Claudio Colmignoli, president of the 130-year-old company.

The first tamari *(soy sauce) brewery to be built outside Japan is located in Henrico County. One reason why San-J International settled on Richmond as the place to establish their processing plant was the similarity of climate to its home base of Kuwana, Japan. The high-quality soy beans needed for the* tamari *are produced locally in great quantity and the environment is essential to the intricate fermentation process.*

RICHMOND'S EMBARRASSMENT OF WEALTH   Where commercial space is concerned, companies coming to Richmond in the 1980s—whether of foreign or domestic origin—had an embarrassment of wealth from which to choose. Undeveloped land, industrial and office park property, existing commercial space, office/warehouse combinations—all were available to immigrant firms at a relatively modest cost.

By the late 1980s a freestanding, zoned-industrial site in the Richmond area could be had for between $20,000 and $30,000 per acre. Costs were generally higher for plots of five or fewer acres, and generally lower for 30 or more acres. Sites in industrial parks for light and medium industry were comparable, with costs running from $30,000 to $60,000 per acre depending on total acreage selected.

Figures compiled by Richmond commercial real-estate firm Harrison & Bates, Inc., reveal that in the light-industrial sector alone, rentable space more

than doubled over a five-year period. In 1984, 1.85 million square feet was available and vacancy rates stood at 24 percent. By 1988 the square footage total was 3.89 million, vacancy had dropped to 12.8 percent, and a record 654,000 square feet had been leased out.

But the largest increase in total square footage was registered in the office-space market. Harrison & Bates' statistics indicate that in 1983, 7.2 million square feet of office space was in use or available for occupancy. By 1988 that figure had reached 13.8 million square feet, with another 2 million under construction. By the year 2000, the firm predicts, 23 million square feet will be listed in the office-space inventory—a 200 percent-plus increase in less than two decades.

The explosive growth and sustained maturation of suburban areas has played encouraging parent to the office-park child. The majority of service-sector jobs, the fastest-growing component of the U.S. labor market, are being created outside the jurisdictional boundaries of traditional urban manufacturing

Mazda Motors of America, Inc., opened its technologically advanced parts warehouse in 1989 and now services some 100 dealers in six neighboring states and the District of Columbia.

areas, bolstering the growth of suburban "outtowns" (see chapter 1). In addition, the development of an interconnected lattice of multilane highways has led to late-twentieth-century versions of nineteenth-century rivers: Along or close to these latter-day concrete tributaries have mushroomed the settlements of the last—and the next—25 years. Like their pioneer predecessors, present-day suburban settlers are electing not to travel too far from hearth and home.

"There's been a lot of residential and office-business migration to the suburbs," says Stevens N. Gentil of Harrison & Bates. "People living in the suburbs say, 'If we're living out here, why don't we work out here?' It gets into commuting times and parking. There are companies that are right for office parks and right for central-business-district space, but 20 or 30 years ago all those companies were downtown."

The appeal of office parks transcends the impeccable landscaping and impressive architectures by which many of them have become known. Companies appreciate beauty, of course, but when choosing a location from which to conduct business, they must carefully eye the bottom line. By that measure, office parks often provide more space for less money.

"You've got to go vertical downtown. By its nature it's more costly, which creates high rental rates," explains E. Bryson Powell, partner in Laveer Properties, Inc. "The reason to go to the suburbs is more land that allows you to spread out . . . Office parks provide an entire environment for the office worker. The suburban areas will continue to thrive because we're all conscious of our life-styles today."

Office space in Richmond is expected to reach 23 million square feet by the turn of the century, culminating in a 200 percent increase in less than two decades.

In Richmond, office-park development began in the 1970s in the northwestern portion of the metropolitan area, but by the 1980s had begun to bloom quickly in the southwest. "Five years ago office development was 75 to 80 percent north of the [James] river in Henrico County," Powell points out. "Twenty-five percent was in Chesterfield. Now it's almost 50-50."

In the Richmond area, as elsewhere, the most noticeable trend in office parks is mixed-use development, the real estate term used to describe a blend of commercial, residential, and retail components. The newer parks contain a wide variety of living and working enticements, including smart shops, upscale eateries, drugstores, apartments, detached homes, fitness centers, jogging/biking trails, and plenty of landscaping to soothe the spirits of the hard-at-work. In one sense, mixed-use office parks are metaphors for a bright future: self-contained, self-reliant, environmentally sound villages whose inhabitants feel as free to work as to play.

Richmond's profusion of office parks—35 alone are projected to be completed in Chesterfield County within the coming decade—may make it seem that the area's developers have gone overboard and overbuilt. But area developers have confidence in the economic strength of the area. As Gentil says, "You can have the prettiest land and buildings, the lowest mortgage rates, the highest quality developer—but if you don't have job creation, the demand side of the equation, that's when it gets scary. It's been a fairly healthy mix of speculative and build-to-suit."

So, if there is such abundance—of convenient, free parking, relatively

short commuting times, large, inexpensive offices near shops and food, all nestled in a bucolic setting of trees, grasses, decorative plants, and shrubbery—why doesn't everyone flee the congestion of the city for the calm of the countryside? First, because not every business wants or is suited to what office parks offer. Second, say the experts, don't discount the appeal of downtown—particularly not the downtown Richmond of the late 1980s and 1990s.

"There's been strong downtown urban office development at the same time as the emergence of a suburban market. That's very healthy," says Laveer's Powell. "One of the great things Richmond has as a headquarters city is an exciting corporate presence in downtown Richmond. But at the same time companies who don't want all their people downtown can be in the suburbs in less expensive space. In Richmond there can be both and both can be successful."

Taking advantage of the available land in Henrico, Chesterfield, and Hanover counties, many of the area's office parks, such as the 880-acre Innsbrook Corporate Center pictured here, are designed to enhance the environment with picturesque landscaping and well-designed open spaces.

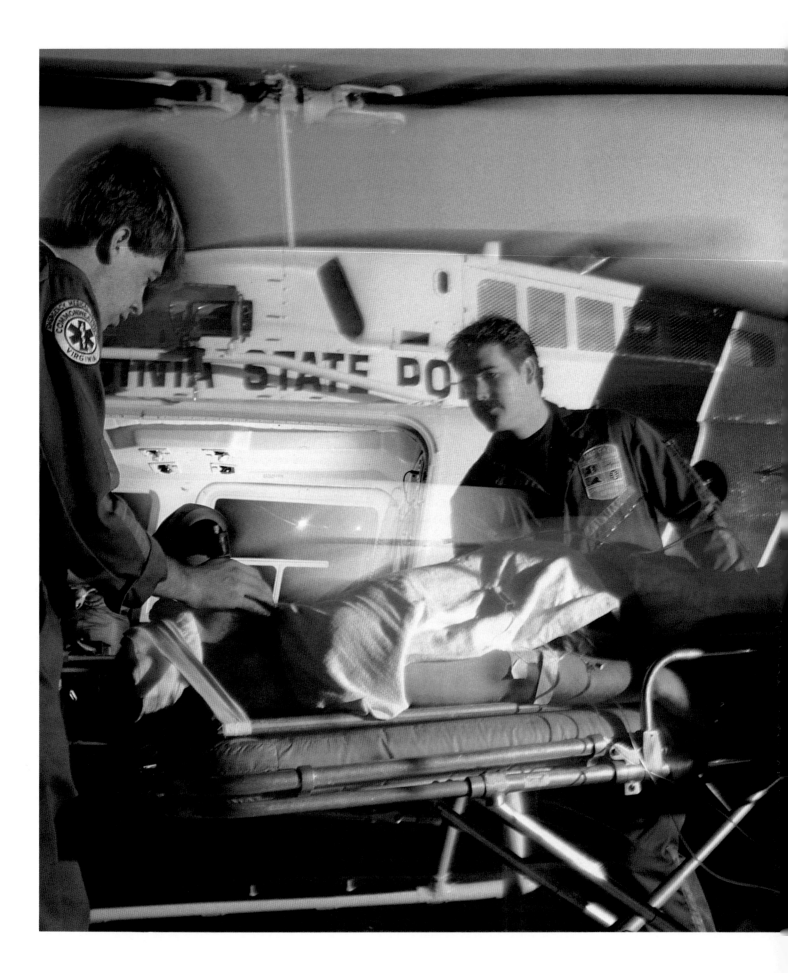

4

BREAD ON
THE WATERS

WITH A NEW CENTURY LESS than a decade away, the field of human health continues a rapid, often breathtaking, advance. By the year 2000 break-throughs in human genetics, biotechnology, and biomedical engineering will have changed the very nature of health care. A new and formidable arsenal of disease-fighting treatments and products will become widely available, made possible by a more complete understanding of fundamental disease-caus-ing—and disease-fighting—mechanisms. While it is quite unlikely that all dis-ease will be completely eliminated, there is little doubt that those living in the next century will be healthier than at any previous time in human history.

The 1980s were an exciting time for medical researchers, in Richmond as elsewhere throughout the country. More than a dozen for-profit and non-profit hospitals in the metropolitan areas provided the latest in medical diag-nosis, treatment, and care, including Children's, Chippenham, Henrico Doctors', Johnston-Willis, Metropolitan, Retreat, Richmond Community, Rich-mond Eye and Ear, Richmond Memorial, St. Luke's, St. Mary's, Sheltering Arms, and Stuart Circle. At Richmond's Medical College of Virginia (MCV) there was considerable progress in the fight against cancer and heart disease; even the new, horrifying, and inevitably fatal disease of AIDS grudgingly yield-ed valuable secrets about the workings of the human immune system. At decade's end disease was far from conquered, but it was under vigorous attack from Richmond's dedicated army of medical professionals.

It has not always been so. Until the first decades of the twentieth century, physicians were pretty much on their own. Medical science understood little about the factors that trigger human illness. Confronted by seemingly intractable medical problems—tuberculosis, typhoid fever, malaria, cholera,

Some 25 emergency medical teams respond swiftly to the area's trauma care needs.

and occasional widespread epidemics of one sort or another—often the best treatment that nineteenth-century doctors could provide was bedside companionship while both physician and patient waited for death to provide the ultimate "cure." So frustrating and formidable were the obstacles that some physicians dealt with disease by sheer force of personality, going about their medical business with the fury of a veritable whirlwind.

In his book, *Virginia Commonwealth University: A Sesquicentennial History,* noted Richmonder and Pulitzer Prize-winning writer Virginius Dabney provides a fascinating account of the physician's modus operandi, as recalled in 1908 by Dr. William H. Taylor, long-time faculty member of the Medical College of Virginia in Richmond:

Some of the famous physicians and surgeons . . . were notorious for their ill-temper and rudeness . . . Domineering insolence was by no means unknown among the old-time doctors of Richmond. It was not a very strange thing for the doctor to take possession of the patient's home, to go storming through it, to demolish with his own hands obnoxious articles of food and drink, plates, dishes, cups and saucers, and even beds . . . [He made] himself such a portent and such a terror that when he hove in sight consternation fell upon the habitation . . . The women rolled themselves together as a scroll and the children fled into a back alley. This sort of thing is no longer tolerated, as it had to be when only one of two practitioners in a community possessed preeminent talent.

Nor were physicians overly fond of one another. Taylor, again quoted by Dabney, speaks of the "clawing and scratching, the rearing and snorting, figuratively speaking, when we got together . . . For the most part the proceedings were restricted to a graphic loquacity and a gentlemanly damning of one another." Today, such acrimony is indeed rare; if physician conflicts occur, they are generally restricted to genteel disputations on the pages of medical journals. These days medical practitioners favor cooperation over confrontation; modern medical technologies and patients' needs require it.

In the Richmond of the 1980s, perhaps the best-known medical facility was the Medical College of Virginia (MCV), part of the Richmond-based Virginia Commonwealth University (VCU). Known by the official acronym of MCV-VCU, the Medical College has a long and illustrious history that stretches back to November 1838, when its doors were first opened at the Union Hotel at 19th and Main streets.

MCV's early years were hard ones, as the facility struggled to enlist enrollees and make ends meet. The Civil War brusquely interrupted the

ABOVE: More than 3,000 doctors and about 47 hospitals and clinics treat the health care requirements of the greater Richmond community.

FACING PAGE: Research into the devastating AIDS virus is just one of the areas being investigated and studied by the trained staff of the Medical College of Virginia Hospitals, part of Virginia Commonwealth University.

Founded in 1838 within the walls of the old Union Hotel, the Medical College of Virginia joined forces with the University College of Medicine in 1913, creating an adjunct part of Virginia Commonwealth University. The resulting facility is still known today as the Medical College of Virginia.

fledgling institution's programs, and the Medical College was forced to close its doors from 1864 through 1867 because of financial and other difficulties. The next three decades also were dicey; the school struggled to reassert itself professionally and administratively even as internal political strife embroiled members of its faculty and Board of Visitors. To make matters worse, by 1893 a competing medical school, the University College of Medicine, was established.

Times, however, began to improve in the early years of the twentieth century. The Medical College merged with University College in 1913, and by the late 1940s the MCV plant was expanding, new treatment and research programs were being introduced, and the curriculum had been revised and strengthened. In 1968 the Medical College was officially joined with VCU, and a scant 20 years later was recognized as one of the nation's foremost medical centers and a leader in the field of medical education.

"MCV is probably the fifth or sixth largest medical school campus in the country," says Dr. Stephen M. Ayres, dean of the MCV-VCU School of Medicine. "Medical centers of our size are usually seen in very large cities. We thus provide a special opportunity to residents of the Richmond area: We are a regional resource, taking care of people not only in Richmond but throughout the southern United States.

"By virtue of the skill of its staff, the Medical College has been a tremendous boon to Richmond. We're pioneers in specialized treatment programs and medical diagnostics. At the end of the '80s we developed strong programs on substance abuse. There's also the emergency room—ambulances come in from a radius of 100 miles. For anyone to be reasonably close to a major medical center such as ours is a real asset. There're very few things we can't do as well as anyone else in the country."

In addition to its prowess in the field of medicine, MCV is becoming nationally known for its faculty's work in the field of health-care economics, and (in cooperation with the University of Virginia in Charlottesville) health law and health-related public policy and ethics issues.

In an excerpt from their 1987 book, *The Best Hospitals in America,* authors Linda Sunshine and John W. Wright independently confirm MCV's status as one of the crown jewels of American medical research:

We discovered that virtually every form of contemporary medical service is available here, including one of the world's largest organ transplantation programs, a first-rate cardiac surgery department (about 800 bypass procedures are performed here annually), a major burn unit, and a regional head trauma center for special neurological and surgical services. There's also a Level I Trauma Center, a Comprehensive Cancer Center housed in its own four-story building, and a nationally famous neonatal intensive care unit, which is a vital regional resource for premature babies.

Wright and Sunshine went on to describe MCV's Massey Cancer Center as "a NIH [National Institutes of Health]-designated cancer center, one of only 20 or so in the country, and a regional referral center for the entire state." They also noted that the Children's Medical Center has the largest comprehensive hemophilia clinic for children in Virginia, and wrote that "the Dementia Clinic is designed as a model for others nationwide [and] is expect-

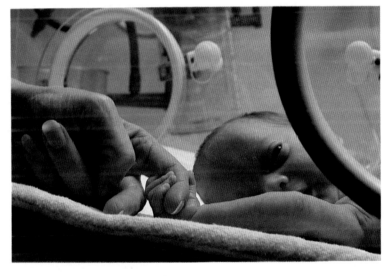

Even the youngest patients benefit from the quality care provided by Richmond health professionals.

ed to provide a prototype treatment for victims of Alzheimer's disease." Ending their assessment of MCV, they observed that "the people of Richmond and the surrounding area regard it as having the most qualified doctors and the best facilities." As one decade ended and another began, it was a comforting thought that first-rate medical care for Richmond-area residents was so close to hand.

AREA COLLEGES AND UNIVERSITIES

The inauguration in Richmond on January 13, 1990, of Virginia's—and the nation's—first elected black governor, L. Douglas Wilder, should bring broad smiles to officials and supporters of Virginia Union University. Wilder is a graduate of the predominantly black institution, located in the City of Richmond's north side. "Having the governor as an alumnus of our institution will give us bragging rights," quips S. Dallas Simmons, Virginia Union University president. "The name of Virginia Union will be more generally known [even though] this has always been a good solid institution with a rich tradition of educational excellence."

Virginia Union is among several universities and community colleges located in the greater Richmond area, and one of the oldest. The university was incorporated in 1867 by University of Chicago faculty member (and fervent abolitionist) Reverend Nathaniel Colver, and was initially situated on the site of an infamous slave market. The property was leased to Colver by a certain Mrs. Lumpkin, widow of the man who ran the slaves' jail that was located

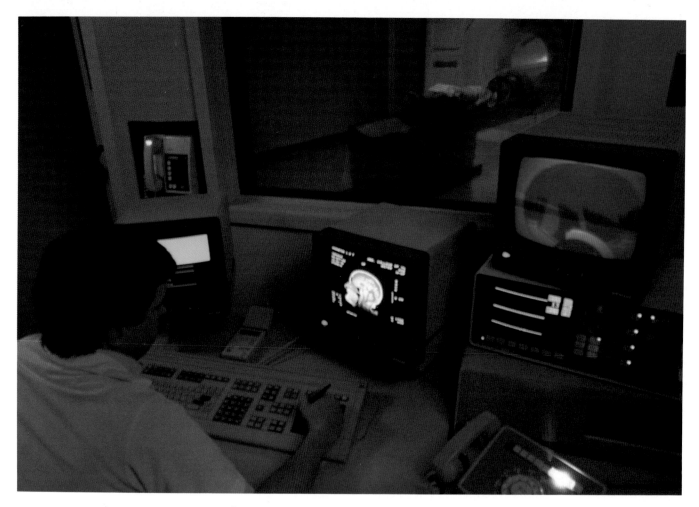

The Medical College of Virginia is one of the country's largest teaching hospitals and is a leading force in medical research and development.

on the same property. Colver's first year was moderately successful, with 88 students enrolled by the end of November 1867. From such modest beginnings would rise one of the nation's most prestigious private black colleges.

Today, with an enrollment of more than 1,300 students, Virginia Union's emphasis continues to be on educational excellence in the liberal arts. The university is adding to its course offerings, and under Simmons' leadership seeks to dramatically bolster its endowment from a current level of $8 million to $75 million by the year 2000. Given the support he sees in the local community, and the enthusiastic support of alumni, Simmons is confident the endeavor will succeed.

"My philosophy is, think for today but plan for the future," he observes. "The biggest challenge confronting us is finding the dollars to fund programs at the level we would like to fund them." Simmons says that one crucial ingredient to Virginia Union's success has been the attitude of the greater Richmond community, which he describes as supportive and encouraging. "Richmond is one of the best places you can find anywhere," Simmons says. "I tell new faculty Richmond is great because of educational opportunities and cultural events—every night of the week, if you wish. I've also found the citizens of Richmond to be very warm. One of the things that really impressed me was that when word got out in 1985 that I was coming, within a couple of days I received a package from the Chamber of Commerce with information on housing, education, health services, and related areas. That said to me that I was welcome. [My family and I] never felt we were strangers.

"Virginia Union will have fewer challenges in Richmond, as opposed to other predominantly black universities in other cities, because Virginia Union has a partnership with the Richmond community. Many other localities do not have such a thing."

Also numbered among the area's prominent colleges and universities is the University of Richmond, founded in 1830. The private, Baptist-affiliated "U of R," as the facility is sometimes called by locals, is actually composed of two colleges: the all-male Richmond College and the all-female Westhampton College. The pair are physically separated by Westhampton Lake, but connected in nearly every other way; both are overseen by the same board of trustees, classes are held on both sides of the lake, and a combined faculty teaches a common academic curriculum. And while each college has an enrollment of approximately 1,200, there is but one administration. The university is particularly recognized for the academic excellence of its E. Claiborne Robins School of Business and its T.C. Williams School of Law.

Other institutions of higher learning in the Richmond area include Virginia State University, Randolph-Macon College, John Tyler and J. Sargeant Reynolds community colleges, Union Theological Seminary, and the Presbyterian School of Christian Education.

But by far the biggest kid on the higher-education block is Virginia Commonwealth University, with a student population in excess of 21,000. Born as the Richmond Professional Institute in 1917, VCU has grown well beyond its humble origins in three unfurnished third-floor bedrooms in a former downtown residence.

"We're an urban doctoral-granting university," says VCU president Edmund F. Ackell. "We're involved in the problems of a mixed community—traffic, health care, urban planning, and so on—from the very rich to the very poor. In some ways, we're the typical large-city university, even though we're the smallest urban university in the country in terms of the size of our enrollment.

"We're involved in Richmond, Richmond meaning the greater Richmond metropolitan area. We have 140 degree offerings, we do research, surveys, consult with local schools and the boards of supervisors in the counties. In essence, we're here to both serve and educate. In that way we hope we've been able to serve the Richmond community and perhaps solve some pressing urban problems."

SMARTER LEARNING, SMARTER SCHOOLS   Perhaps no phrase better sums up the sensibility of a decade worried by the apparent decline of educational standards than the four-word question, "Why can't Johnny read?" In the 1980s "Johnny's" lack of skill—be it literary, mathematical, scientific, or geographical—was the subject of intense national discussion. Why were test scores declining? Why couldn't high school graduates fill out job applications or balance a checkbook? And who was to blame? The answers weren't simple ones.

"In the '80s education received a great deal of negative national press," says Stephen M. Baker, superintendent of Hanover County Public Schools. "Our economy has changed from a national to a global economy, and people have started making comparisons. Not all the [country-to-country] comparisons are fair. Education has become the scapegoat for a lot of our ills. Not that education doesn't need to improve. But we try to educate each and every child and I don't think our educational programs are as ineffective as they are painted to be."

For its part, and in terms of defining and meeting education needs, the

Established in 1917 as the Richmond Professional Institute, Virginia Commonwealth University now boasts an enrollment of more than 21,000 students and maintains a close involvement with the greater Richmond community.

computer science. On the campus of the center are a number of special study areas, including the Aquarium, the Spider Room, and the A.H. Robins Chemistry Laboratory.

In 1987, supported by a grant from the Virginia Environmental Endowment channeled through the non-profit Richmond Renaissance, the center published "River Times," a science and social-studies curriculum for grades four through nine. The focus of "River Times" is the history and ecology of the James River, and in 1988 it received the Environmental Protection Agency's Center for Environmental Learning Award. In November 1989 Signet Bank donated $200,000 to the Math and Science Center and became the first corporate sponsor of the Challenger Center, a simulated space station dedicated to the memory of the crew of the space shuttle of the same name.

"A lot of kids come to school excited about science, but something happens and by the time they graduate they're no longer interested. I like to think of us as keeping the flame alive," says Elizabeth Waring, Math and Science Center director. "What people find difficult to believe is that our total operat-

ing budget comes out of five school jurisdictions as a line item in their budgets. The center is not being funded with state or federal funds. We're not aware of any like venture in this area of the country. It's an exemplary model of regional cooperation. We have no written contract with these school systems—the reason we're still here is that we provide a useful, quality service, one that's cost effective."

In decades to come, endeavors like the Math and Science Center will probably become more common. As the general pace of change accelerates, so too must education. In order to meet current and future challenges, schooling will undergo profound, perhaps radical, transformation. Richmond-area educators believe that most of that change, if thought through and planned for, will be to the good.

"Three things are fairly obvious," says E.E. Davis, superintendent of the Chesterfield County public school system. "First, given the environment in which we're operating and the national emphasis on competition with foreign governments, probably the biggest issue for the '90s is local control and local

RIGHT: Captivated students intently watch their teacher perform an engaging laboratory experiment during science class at Byrd Middle School.

ABOVE: For these young students at Donahue Elementary in Henrico County, art class helps to promote creative expression as well as providing a relaxed atmosphere in which to establish lasting friendships with their schoolmates.

decision making—and defining what exactly that is. The second issue is what some would call the 'plastic curriculum.' We keep putting things in and nothing gets taken out; there's too much in the school day now as it is.

"Third, the management for the twenty-first century has to be results-oriented management. Someone tells you where the goal line is—but they don't tell you to achieve it. The name of this game is clients. The kids and their parents are our clients. [School systems] have to be less dictatorial and more oriented to the needs of the kids.

"Historically, schools have been selecting and sorting institutions. Now we're in the business of total population education. Ability grouping is not what's needed in society today."

For the Richmond area, as elsewhere, the key to effective education will be the ability of school systems to inspire and motivate their pupils to learn more than just facts and figures. Clearly, the time of rote learning for rote learning's sake is long past. Teaching children to put what they have learned into a proper and understandable context will be one major goal. Another will be to create an enriching environment for each and every student, regardless of economic or social status.

"That which is an asset—diversity—is also a challenge. Our population is heterogeneous," says Henrico County Schools superintendent William C. Bosher, Jr. "We need to work at developing programs which will aid young people from poor backgrounds, as well as develop programs for young people from well-to-do backgrounds. The only place they come together is that place known as a school."

THE CHANGING FACE OF CHARITY   A renewed emphasis on educational excellence comes as welcome news to the nation's business community, concerned as it is with the aptitudes and abilities of young people. For business, involvement with education is ultimately a case of enlightened self-interest: Today's student will be tomorrow's entry-level worker. As the U.S. economy becomes truly global, competition is forcing companies to dedicate corporate monies to the development of its most valuable resource: its people. Human-resource investment is wise investment, for in decades to come a company's success will hinge on how well its work force is able to navigate and master the swift currents of change sweeping the international economy.

But that work force can't simply be enthusiastic about new products or processes. To help their employer stay competitive, employees must have at least a basic understanding of the workings of their respective firms. Furthermore, the introduction of new technologies is bound to continue. Staying put will mean falling behind. The new reality is one of lifelong learning.

In metropolitan Richmond, concerns over the economic future led the corporate community in the 1980s to increase its philanthropic level of support for education. Richmond businesses have historically been enthusiastic sponsors of various educational programs, but in the 1980s their patronage assumed unprecedented importance. It was then, employers report, that they came face to face with a stark reality: Would-be—especially younger—employees didn't have adequate reading, writing, and arithmetic skills. For whatever reason, they couldn't measure up to companies' basic hiring standards.

"In my mind, education became a major issue in the 1980s," says Bill White, C&P Telephone Company director for central Virginia. "It caused a whale of a lot of concern. If you've got kids dropping out of school, chances are they're not going to contribute. They're unable to fulfill their full potential, to obtain a job that would help them pay for their own health needs or provide for their families—to fit into the job market. You either train people now or train them later."

Particularly for a firm like C&P, the gallop of technology demands technical proficiency. His company became concerned in the mid-1980s, White recalls, when C&P began to notice that growing numbers of applicants were unable to pass entrance tests. "The technological changes are very exciting

Jacobs Road Elementary in Chesterfield County is just one of the many schools in the greater Richmond area that provide a strong educational base for the region's school-age population.

and it's all happening very quickly," says White. "But different skills will be required. Somewhere, somehow, these skills need to be picked up."

Education was but one of a host of areas in the Richmond region that cried out for charitable attention in the 1980s. The political climate had changed, as had the national consensus about the necessity of broad federal support for social programs. Federal outlays for social programs were sharply curtailed. As the dollars dried up, programs were cut back or completely eliminated. Localities began to bear a bigger burden of charitable care, even as charities looked to corporate and individual giving to make up budget shortfalls.

Sometimes education steps outside of the classroom and into a divergent environment in an effort to help stimulate the learning process. Here, children come face-to-face with live animals at the petting zoo of Maymont Park.

"President Reagan came in the beginning of the 1980s and looked at cutting social-services delivery in a significant way. The belief was that the private sector would take up the slack," says John Burke, James River Corporation manager of government and public relations. "Sure enough, [the cuts] increased the number of people who came to our door. As far as charities were concerned, it's done two things: put a lot more pressure on people to fund-raise and prove their worth in the community. They have to prove it to us and they have to prove it to their boards. Those that don't, go away. It's sort of the Darwinian approach—but you need a constituency to stay around."

At the beginning of the decade, new needs were serious indeed. Counted among their number were homelessness, the spread of the AIDS virus, seemingly intractable drug dependency, and the emergence of a permanently unemployed "underclass." More than rhetoric was needed to combat such serious ills. The

responsibility for doing so increasingly fell in the 1980s on the so-called mainstream charities like the United Way.

"If you had asked somebody in the late 1970s what the United Way funds, the answer would likely have been the Red Cross, the Girl and Boy Scouts, maybe the YMCA and YWCA," says Craig E. Lafferty, former senior vice president of community resources and planning for United Way Services in Richmond. "Now the United Way is taking on contemporary problems: AIDS, homelessness, literacy. They were new issues creating new demands for services."

Happily for the United Way and her sister charities, Richmond-area companies were generous in their philanthropic support. While *Fortune* 1,000 corporate donations could not replace all of the lost federal revenues, in a number of cases they did much to ease the economic pressure. For instance, in 1988 the annual United Way campaign brought in $14.7 million, an increase of nearly 10 percent over the 1987 total and the highest percentage increase since 1983. The following year, 1989, broke another percentage record as year-end giving vaulted past the $17-million mark.

"Richmond has had a long tradition of charitable giving, both from the individual and corporate giving sides," says A. Prescott Rowe, Ethyl Corporation vice president of corporate communications. "The Richmond-area corporate community is generous to a wide variety of causes. It's the very nature of Richmond, which has a small-town spirit in a large-town body. It's a friendly, warm place. Because those in the corporate leadership know one another well and socialize together, it is perhaps easier to come together as a community in generous support of a wide variety of causes."

A result of the cooperation between Richmond's school districts is the Mathematics and Science Center, which provides after-school and weekend classes in the exciting fields of basic and applied science. One such offering is this rocketry class, which teaches children about the dynamics of space.

"It's that Jeffersonian sense—to whom much is given much is expected," observes Burke of James River. "Many around here [in Richmond] believe that Jefferson said that last week. It's not quite a sense of noblesse oblige per se, but a sense of giving something back to the community and not just in dollars and sense."

In addition to corporate donations, Richmonders also were generous in their individual giving. While Richmonders contributed their time to a number of worthy causes, they were also willing to come through in a financial pinch. For instance, when much-beloved Richmonder Gilbert "Flower Man" Robertson died penniless in October 1988, leaving behind his elderly wife Virginia, the Richmond community was, in the words of *Richmond Times-Dispatch*

Along with the more traditional areas of study and research, Virginia Commonwealth students are exposed to the fields of the visual and performing arts.

writer Mark Holmberg, "on the move . . . In the end, $11,179.85 went into a permanent fund known as the John Gilbert Robertson Memorial Endowment, established to assist low-income elderly or disabled persons (like Robertson) residing in the metropolitan Richmond area."

Darcy S. Oman, executive director of the Greater Richmond Community Foundation, the organization that administers the Robertson Endowment, believes that such an outpouring of financial support proves anew that Richmonders are ardent in their support of worthy causes. "The Robertson Endowment talks to how people in this community respond to perceived needs. There's a very strong tradition of personal giving in the Richmond community."

But as generous as Richmonders are, the philanthropic pocket is only so large. Large companies in particular warn that their largess isn't limitless. They say that, given the extremely competitive economic environment, a finite number of dollars will be earmarked for charitable purposes. "There seems to be an enormous increase in requests for charitable giving. We can't keep up with it all," says Ethyl's Rowe. "There's a perception that [large corporations] have endless amounts of money to give away—but it has to be understood that corporations are not endowed with unlimited funds. We've been telling recipients and potential recipients that it's a very competitive environment and we can't give them everything they ask for. The age has changed. There are so many askers and we can't cover all the bases."

"By our very visibility people will come to us for help," adds Burke. "Like it or not, everybody sees Paul Bunyan. The demands will continue and grow. The challenge for us is to become more sophisticated in the way we administer our contributions. We've put in place the technology we need, and we'll want to hone our aptitude in analyzing grants."

In the 1990s the charitable decisions made by companies and individuals will likely determine the fate of many a worthwhile cause. In the case of Richmond, though, the news is fairly good: A strong sense of connectedness and interdependence will enable the tough social problems to be confronted and perhaps even corrected.

"The challenge of the '90s isn't too different from the needs of the '80s," Lafferty says. "We will still have people who'll be in need of help. The challenge of the '90s is making sure that quality human services are made available. Fortunately, in Richmond people come together to address community problems. In Richmond, our community has responded. Yes, we still have such problems as affordable housing, but that's not something that happened overnight and will not be solved overnight. What encourages me is that here in Richmond, there's a sense of pride—this is home and the feeling is we have responsibility for our community."

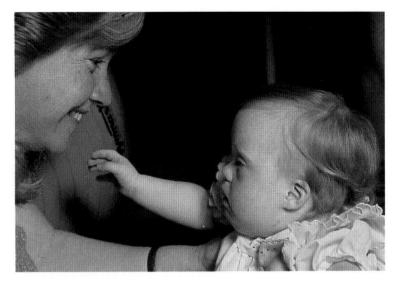

The Richmond Area Association for Retarded Citizens is just one of the many United Way of Greater Richmond agencies that provide support and services for the entire community. Photo by T.A. Stephens/United Way Services Marketing Resources Division

Generous donations of time and financial contributions by both individuals and the corporate community to charitable organizations in the greater Richmond region benefit many worthy causes, including the William Byrd Community House, which provides a variety of services such as nutrition for the elderly, adult counseling, and youth activities. Photo by King David Webb/United Way Services Marketing Resources Division

5

HIGH TIDE FOR THE ARTS

BY ANY STANDARD, AND especially considering Richmond's past, the exhibition that opened in February 1989 at the Valentine Museum was a stark one. Entitled "Jim Crow: Racism and Reaction in the New South, Richmond, 1865-1940," the program presented, in unrelenting detail—down to sets of battered keys tagged according to race and used to open segregated bathrooms—the attempts made by Richmond's white population to control and dominate black citizens. Even with the passage of nearly 50 years, the Valentine's foray into formerly forbidden territory was a bold move.

"The Valentine is seen by some as the most important place for interracial conversation in Richmond," says Valentine Museum director Frank Jewell. "The Jim Crow show was one of a series and it came after the 'In Bondage and Freedom' show, which was known in-house as IBAF. IBAF emotionally affected the black community by physically restoring the past [with a variety of exhibited artifacts], and it was also our most heavily visited show. In most respects, Jim Crow was the most upsetting, but it cemented our credibility in the black community. Assuming a solid and responsible scholarship, there are no longer any issues in Richmond that cannot be talked about. That's a very big change." As Sue Robinson, writing in *Style Weekly* in January 1989, wryly observed, "This is not your father's Valentine . . . Within the past five years . . . the museum [has been] pulled in new directions. The prim blue-haired dowager has the fresh, dewy look of a Gibson Girl." The Valentine was not alone in its rejuvenated approach. In the 1980s arts and cultural institutions matured and flourished throughout the Richmond area, bringing unprecedented variety and vitality in the fine and performing arts.

From an afternoon of summertime enjoyment with the Richmond Symphony to an evening's entertainment of dance and theater, the Richmond community is truly committed to the arts.

FACING PAGE: Through the invaluable contributions and financial support of Sydney and Frances Lewis, the Virginia Museum of Fine Arts has achieved national fame for its comprehensive collections and innovative arts programs.

BELOW: The Richmond Pops play to capacity crowds at The Boulders office park in Chesterfield County each year, just one of many outdoor concerts performed for Richmond audiences during the spring and summer months.

Museums intensified their educational efforts, expanding their range well beyond the confines of the exhibit case. Theater blossomed, bringing more plays, more performers, and better productions to Richmond than ever before. There was an abundance of music and dance programs of every kind. The arts organizations that had sprung up in previous years matured. For Richmonders, the 1980s was a time in which nearly every cultural taste could be accommodated.

"About 15 years ago we began to see sustained growth of arts organizations," says Adrienne G. Hines, executive director of The Arts Council of Richmond, Inc. "By the '80s the growth had become dramatic. The arts became hot everywhere, not just in Richmond, but throughout the country.

"First and foremost," Hines says, "people began to realize what the arts offered to the quality of life. Quality of life is such a hackneyed term, but it has real meaning; when you add the extra dimension of outstanding arts—and for an area our size they are outstanding—then the quality of life is appreciably improved. In particular, Richmond's business community became very committed to the arts because they realized what the arts offered to the quality of life.

"Secondly, metro Richmond residents have always had a good feeling about where they live. People here recognize that the arts at all levels are valuable, and say 'We want our children to know the arts.' That's really important, because that's given us a new audience and a new enthusiasm for the arts. The

youth audience is going to carry us through the next 10 years.

"Third, most of our major cultural institutions—TheatreVirginia, the Richmond Ballet, the Richmond Symphony, the Virginia Opera Association, Theatre IV, the Richmond Children's Museum, the Arts Council, and others—had reached critical mass whereby they had a professional staff. When you have professional arts administrators running organizations, those organizations will grow and prosper. That opened the door for the small arts organizations engaged in dance, music, and the arts. Taken together, arts gave people a sense of place and brought the greater community together."

"Many of Richmond's major arts organizations were founded in the mid-to late '50s by great artistic entrepreneurs, who then held them together by hook or by crook through the early '70s," explains Edwin J. Slipek, Jr., a Richmond-area public relations consultant and arts activist. "Then a new generation came in, took a look at the organizational charts, and figured a way to get to the next plateau. In every instance, a point of no return had been reached. The audiences had gotten built, there were salaries to pay, mouths to feed, staff to hire, and buildings to heat. There was no more of 'Daddy says we can have the barn for the show.' Now Daddy was saying 'We need to raise a million dollars this year.' Being a board member of arts organizations became a major commitment.

"Since big bucks are needed to feed the hungry [arts] monster, major corporations began to make major contributions. Representatives of those corporations began to sit on arts boards. Corporate largesse can be a mixed blessing; knowing when to stick your nose into the day-to-day operations and knowing how to wait takes a great bit of gracefulness. Fortunately, in the Richmond area, the artistic side and the board-oversight relationship have been kept free of conflict and in good balance."

Intensifying the involvement of Richmond's business community in cultural growth had perhaps its most visible precedent in the three-plus decades of support given to the arts by the Richmond-based Best Products Company, Inc. Founded in 1957 by the husband-and-wife team of Sydney and Frances Lewis (themselves enthusiastic private collectors of modern art), Best became nationally renowned in the 1970s for the unusual facades on company stores. Wildly original and occasionally disconcerting, the facades cemented Best's image in the minds of consumers. As the company's profits grew, so did the fortunes of its founders. Whether by barter, check, or cash, the Lewises amassed a huge collection of contemporary art, a large portion of which actually ended up on display in the Best corporate headquarters in Henrico County.

"There have been two very significant things to happen to Richmond culturally," says Robert L. Burrus, Jr. an attorney and partner in the well-known law firm of McGuire Woods Battle & Boothe. Burrus has sat on the board of several Richmond-area arts organizations. "One is Sydney and Frances Lewis—it's hard to overstate the value of the collections the Lewises donated to the Virginia Museum. The other is the growth of the VCU School of the Arts. Both have collectively resulted in Richmond developing an appreciation for the arts."

In the Lewises' case, their first formal involvement with the Virginia

Museum came in 1969, when they donated three prints by Andy Warhol to the museum's permanent collection. An Earnest Trova painting, *Falling Man,* followed one year later. In 1971, in order to enlarge the facility's contemporary collection, the couple gave the Museum a grant of $100,000 to acquire post-World War II American art. Additional gifts of works by Warhol and Roy Lichtenstein followed, as did a second grant of $500,000 in 1972. But the best was yet to come; in celebration of the opening of a new museum wing in 1985, the Lewises made an outright gift of close to 1,000 pieces of painting, sculpture, and decorative art.

The Lewises' generosity catapulted the Virginia Museum, already nationally known, even more into the limelight. In Richmond, there was something of a domino effect: As area residents became aware that something culturally important was afoot, there was more interest in the arts and a subsequent desire for participation. The arts medium had become the cultural message and the message was that there was much to see and appreciate in Richmond, a place that for years had been seen—even by its most fervent supporters—as rather placid and self-satisfied.

"There's been a tremendous change. There's so much more going on," says Frances Lewis. "The symphony now has three series. You have new

The Virginia Museum of Fine Arts is home to the TheatreVirginia company where performances such as the lively production of Tom Foolery *can be seen at the 500-seat theater. Courtesy, TheatreVirginia*

music—Fast Forward at the Virginia Museum, for example. Theater seems to be booming. On the visual arts side, what I think is terrific is that local artists are selling their work. That definitely didn't exist when we started. Buying art has become a part of many, many people's lives. People seem more open-minded about what they see and hear."

"When [the Virginia Museum music series] Fast Forward first came to Richmond," observes Sydney Lewis, "it blew the minds of some of the people who had to be cajoled to go there. Now it's become a standard in the community. And most are sold out. I can't imagine that cultural involvement [in Richmond] will do anything but go forward."

Richmond's cultural resurgence has been enthusiastically embraced and encouraged by the emergence of new generations of artists, performers, and musicians, many of whom graduate from or teach at the VCU School of the Arts. A number of the school's graduates have gone on to nationally prominent careers in fine arts, fashion design, music, theater, television, and

The Virginia Commonwealth University School of the Arts helps to introduce new generations of artists and performers into the Richmond arts community, some of whom have achieved national recognition in their respective fields.

dance. The fortunate fact for Richmond is that, upon graduation, many decide to make their homes where they had learned their lessons.

"In many respects the School of the Arts is a pacesetter," says Murry N. DePillars, dean of the VCU School of the Arts. "It acts as a catalyst for future arts as well as for cultural programming throughout the area. Many of our graduates elect to stay in the Richmond area. In a larger context, when you have a large arts community working, it adds a sense of vitality to an area. Art can shape one's frame of reference. It's fair to say that, because of what VCU graduates have accomplished and continue to accomplish, Richmond's cultural reputation has been enhanced well beyond her borders."

MUSEUMS AND GALLERIES   For several generations of Americans, museums were considered places to go to gaze upon ancient objects donated by dead people. A museum visit was akin to attending a particularly demanding school—a dreary, if necessary, lesson on the complexity of culture. Fortunately, that image is itself antiquated; the museums of today are designed to stimulate one's imagination, not stymie it. Modern museums, advocates maintain, are dynamic, exciting places to be. Moreover, they say, the emergence of the museum as a vital cultural force can be explained by the need for people to understand where they came from and where they're going.

"What happened in the '70s and then the '80s was a great awakening to

the past, a desire for a sense of place and a return to the understanding of the need for ecological balance," says Paul N. Perrot, director of the Virginia Museum of Fine Arts. "Museums are places that provide perspective and involve the visitor in a certain tactile reality. Objects in a museum are not just the products of a rarified human being separate from society. Rather, they are the result of cultural, economic, and historical interactions—a fact that makes museums exciting generally.

"For a long time," Perrot says, "this and other museums were considered citadels of black tie. It was perceived that the rest of the community didn't belong. That has all gone by the wayside. A museum belongs to everyone. Our programming efforts here at the Virginia Museum are focused on making this a place as accessible as can be to all economic and cultural groups. That's why we have a varied musical program during the summers and are opening a children's resource center. We need to overcome this sense of museum as temple and, instead, be seen as a center of exploration, enjoyment, learning, and relaxation."

Always a prominent participant in the development of Richmond's cul-

The largest museum in the Southeast, the Virginia Museum of Fine Arts features more than 30 permanent galleries, which house an almost indescribable amount of fine works that include the decorative arts, pop art, French Impressionists, medieval tapestries, Fabergé eggs, and paintings, drawings, sculptures, and prints from the past three centuries.

ABOVE: Children of all ages can learn about the exciting world of science and technology through the many hands-on exhibits at the Science Museum of Virginia.

RIGHT: The Virginia Aviation Museum, located at the Richmond International Airport, features an extensive collection of vintage aircraft, navigation devices, and memorabilia that dates from 1914 to World War II. Pictured here at the museum is former aviator Ivor Massey, dressed in the classic flying gear of that era.

tural life, the Virginia Museum assumed an even bigger role with its 1985 inauguration of a $22-million, 90,000-square-foot West Wing. The museum's permanent collections—its French impressionist and postimpressionist art, the dazzling Pratt Collection of Russian Imperial Easter and Fabergé eggs, its sculpture and tapestries and nationally acclaimed collections of Indian, Nepalese, and Tibetan art—were greatly enhanced by the West Wing addition. Upon seeing the West Wing and its attendant Lewis and Mellon Collections, *Washington Post* art critic Paul Richard was moved to write, "Most curators of modern art—those, for instance, at the Hirshhorn—would give their eyeteeth for the best new things in Richmond."

Another Richmond-area museum that breaks the traditional definition of a museum is the Science Museum of Virginia. Housed in the former Union Train Station, the Science Museum is a hands-on facility, with a myriad of exhibits designed to provoke the curiosity and increase the scientific literacy of young and old alike. Whether one's interest leans toward biology, astronomy, physics, computer science, or the daily habits of dinosaurs, the Science Museum was the place to be in the 1980s.

In 1983 construction was completed on the facility's UNIVERSE planetarium/space theater, doubling Science Museum attendance in its first month of operation. The subsequent opening of the UNIVERSE Theater brought the museum international acclaim as operators of the world's first Digistar computer-projection system and of Omnimax, the world's largest projector. At the

Situated among the landscaped grounds of the 150-acre Crump Park in northern Henrico County, the Meadow Farm Museum is a living testament to the fascinating history of Richmond in the mid-1800s, depicting a working nineteenth-century farm. Enhanced by guides in period costumes, some of the highlights of Meadow Farm include the farmhouse, smokehouse, gardens, and farm animals, plus Civil War reenactments as shown here.

Cultural history abounds along the James River in the shape of stately homes and plantations built during a bygone era. Home of the Carter family since 1723, the Shirley plantation features original furnishings, family portraits, and other decorative arts in the Queen Anne-style mansion, which was once the home of Anne Hill Carter, mother of General Robert E. Lee.

time of its completion, UNIVERSE's 280-seat domed theater had the largest wraparound projection surface of any planetarium in the world. In 1987, as part of Ethyl Corporation's centennial observance, the company donated $2 million to the Science Museum. In honor of the fact, the planetarium was renamed the Ethyl UNIVERSE Planetarium and Space Theater.

"We're competing for people's free time. We've got to position ourselves to draw folks into the museum," says Paul H. Knappenberger, Jr., Science Museum director. "We want to stimulate and motivate people to become more interested in science and technology. We recognize that the kind of education we do is of necessity very different from that which goes on in classrooms. Here people come for one visit a year and spend two hours at a time. They're in a different environment; it's definitely not a sit-at-the-desk-and-listen-to-the-teacher situation.

"We present an exciting, entertaining, fun time. While you're here you're going to learn something. Science museums like ours are not simply repositories of artifacts from the past—we're on the leading edge of science literacy. We want our visitors to gain understanding of not just where we were, but also where we are and where we're going."

Other museums in Richmond expanded their offerings in the 1980s. There was much to see and learn at the Richmond Children's Museum, the Federal Reserve Bank's Money Museum, the Black History Museum and Cultural Center, the Museum of the Confederacy, the Chesterfield County Museum, Meadow Farm Museum and Crump Park in Henrico County, and the Edgar Allan Poe Museum in the Church Hill section of Richmond. There was also the captivating—and, at one time, the world's only—Spider Museum, located at the Mathematics and Science Center.

The Richmond area also is home to more than two dozen commercial and not-for-profit art galleries. Although not museums in the strict sense of the word, these galleries nonetheless showcase the work of artists who, genera-

The Museum of the Confederacy houses the largest collection of Confederate memorabilia in the world, which includes the gear of the brilliant Civil War cavalry hero James E.B. (Jeb) Stuart.

tions hence, may be extolled as among the best in their time.

Diversity has served to bring Richmond's cultural pot from a simmer to a boil. For many, like the Valentine's Frank Jewell, the proliferation and maturation of cultural organizations in the area has signaled the development of new attitudes and fresh perspectives. "I'm fairly certain that the intellectual agenda I brought—an examination of American urban and social history and Richmond's place in it—wouldn't have interested the greater Richmond community in the '60s or '70s," he ventures. "The community has changed. To some extent they want to make a sharp break with [the practices of] the past. People in Richmond were willing to hear and see things in the '80s that they weren't previously."

MUSIC, DANCE, AND THEATER   In many respects, a photograph appearing in the July 24, 1989, edition of the *Richmond News Leader* was emblematic of the ways Richmond had evolved—artistically and otherwise—in the 1980s. In the picture, against a backdrop of the new office buildings of a reinvigorated downtown and next to the James River on a relandscaped Brown's Island, two thousand people lolled on lawn chairs and clustered on blankets as they listened to the last of the concerts presented by the two-year-old Richmond International Festival of Music. *News Leader* music critic Francis Church, commenting on the performance, called it "a cornucopia of musical Americana . . . a splendid finish to a splendid festival of music." After nearly three weeks and more than 20 concerts, the festival had successfully completed its eclectic run of jazz, classical, symphonic, folk, big-band, and popular music.

The popularity of the festival underscored Richmonders' fondness for all things musical, of which there was an abundance in the 1980s. By any stan-

RIGHT: Monroe Park was the site for an impromptu concert by this Virginia Commonwealth University jazz quartet.

FACING PAGE: The relaxed atmosphere and musical variety of the outdoor Brookfield Concert series attract thousands of music lovers every year.

dard, it was a rich decade. "Jumpin' In July," an often-offbeat offering, premiered at the Virginia Museum to great acclaim. The VCU School of the Arts organized a Jazz Festival and cosponsored, with the John F. Kennedy Center for the Performing Arts in Washington, D.C., a series of Terrace Concerts on its campus. The Richmond Jazz Society swung into high gear, promoting Richmond's homegrown jazz artists and sponsoring concerts by jazz greats, some of whom were Richmond natives. The Virginia Opera Association, based in Norfolk, established a four-production Richmond season that played to enthusiastic audiences.

Lunchtime music abounded in a variety of locations in metropolitan Richmond, from the Brookfield office-park complex in Henrico County to Plaza Pizazz downtown. In Chesterfield County, the Boulders Concert was an annual hit. The Richmond Symphony expanded its offerings and frequency of performances, while groups as diverse as the Richmond Renaissance Singers, the Richmond Concert Band, the Richmond Chamber Players, the

Richmond Community Orchestra, the CAFUR Chorus, the Harry Savage Chorale, the Tobaccoland Chorus and the Sweet Adelines also were popular. Few musical idioms were left unheard in live performance in the Richmond area in the 1980s.

"In terms of musical taste, Richmond's a pretty good place," says Thomas Philion, executive director of the Richmond Symphony and Sinfonia. "You have a concentration of educated, discriminating individuals who know what they like. It's also a good place for a musician to live—$25,000 means a lot more here for a seasonal job of the sort the Symphony provides than it does in a place like New York."

In the particular case of the 30-year-old symphony, which was shaken by an acrimonious strike by its musicians in 1985, Philion says that extensive community support in the latter half of the decade made his organization more fiscally prudent and administratively stronger. The change was most apparent

ABOVE: Now under the direction of conductor George Manahan, who is pictured here at the beautifully renovated 2,000-seat Carpenter Center, the Richmond Symphony has achieved critical acclaim in recent years and now reaches a broader audience by performing an expanded range of musical offerings.

FACING PAGE: Dogwood Dell in Byrd Park is a favorite location for concerts, plays, and other exhibitions.

after the symphony's labor dispute was settled. "Management was reorganized. It was a cataclysmic change. Members wanted, and got, a better organization and a better orchestra. The formula changed and we diversified. We just don't play Mozart, Beethoven, and Brahms. You name it, we play it, from Duke Ellington to Emmylou Harris. We've targeted our audience and in the past three years have doubled revenue from our concerts. And thanks to our board, who in the '70s built an endowment and who in the '80s established another, we're supporting living, breathing artists who make an economic contribution to the area."

Established as a professional company in 1984, the Richmond Ballet now attracts dancers from across the nation and abroad, and boasts an impressive repertoire for its statewide audience.

Another strong contributor to the Richmond arts scene in the 1980s was the Richmond Ballet, the only professional corps de ballet in Virginia. Its company regularly crisscrosses the state, literally from the mountains to the shore, bringing ballet to audiences who otherwise would have no opportunity to see this most graceful form of dance.

"When I came in 1980, the Richmond Ballet was a civic student company and contained the most proficient student dancers," says Ballet director Stoner Winslett. "But our best students were leaving to join nationally and internationally prominent companies because there was no place in this state that a dancer could go and dance for a living. So in 1984 we established a professional company and opened up the Richmond Ballet through national auditions.

"Professional orchestra and professional theater had been in town for some time," Winslett says. "We gained support from people who wanted to see something new. Since 1984 we've been striving for national excellence. We're slowly getting there. A lot of people still perceive ballet as a bunch of pretty girls in pink tutus, but ballet itself is just a way of moving. It's a very versatile form of artistic expression that can be sexy, athletic, and dramatic. It tells a story to an audience."

Telling a story is the primary aim of theatrical expression, and in the 1980s theater was alive and well throughout the Richmond area. No better symbol of that came with the spectacular mid-1980s transformation of the former Loew's Theater in downtown Richmond into the impeccably appointed Carpenter Center for the Performing Arts. Official home to the Richmond Symphony, the 2,000-seat Carpenter Center also welcomed first-rate touring theater and musical productions. More than any other structure (including its older "sister" facility, The Mosque, which also hosted its fair share of performing and other events), the Carpenter Center was a focal point of performing-arts excellence.

At the beginning of the decade TheatreVirginia, Richmond's only professional regional theater, towered over the competition. To be sure, there were other established companies. Renowned dinner theaters like Barksdale, Swift Creek Mill, and Haymarket; collegiate companies like Theatre VCU and the University of Richmond's University Players; community theaters like the Henrico Theatre Company, Chamberlayne Actors' Theatre, and the John Rolfe Players: all had performed regularly and popularly throughout the 1970s. But the 1980s brought with it an increase in the total number of troupes trotting the boards. Among these, Theatre IV, The Production Company, As Yet Unnamed Theatre Company and Studio Theatre of Richmond (formerly Actors Studio of Richmond) were the best known.

"Richmond has an extraordinary amount of theater for a community its size. And the quality is high," says TheatreVirginia artistic director Terry Burgler. Part of the reason for the theatrical vitality, Burgler and others say, may be due to personal choice. Actors can quickly tire of the stresses and strains of big city living; when they discover the agreeable ambience of a place like Richmond, they often decide to make the area their home, thereby maintaining a lively theatrical tempo.

"Simply in what it costs to survive, New York is starting to become an overwhelming challenge for an unestablished actor. It's outrageous," Burgler says. "You'll spend all your time trying to meet expenses and have no time left to audition. Richmond may have fewer job opportunities [in professional theater],

The Barksdale Theatre, housed in the eighteenth-century Hanover Tavern, is renowned as the country's first established dinner theater. Dramas, musicals, and lighthearted comedies are performed to the continuing delight of local audiences.

but at least you're not faced with such formidable financial obstacles. And the quality of life is good. But I do think a certain amount of the acting community is making a living acting here in this area. I hope the trend continues."

"It used to be that everybody wanted to go to New York City," agrees Robert Merritt, principal arts writer for the *Richmond Times-Dispatch.* "In the '80s you find people not wanting to go to New York. There has been a show of people coming to Richmond. They love living in a real city. On the other hand, while opportunities have improved a little here, theater at the local level mostly remains an avocation for everyone involved. The exception is Theatre-Virginia, and to a lesser extent Theatre IV, both of which pay a decent salary relatively speaking."

One former Richmond resident who has returned is Randy Strawderman. A graduate of VCU, Strawderman has directed a number of plays in the Richmond area and has also lived and worked in New York and Los Angeles. In 1983

Professional regional theater is applauded in the form of TheatreVirginia, whose recent production of the ever-popular Guys & Dolls *musical is shown here. Courtesy, TheatreVirginia*

he founded Actors Studio of Richmond, which by March 1988 had been reorganized into Studio Theatre of Richmond. The company's primary goal is to literally provide a stage for the work of emerging American playwrights: once a play has been produced and polished, it would then be "shopped" to on- or off-Broadway and regional theaters throughout the country.

Strawderman has recently been working on a musical stage adaptation of Stephen Crane's novel, *The Red Badge of Courage.* He hopes that it will follow in the tradition of such adaptations as *Cats, Phantom of the Opera,* and *Les Miserables,* and become a big hit nationally, perhaps internationally. Whatever the outcome, Strawderman has concluded that Richmond is the place to build a strong theatrical future.

"I came back because I really began to notice how Richmond had grown, how much more vital it had become in terms of the arts. Many more

people were staying around. There are now actors making a living in film working in Virginia; when I left [in the 1970s] that was unheard of. I directed *Joseph and the Amazing Technicolor Dreamcoat* at Barksdale and it ran for two whole years, a phenomenal amount of time. The fact that long runs could happen here was a good sign. Richmond seemed a good place to jump into the regional theater movement.

"I don't want to run to New York. I want to stay in this area. I want to live in a city you can breathe in, one that has a lot of charm. We're really lucky to be as close as we are to Washington, D.C., to the mountains, to the beach. It's still a little too lethargic and we need to take more risks. But I feel like I'm in an environment that's good for me professionally. I'd rather be a fish in a big pond and be challenged. Richmond is gaining that atmosphere. It's exciting. The vitality, energy, and talent are all here."

The Performing Arts Center at Virginia Commonwealth University is an active center of college theater.

6

SHOOTING THE
RECREATIONAL RAPIDS

WEARY OF THE HEAT OF summer and seeking a respite from hectic city living, Richmond residents in the nineteenth century discovered a bucolic retreat a short train trip from their homes. Known first as Brown's Summit, this Chesterfield County spot eventually became the resort of Bon Air, a community of vacation hideaways and genteel hotels a short distance from the cool waters of the James River. Visitors—far removed from the mechanized thrumming of the Industrial Revolution—could retire for a few days or a few weeks to more sedate surroundings for relaxation and recreation.

The Information Age has since brought with it a metamorphosis in notions of leisure—physical activity, for example, is currently seen by many modern-day recreationists as a virtue, not a vice—but recreation continues to matter. For Richmonders, the 1980s proved to be one abustle with diversions of every kind. It was, observers say, a departure from earlier times in the sheer quantity of available options alone.

"I remember how it was when I arrived in 1975. Really, there's no comparison," says Bernie Simmons, community affairs director for Richmond television station WWBT-12. Simmons reports and produces the channel's popular Monday-through-Friday feature, "12 About Town." "There are more things to do in the Richmond area than there have ever been. Around the early '80s it seemed that many different kinds of entertainment gathered impetus, and the impetus became infectious. Personally and professionally there are so many activities and projects in which individuals can involve themselves that there's absolutely no reason why *anyone* shouldn't find something in Richmond that will interest them."

White-water rafting on the James River is a must for outdoor enthusiasts, and the Richmond Rafting Company accomodates those with a flair for this exciting water sport.

From basketball and football to rugby and lacrosse, college athletics are an integral part of the dynamic Richmond sports scene.

Sports was the chief diversion in the 1980s for both fans and weekend athletes in the Richmond area. There were exciting professional tennis and golf matches to attend, pulse-pounding NASCAR and Winston-Cup series auto races to experience, marathons to run, and slow- and fast-pitch softball leagues in which to play. Fans of college sports could watch the University of Richmond Spiders football team battle opponents, see the VCU Rams basketball team go hoop-to-hoop with their adversaries, or watch Virginia Union and Virginia State sports teams take on each other and the nationally ranked CIAA competition. Soccer, rugby, karate, and lacrosse matches were held, and there was even an annual polo competition. In March 1990 Richmond welcomed a new professional hockey team, the Richmond Renegades of the East Coast Hockey League, to the area.

In 1988 Richmond-area baseball fans had something to cheer about when the area's very own professional baseball team, the Richmond Braves of the International League, moved into their brand-new baseball park, the Diamond. The $8-million facility, one of the most handsome ballparks of its size (12,500 seats and 300,000 yearly attendance) in the country, was the result of a concerted and highly successful fund-raising effort initiated by Richmond's business community.

By 1987, 34 swimming pools, 394 tennis courts, 130 playgrounds, 18 golf courses, and 661 outdoor playing fields had been set aside for public use within the metropolitan area. In their off-hours Richmonders could go hunting and camping, or fishing, boating, and white-water kayaking on the James. The great outdoors was made available to Richmonders in the form of more than 35,000 acres designated for recreational use in the greater metropolitan area. Of the total, Pocahontas State Park and Forest alone comprised 7,813 acres; within its boundaries are 43 miles of hiking and bicycling trails and opportunities for swimming, fishing, boating, and horseback riding.

Other facilities host major outdoor and indoor leisure-oriented activities. Dogwood Dell is in the former category—an open-air amphitheater located in Byrd Park where concerts, exhibitions, and plays are presented. In downtown the Richmond Coliseum, a 12,176-seat indoor domed structure, hosts stage shows and concerts, college and professional basketball, tennis exhibitions and matches, ice shows, circuses, trade shows, and professional wrestling matches. In addition, the Virginia State Fairgrounds in Henrico County is the

LEFT: More than 600 playing fields and playgrounds provide Richmond citizens with plenty of recreational outdoor opportunities.

BELOW: The area's very own professional AAA baseball team, the Richmond Braves, now play to enthusiastic crowds at the new $8-million Diamond ballpark, attracting more than 300,000 fans each season.

site of the annual fair of the same name, beginning in September. The fairgrounds' recently enlarged Richmond International Raceway remains Richmond's host for several major NASCAR events; the grounds also are the scene for motorcycle racing, horse shows, Richmond's famed Strawberry Hill Races, the Virginia State Horse Show, dog shows, home shows, van and four-wheel-drive shows, country music performances, and crafts exhibits.

Two-wheel drive sprinted into Richmond in a big way in 1989 with the arrival of a leg of the Tour de Trump. A 10-day, 837-mile cycling contest named in honor of flamboyant New York real-estate mogul Donald Trump, the Tour brought hundreds of professional cyclists—as well as national media attention—into Richmond. In years to come the Tour de Trump promises to remain one of the premiere events on the professional cycling circuit.

In the 1980s—as the largest segment of the American population, the so-called "baby boomers," began to age and prosper—the biggest recreational trend in Richmond, as throughout the United States, was a preoccupation with and desire for fitness-related activities.

"There weren't 'fitness' clubs before the '80s; they were health clubs," says Lorna Wychoff, publisher of *Style Weekly* magazine. "Biking, walking, swimming and river activities: they were always popular, but in the '80s they became even more so as the baby boomers came of age. Two-career boomer couples are working more, not less, and there's more affluence, more hunger for new experience. The baby boomers insist on fun and experience, but they also

The exhilaration of a steeplechase plus a warm and gracious ambiance has helped to transform the Strawberry Hill Races into a traditional springtime event.

insist on convenience. To fill that need there's been a substantial increase in the number of activities and the organizations or companies that coordinate those activities."

After-hours entertainment increased in the 1980s with the emergence of Shockoe Slip as a center of Richmond-area nightlife. There were restaurants, musical entertainment, places to see and be seen, and one other thing: laughter. Comedy was suddenly king for a number of people in Richmond.

"Comedy had a resurgence in the late '70s. All of a sudden people said, 'Hey, we need a break: We need to laugh,'" says Garet Chester, a long-time Richmond resident, former stand-up comic, and local radio and television personality. "Richmond was a good town because it was starved for that kind of entertainment. Comics that played the whole East Coast said that Richmond was a great audience. In fact, Richmond even spawned a few good comedians who've now gone on the national circuit."

For native Richmonders, the abundance of entertainment was as welcome as it was unprecedented. Whether one's tastes ran to kayaking or concertizing, the 1980s was a time of almost bewildering variety.

"Richmond's social life was essentially nonexistent until about 12 or so years ago," says Donne Storino, a Richmond native and high-school English teacher. "If you wanted a social life, you had to belong to one of the old social cliques. There was very little for young people to do. There was no nightlife to speak of. Now there's definitely one. I also know that every weekend there will be something to do. In fact, there's so much to do that I'm lost—I need [an entertainment] guide to my own city."

OF FESTIVALS AND FAIRS   Of all the things that Richmonders do to amuse themselves during their nonworking hours, attending large-scale events is among the most popular. As elsewhere, the discovery of the last decade in the Richmond area was of the fun to be had at fairs and festivals.

"Festivals are very important to an area. These days everything has the word 'festival' on the beginning or end of it," contends the Arts Council's Adrienne Hines. "The public's looking for it. It's affordable and it's fun without the reputation of being threatening. 'Festival' sounds more accessible and entertaining; it's not a heavy dose of education. Festivals are real sexy.

"Richmond-area residents are like residents anywhere else: They want to get out and see who's there. They want to get together, rub shoulders, and celebrate who and what they are."

The granddaddy of Richmond's outdoor music festivals is June Jubilee, which celebrated its 15th anniversary in June 1990. Brainchild of the Arts Council of Richmond, the Jubilee is a celebration of art, music, and popular culture. Every June thousands of Richmonders flock together for a weekend celebration of cultural vitality and diversity. That it has become a virtual institution in such a short period of time attests to Richmonders' pride in and support of their community.

In 1986 the Arts Council has also introduced the Children's Festival to Richmond. The Festival celebrates the presence in the lives of children of art, reading, dance, music, story-telling, and theater, presenting its assorted events in ways specifically intended to excite a child's imagination. According to the Arts Council, the Children's Festival has gone on to become the best of its kind in the United States. The council is regularly deluged with requests from across the country and internationally on how to go about organizing such an event.

Ten days and 837 miles comprise the new Tour de Trump cycling race, which blew into Richmond in 1989, attracting hundreds of professional cyclists and national media attention when one leg of the course raced through the city.

There is an abundance of other festivals as well. Arts in the Park, sponsored by the Carillon Civic Association, brings out Richmonders by the thousands for more than three decades to see fine arts and handsome crafts. The Strawberry Faire, the Chesterfield County Fair, the Great Pumpkin Festival, the Great James River Bateau Race, Richmond's Delicious Weekend International Festival, various parades, and a number of smaller taste fests, food festi-

vals, and crafts fairs complete the fairs-and-festivals ensemble.

Two landmark smaller-scale festivals developed during the 1980s are Friday Cheers, sponsored by Downtown Presents, and Jumpin' in July at the Virginia Museum. Both cater to the professional crowd eager to unwind after a hard day or hard week at work, and both are places where the young in particular can go to hob-nob and socialize, listen to music, nibble on snacks and sip favorite beverages. WWBT's Simmons refers to both as "nosh 'n talk" events.

"From the very beginning there were two very successful events: Jumpin' in July and Friday Cheers," Simmons says. "Both drew a group of people who hithertofore had not frequently congregated together. Those two events let the community know there are people out there who have disposable income and who want a good time."

Garet Chester, whose radio work sometimes led to master-of-ceremonies duty at Friday Cheers, agrees that festival-like happenings are a good thing. Such happenings, along with similar events that proliferated in the 1980s in Richmond, confirm his opinion that the area has few quality-of-life equals. "The Richmond area is just a great place to live. Every week I meet at least one person who's moved here and has lived in a number of other places. They move to Richmond and they want to stay here. This is the last move for a lot of people. To me that says something."

ABOVE: A quiet afternoon of sailing along the waters of the Swift Creek Reservoir rejuvenates the mind and spirit.

FACING PAGE: One of the more popular athletic competitions in recent years has been the Richmond Newspapers Marathon—a challenging and inspiring event that attracts hundreds of devoted runners every October.

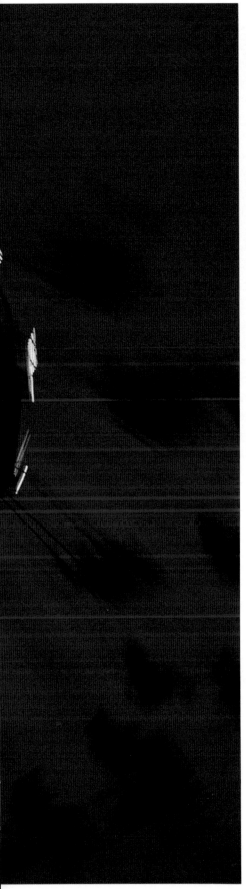

ABOVE: Since its inception in 1976, June Jubilee has evolved into a week-long summertime extravaganza of arts, music, and culture. Established by the nonprofit Arts Council of Richmond, this festival features star-studded performances, arts and crafts displays, delicious foods, and engaging activities for children.

LEFT: Thrilling rides, intriguing exhibits, and challenging games of skill abound at the Virginia State Fair, which is held each year at the State Fairgrounds in Henrico County.

DOWN BY THE RIVER   The James River runs more than through the literal heart of Richmond. It also plays a potent role as unifying symbol, linking counties to city, commuters to commerce, and leisure to life-style. Its very appearance, evocative almost of human moods—deep brown in times of heavy spring rain, blue and dazzling on clear winter days, languid and smooth in the heat of summer—is a subliminal reminder that there is more to the James, and thus to Richmond, than meets the casual eye. It is appropriate, then, that Richmonders appear to be headed back down to the river.

"It is dawning on us now that the riverfront is a marvelous recreational and—in the nicest sense of the word—a commercial area," says Mary Tyler Cheek, a prominent Richmond resident active in the arts and civic affairs. "It is one of our unrealized, undeveloped assets. Belle Isle is a priceless recreational area. And the canal, when it is reopened, will be a delight."

Cheek refers to preliminary efforts under way to reconstruct a portion of the James River and Kanawha Canal system (the original version was navigable for about 200 miles, all the way to Buchanan County in Southwest Virginia). Advocates, including the Historic Richmond Foundation and Richmond Renaissance, would like to see a reconstructed canal running a mile and a half from downtown Richmond upriver to Maymont Park, a former nineteenth-century estate that is now a city park and animal preserve. Eventually, shallow-bottomed bateaux may again ply a part of the same water route they did more than a century earlier, carrying modern-day sightseers on new voyages of discovery.

"The James River is a tremendous resource. Riverfront development would give the city an identity that will resonate with citizens and visitors alike," says attorney Robert Burrus. "It's a very important undertaking. People want to see things they can't see anywhere else. In my opinion, the opening and development of the riverfront will happen."

"Riverfront development is inevitable," agrees Adrienne Hines. "The reason it will happen is because people and corporations are willing to share their money to make sure it will happen. That it will be accessible to the public is also inevitable. But it will be slow going. First you need appropriate facilities. The amenities just aren't there yet."

Riverfront redevelopment would not be limited to those catching a slow boat to Maymont. There is every indication that improvements will continue on Brown and Belle islands, making them even more attractive as recreation

BELOW: In the lush surroundings of Byrd Park, the delightful Arts in the Park festival features the fine works of local artists and craftsmen.

FACING PAGE: Produced by Barnstormers Airshows, the annual Virginia State Balloon Championship sails over the Richmond countryside from its starting point at Hanover Airport.

The magnificent James River is an inviting location for a host of waterside activities in James River Park, along with a range of boating activities that include canoeing, kayaking, and white-water rafting.

FACING PAGE: A radiant sun casts its warm glow over the languid James River—a vital and endearing cornerstone of life in Richmond.

LEFT: More than 25 public and private golf courses dot the metropolitan landscape of Richmond.

BELOW: The spectacular Richmond countryside affords the chance to get out from under the hustle and bustle of mainstream city life to enjoy a quiet horseback ride through the handsome scenery of the area's rural lands.

destinations. More ambitious planning is already under way, and could eventually involve the complete transformation of the downtown expanse fronting the James River into an area of parks, dwellings, shops, stores and exhibits.

In the immediate future, the Valentine Museum intends to construct a complex on near-riverfront property provided by the Ethyl Corporation. Director Frank Jewell says that the new structure will house important artifacts and exhibits bearing directly on Richmond's history and development as a river city. Jewell, however, feels the Valentine's latest venture will have an impact beyond social or urban history. He says his museum's presence could well be the spark that ignites future riverfront development.

FACING PAGE: Byrd Park's 300 acres of rolling hills, wooded trails, and scenic lakes have created a central focus of outdoor fun and recreation in the heart of the city.

"We're the anchor tenant of development directly on the James River. That's a very traditional role for arts and cultural organizations in reclaiming American urban areas. This investment is going to make it more attractive for commercial dollars to follow. To some extent, it will also flip the balance in the feeling for the riverfront; it will transform an area now empty of people into [one] full of people. We'll be a magnet for further development."

The downtown portion of the James is not the only part of Richmond that is being rediscovered. So too is Jackson Ward, for decades the center of black cultural and community life in Richmond. Its renovation in coming years will affirm the primacy of black involvement in the history of Richmond and underscore the gains made in biracial cooperation and participation.

As the twentieth century ends, Richmond in one sense has readied herself for a leap back to the

future—an appreciation of the best of the past and a clearer vision of the challenges of decades yet to come. Redoing the river's edge is one step in the process, as is the restoration of Jackson Ward. A generation hence Richmond residents, black and white, may crowd into Jackson Ward jazz clubs or regularly come down to the James to gaze, as the German traveler Dr. Johann Schopf did in 1783, "on one of the greatest and most beautiful of American streams." That the Richmond of the year 2000 will be a different Richmond there is little doubt; it will be one built upon the efforts of the dedicated people who labored in the 1980s to make the area the best possible place to work and live.

ABOVE: An active and healthy style of living is a top priority for most Richmond residents and the broad assortment of the recreational opportunities and facilities available helps them to achieve this important goal.

In recent years, the vibrant economy of Richmond has exploded into a flurry of activity for the city's commercial and industrial sectors.

7

NETWORKS

RICHMOND'S ENERGY, COMMUNICATION, and transportation providers keep power, information, and products circulating inside and outside the area.

Photo courtesy, Henley & Savage

PORT OF RICHMOND

OCEAN FREIGHTERS ARRIVE at and depart from the Port of Richmond Terminal (PORT) daily. They are loaded with products bound to and from Virginia and her neighboring states. At the PORT, these hardworking ships receive the efficient, cost-effective handling that has earned this Virginia facility an impressive international reputation as a port alternative.

Richmond, with its location at the fall line of the James River, has always hosted an active waterfront. Since PORT was established, its combination of easy access to Virginia and the mid-Atlantic area has attracted countless oceangoing vessels.

Richmond's network of arterial highways (including Interstate 95 and Interstate 64), outstanding rail-cargo service provided by CSX, and the rapid growth and development of Richmond International Airport have heightened its natural advantages. They have helped transform the PORT into a key transportation and distribution hub.

The harbor handles a wide variety of products: synthetics and chemicals, paper, tobacco and tobacco products, lumber, cocoa beans, rubber, copper, steel, aluminum and scrap metal, machinery and rolling stock, alcoholic beverages, and livestock. These and more are shipped by way of regularly scheduled container-line service to Europe and the Mediterranean and by break-bulk liner service to South America, West Africa, and the Red Sea.

Some of the world's most famous corporations ship their familiar products through the port at Richmond. They include Philip Morris, Du Pont, R.J. Reynolds, American Tobacco, Allied-Signal, Union Carbide, and Van Munching & Company, Inc., importer of Heineken beer.

The PORT has several unique advantageous features that are especially important. Personalized service and an outstanding labor force are two of those features. Stevedoring and terminal-operating employees are represented by the Teamsters Warehouse Employees Local No. 322. Service at the PORT has never been interrupted by strikes.

Over the past three years the terminal has increased its tonnage handling by more than 60 percent. To continue providing quality services for its growing list of international clients, PORT has undertaken

An aerial view of the Port of Richmond terminal. Its easy access to Virginia and the mid-Atlantic area has attracted countless oceangoing vessels.

several new projects. These include widening the channel between Richmond and Hopewell, extending the dock wall to accommodate larger vessels, expanding its warehouse capacity, and an innovative cross-channel lighting program to allow ships to sail the James River at night, facilitating a more rapid turnaround.

The Port of Richmond Terminal is owned by the City of Richmond and operated under the authority of the Port of Richmond Commission by Meehan Overseas Terminal, Ltd.

COMMONWEALTH GAS SERVICES, INC.

COMMONWEALTH GAS SERVICES, Inc., is Virginia's third-largest distributor of natural gas services. A unit of the Columbia Gas System, Commonwealth Gas provides safe, reliable service at competitive pricing to about 130,000 residential, commercial, and industrial customers.

Commonwealth delivers more than 39 billion cubic feet of clean, efficient natural gas each year through its more than 2,800 linear miles of pipeline. Its combined revenues from sales of natural gas and transportation services (delivery of gas owned by others) are more than $130 million per year. In 1989 Commonwealth invested $19 million in capital improvements. The value of its plant facilities now exceeds $150 million.

Commonwealth, headquartered in Chesterfield County, operates in 52 counties of central, Southside, and Tidewater Virginia, and west into the Shenandoah Valley. Its service is handled through three operating divisions: the northern region, based at Manassas and including the Culpeper, Warrenton, and Fredericksburg areas; the western region, based at Lynchburg and serving the Covington, Harrisonburg, Waynesboro, Buena Vista, Lexington, and Pearisburg areas; and the southern region, based at Portsmouth and including the Petersburg and Chesterfield County areas.

Commonwealth Gas boasts a long history. It represents a composite of several formerly independent entities with roots back to the decades preceding the Civil War. One of the original companies, the Petersburg and Hopewell Gas Co., began providing manufactured gas (produced from coal) to its customers in the mid-1840s, when its primary use was to provide gas lighting. In 1854 the Portsmouth Gas Co. was granted a franchise to provide manufactured gas to residents of Portsmouth. At about the same time, the Natural Gas Service Co. of Fredericksburg was formed.

Portsmouth Gas Co. was acquired by Commonwealth Gas Pipeline Corporation in 1950—the same year in which pipeline-delivered natural gas service was introduced in Virginia. Commonwealth Gas Distribution Corporation was formed in 1955 as a subsidiary of Common-

Commonwealth Gas Services' general office, at the Moorefield Park office complex in Chesterfield County, provides executive and staff support for the utility's residential, commercial, and industrial operations across Virginia.

wealth Gas Pipeline. It provided natural gas service to industrial customers in areas along the intrastate transmission line that were not served by other distributors. The distribution company eventually became part of Commonwealth Gas Services.

The pipeline company's distribution operations were further expanded with acquisitions of the Fredericksburg firm (1965) and the Petersburg and Hopewell company (1969).

In 1980 the companies came to be known as Commonwealth Gas Services, Inc., with headquarters in Richmond. In August 1981 Commonwealth merged with the Columbia Gas System. Columbia Gas of Virginia, which began in the western part of the state in 1931, was merged with Commonwealth Gas Services on January 1, 1989. Commonwealth acquired Lynchburg Gas later that year.

The firm has always provided energy for the state's growth. Now, in combination with Columbia's other gas-distribution properties in Virginia, Commonwealth is strengthening and streamlining its operations.

For the new decade and the new century, Commonwealth Gas Services, Inc., will be a vigorous contributor to the growth and economic development of Virginia.

CONTINENTAL CABLEVISION OF VIRGINIA

THE PROVIDER OF cable television services to the city of Richmond, Henrico, Hanover, Ashland, Goochland, as well as James City, and York Counties, Continental Cablevision has been serving Virginia residents since 1979. In central Virginia Continental Cablevision of Virginia serves 126,000 households.

Continental Cablevision's success in Virginia comes from focusing on the fundamentals of quality customer service and making sure each employee has the responsibility and

makes all of its operating decisions and sets all local policies."

"We're not here as speculators," says H.W. "Buzz" Goodall, senior vice president of Continental Cablevision and the chief operating officer of the Virginia region. "We're here for the long haul." Goodall is a past president of the Virginia Cable Television Association. He is also deeply involved in Richmond's civic affairs; he is president of Ronald McDonald House, and is active with the Metro Chamber and in regional educational affairs.

graphically mobile citizens—all excellent prospective subscribers for cable television service—from the city center to the surrounding counties.

Henrico County is one of the fast growing municipalities in Virginia. With 66,000 customers, the Henrico office faces a rigorous building schedule while delivering superior service to a demanding customer base.

The Williamsburg area offices are based in rapidly growing communities with highly upscale demograph-

authority to take action. This assures a high level of customer satisfaction. Continental's executives regard the "can-do" attitude of service-oriented employees as one of the company's most valuable assets.

Continental Cablevision is a Boston-based corporation with 10 operating regions serving 16 states. Continental is the largest privately held cable company in the world and the fourth largest overall.

Each of Continental's regions operates autonomously. "It's company policy to keep the decision-making process as close to the customer as possible," says Kenneth M. Dye, marketing director for Continental Cablevision of Virginia. "The local office

Satellite dishes at Continental's "headend" facility receive cable networks such as HBO, ESPN, and Cable News Network.

Continental Cablevision of Virginia operates through four independent cable systems, one serving the city of Richmond, one for Henrico County and adjacent communities and systems serving the counties of James City and York.

Each local system serves a distinct community with its own unique challenges. The city of Richmond, like many other urban centers throughout America, faces a relatively flat population curve and the continued movement of socially and geo-

ics. More than 85 percent of the potential households in this area are served. With their lower residential densities, the James City County and York County offices face unique needs to develop highly efficient building programs in order to meet profitability goals.

In part through The Subscriber Account Management (SAM) system, a computer system developed in house by Continental Cablevision of Virginia, Richmond has managed impressive subscriber growth even though no new homes have been added to the franchise in many years. With more than 40,000 customers, the Richmond office now serves about 45 percent of all homes in its

Continental's 300-foot tower allows clear reception of all local broadcast stations.

training and development, motivation and performance incentives, and internal communications) as on external (consumer-oriented) efforts.

All four local offices benefit from Continental Cablevision's commitment to experienced, homegrown management. Continental's vice presidents/ district managers average more than eight years of experience with the company. All are Virginia natives and committed to their communities.

Amos Hostetter is chairman of Continental Cablevision. He has built Continental into a company widely admired by analysts as a model for the industry. "It serves customers efficiently, it manages effectively, and it delivers steady profits to private investors and its owner/managers," says a spokesman for Dow Jones & Company, a former partner in the company.

Readers of CableVision magazine, a major industry publication, feel the same way. A recent survey ranked Continental Cablevision as the industry leader for quality of management, quality of service, quality of work environment, and community relations. "The product of Hostetter's efforts," concluded the magazine, "is Continental's reputation as the premier provider of cable television service."

"I once described my management philosophy as feeling that it's more important to recruit well than to manage well," replies Hostetter. "You really get the best out of people when you make them understand that their fate is in their own hands—that they control their destiny."

franchise area.

SAM delivers complete cable television data-base management services. In developing SAM software, designers paid special attention to features that personalize customer communications. Inquiry logging lets employees know about previous customer contacts, and a reminder facility encourages follow-up calls.

At the same time, local Continental Cablevision of Virginia management places as much emphasis on internal marketing tactics (employee

COLUMBIA GAS TRANSMISSION CORPORATION

THE COLUMBIA GAS System has served the Commonwealth of Virginia since the early 1930s, playing a vital role in providing clean-burning natural gas for use by Virginia's homes, industries, and businesses. In 1981 Commonwealth Gas Pipeline Corporation of Richmond became a member of the Columbia family. Nine years later Commonwealth Pipeline became a part of another Columbia System company, Columbia Gas Transmission Corporation.

As a leader in energy, Columbia Gas Transmission is providing the opportunity for the economic development and growth of the Richmond area and the entire Commonwealth of Virginia. The sustained economic expansion in Virginia and the increased use of natural gas for electric power generation already has created substantial new demands for natural gas

Columbia Transmission's Richmond marketing team stays in close contact with Virginia customers, informing them of changing market conditions and promoting the increased use of clean-burning natural gas.

throughout the central, South Side, and Tidewater areas. Columbia stands ready to meet these demands and has already committed $30.7 million in 1990 for natural gas facilities.

Columbia Gas Transmission sells and transports natural gas to affiliated and nonaffiliated customers through a 20,000-mile pipeline network that services parts of 13 northeastern, mid-Atlantic, midwestern, and southern states and the District of Columbia. Approximately 1,200 miles of underground natural gas pipeline are in Virginia, and Columbia Transmission's six Virginia

distribution customers serve 391,000 homes, businesses, and industries in the commonwealth. Systemwide, Columbia Transmission ultimately serves more than 5.6 million residential, commercial, and industrial natural gas consumers.

Because natural gas is the cleanest burning fossil fuel and emits virtually no sulfur dioxide or particulate matter, major components of air pollution, Columbia Transmission's customers can take advantage of increasing opportunities for its use in the 1990s and beyond as more industries strive to meet federal and state air quality standards.

Columbia Gas has been a good corporate citizen in Virginia for a half-century, and Columbia Gas Transmission Corporation continues that tradition as an environmentally concerned partner in economic development and progress.

VIRGINIA POWER

VIRGINIA POWER HAS been part of Richmond and its growth for more than a century. In 1888 a small, new company completed construction of Richmond's first electric street-trolley system—the first successful system of its type in the nation.

That company, now known as Virginia Power, remains a national leader—the nation's 11th-largest electric utility—and clearly out in front in a dynamic industry responding to increasingly competitive forces.

Like the city of Richmond itself, Virginia Power at first relied heavily on the James River, which powered its first generating stations. (One of those early hydroelectric stations, now retired from service, stands near the center of today's downtown.)

Although the hydroelectric stations are gone, the river continues to provide cooling waters for Virginia Power's largest coal-fired power station, just south of Richmond, and one of its two nuclear generating stations.

Today Virginia Power, still headquartered in Richmond, serves more than 1.7 million customers in a 30,000-square-mile area covering most of Virginia and northeastern North Carolina. Virginia Power has 29 major generating units using a wide variety of fuels. About 80 percent of its energy comes from economical nuclear and coal units. The system can provide its customers with well over 13 million kilowatts of power.

The company distributes electricity through more than 42,000 miles of above-ground power lines and another 16,000 miles of buried cable. In the 1980s Virginia Power sales rose almost 40 percent, to more than 53 billion kilowatt-hours per year. The strong economy of the firm's market area is expected to continue attracting new businesses, new industries, and new jobs—producing ever-increasing demands on company facilities.

Virginia Power has adopted a strategy of building new power stations only after trying to obtain more economical power from outside suppliers. The company actively encourages customers to conserve energy. It offers residential and commercial programs that provide financial incentives promoting wise energy management to reduce peak demands.

Virginia Power is organized into five geographic divisions and 39 districts. Four districts serve the Richmond metropolitan area and provide local customer and emergency service.

The firm and its employees have long played an active role in

Virginia Power is the nation's 11th-largest electric utility and serves more than 1.7 million customers.

Richmond's civic and charitable life. It has an employee volunteer program that responds to community needs with volunteers, equipment, and money—and has been repeatedly cited as among the best such corporate programs in the United States.

Virginia Power also established and supports the EnergyShare fuel-assistance program. This program provides assistance to those needing coal, oil, gas, wood, or electricity to stay warm—and who have no place else to go for help.

Virginia Power employees participate in these and many other programs, on the job and off, as part of a constant effort to improve the quality of life in the communities the company serves.

WRIC-TV

TV8, Richmond's ABC television network affiliate, has just completed a metamorphosis. The station's new life is symbolized by its new identity. It has a new name, WRIC-TV, and striking new studios at the Arboretum, just across the Richmond city limit in Chesterfield County.

TV8's new home is a state-of-the-art facility housing the station's entire operation. The 34,500-square-foot structure contains two production studios, computerized editing facilities, and new offices for the entire TV8 staff.

Part of the new TV8 is the station's new name. Licensed to Petersburg, Virginia, in 1955 as WXEX, TV8's new call letters became official in April 1990. The change reflects the station's evolution and growth in its

ABOVE: The WRIC-TV studios, located in the Arboretum at the intersection of Midlothian Turnpike and the Powhite Parkway.

BELOW: The Eyewitness News room.

central Virginia market.

TV8's Eyewitness News has become an award-winning operation honored by the Virginia Associated Press Broadcasters and the Radio and Television News Directors' Association. Professional excellence, coupled

WRIC-TV's new studios were designed by Rees Associates Inc., architects specializing in broadcast facilities.

Building on a 35-year tradition of serving central Virginia, WRIC-TV supports dozens of nonprofit efforts. These include the TV8/Jerry Lewis Labor Day Telethon benefiting the Muscular Dystrophy Association, the UNCF Telethon, and the March Of Dimes' annual WalkAmerica.

TV8 continues to support the United Way, the Arts Council of Richmond, literacy efforts throughout the city and the state, and a myriad of public and private initiatives dedicated to the community. In fact, WRIC-TV formally dedicated its new facilities to the thousands of caring volunteers who work countless hours for the community.

The management and staff of WRIC-TV8 greet the 1990s with anticipation and a mission: to be the leading television station serving the Richmond market by providing distinctive, innovative news, information, and entertainment programming. It is the goal of each WRIC-TV staff member to achieve that objective.

with news programming innovations, have made the TV8 Eyewitness News operation a dynamic force throughout the Richmond metropolitan area.

In-depth news series, compelling investigative reports, and an intense commitment to community issues have gained Eyewitness News industry acclaim. Innovations such as "Eleven At 11p.m." and "Eyewitness News on the Hour" (local hourly news updates that air throughout the day) have set new standards in news programming in the Richmond market. "TV8 Town Meetings," telecast quarterly, have brought viewers a better awareness of community issues.

The new on-air look of WRIC-TV8.

WRVA RADIO

"IT IS OUR desire to render service to Richmond and Virginia," said William T. Reed, president of Larus and Brother Company, the original owners of WRVA Radio. The occasion was WRVA's first day of broadcasting, November 2, 1925.

Now, as then, service and com-

L.G. "Bob" Jones, vice president and general manager of WRVA.

munity involvement continue to be WRVA Radio's commitment to its listeners and its region. Richmond-area residents know that for the best in live radio broadcasting and the most complete, up-to-the-minute news reports, they should keep their radios tuned to 1140 on the AM dial.

The WRVA offices and studios sit atop Church Hill, overlooking the city of Richmond. The strikingly modern complex is an architectural monument designed by Phillip Johnson. Virginia's only 50,000-watt clear-channel station, WRVA has been a broadcasting pioneer throughout its history.

WRVA was the first in the region to adopt helicopter traffic reports, which it inaugurated more than 25 years ago, and is the only station offering such a service today. As the city has grown, so has that service. Recently the station switched to a jet-powered helicopter to keep up with the mushrooming development of greater Richmond's highway network.

Since 1940 all of central Virginia's schools have depended on WRVA's specially coded school

Designed by Phillip Johnson, the office and studio complex of WRVA has become an award-winning Richmond landmark.

closing announcements during severe weather conditions. Leading businesses in the area also depend on this critical service.

WRVA operates 24 hours per day and maintains Virginia's largest radio news staff. Satellite connections link the station to the CBS Radio Network, Associated Press, United Press International, and the National Weather Service.

Guests at WRVA are often

Satellite communications link WRVA with its network and news sources.

amazed to see one entire wall of the reception area covered with plaques and certificates. WRVA News has won more news and public service awards than any other station in Virginia, including three coveted Douglas Southall Freeman awards for public service through radio journalism. WRVA News has also received the highest national news awards from the Society of Professional Journalists and the Radio Television News Director's Association.

WRVA's support for community activities is beyond compare, as exemplified by the WRVA Salvation Army

Shoe Fund. Since its inception in 1968, the Shoe Fund has raised more than $2.674 million for shoes for needy children.

The station is also an active supporter of Maymont Park's Adopt-a-Living-Thing, the restoration of the Byrd Park Carillon, Children's Hospital, and many other community activities. The management and staff of WRVA all take deep pride in the station's reputation as a leader in Richmond community involvement.

WRVA's present owner, Edens Broadcasting Company, one of the nation's leading broadcast groups, continues WRVA's service to the community under the leadership of L.G. "Bob" Jones, WRVA Radio's vice president and general manager since 1981.

BELOW: The Salvation Army Shoe Fund is one of WRVA's favorite causes.

8

MANUFACTURING

PRODUCING AND DISTRIBUTING goods for individuals and industry, manufacturing firms provide employment for Richmond-area residents.

Photo courtesy, Henley & Savage

ROBERTSHAW CONTROLS COMPANY

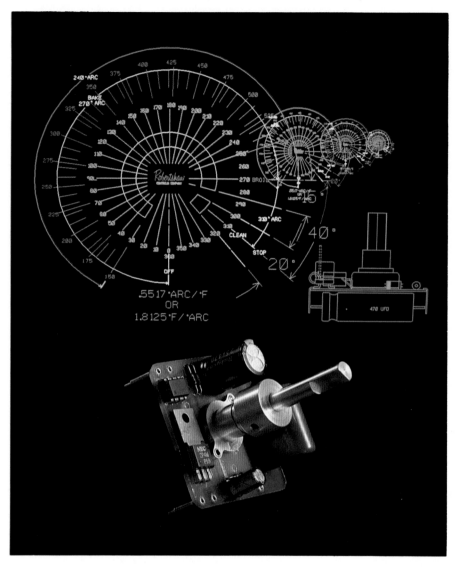

Robertshaw focuses a great deal of energy on its research and development departments, finding new ways to use its technology throughout the world.

TODAY IT SEEMS so logical and simple. Set the temperature on the hot water heater and the water will be the desired temperature. But a century ago, things were not that simple. It took the innovative genius of Frederick W. Robertshaw to invent the mechanism that would regulate the precise amount of gas flowing into the gas heater so the water would never be too hot or too cold.

What Frederick Robertshaw had invented was the hot water thermostat. And the concept of the thermostat was destined to become one of the world's most technologically sophisticated systems for controlling energy.

It has been that same ingenuity and logic, coupled with a dedication to progress and a desire for excellence and innovation, that has made Robertshaw Controls Company a global leader in the manufacture of automatic controls and control systems for industry, commercial buildings, and the home. The firm held more than 400 patents in 1947; today that figure exceeds 2,250.

Domination of the world's controls market began in 1907, in Pittsburgh, Pennsylvania, when demand for the efficient and convenient water-heater thermostat became so great that Frederick Robertshaw formed House Service Utilities Manufacturing Company to market the device. Seven years later the booming plumbing supplies firm moved to Youngwood, Pennsylvania, and that same year changed its name to Robertshaw Manufacturing Company.

Now that temperatures could be controlled automatically, the manufacturers of gas ranges were quick to exploit this extraordinary capability and commissioned Robertshaw to develop a temperature control for gas ranges. By 1922 the firm decided to concentrate solely on thermostats, and that same year it began its successful lifetime alliance with the gas-range industry.

It did not take long for the innovative and thriving thermostat company to come to the attention of another of America's famous entrepreneurs, Richard S. Reynolds. Reynolds Metal Company acquired Robertshaw in 1928 as an independent subsidiary and soon added to its prospering conglomerate the Knoxville, Tennessee, Fulton Sylphon Company, developer of the first bellows for use in water heating systems. In the mid-1930s Grayson Heat Control Limited, a successful California manufacturer of control devices, was acquired by Robertshaw Thermostat.

The energy control industry was now truly coast to coast. The three independent companies continued to expand, innovate, prosper, and meet the energy control needs of an enterprising country.

By 1946 Robertshaw began streamlining and consolidating the companies and production facilities it had acquired for its expanding line of temperature controls for electric appliances.

That spirit of innovation carried the firm successfully into the 1950s, when an international department was formed to coordinate sales to a rapidly expanding worldwide market. In 1957 Robertshaw moved its headquarters to Richmond, and a year later changed its name to Robertshaw Controls Company.

Throughout the next two decades the company effectively

expanded its operations into the temperature control markets for homes and commercial buildings. It developed and marketed a highly sophisticated line of room status and control systems for hotels, motels, and hospitals. And when specialized electronic control devices became essential to the aviation and aerospace industries, the company set up an instrumentation division. In the 1980s the firm continued to make substantial investments for new machinery and tooling to assure its future growth with further expansion planned for the 1990s.

As a man of vision, innovation, and dedication, Frederick W. Robertshaw probably would not be surprised that his company now sets the standards for excellence in the controls industry and manufactures more than 10,000 products—or amazed that his company now owns and operates more than 30 manufacturing sites nationwide and that his subsidiaries and affiliates can now be found in many countries spanning four continents.

Robertshaw Controls is proud to be the quiet giant that supplies the technology to some of the world's largest original equipment manufacturers and aftermarkets.

From Maytag to K mart, General Electric to General Motors, Bradford White to Burke Engineering, plus

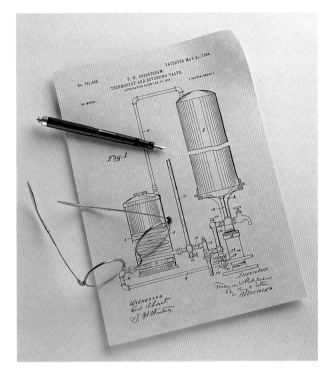

Nearly 100 years ago Frederick W. Robertshaw invented the thermostat. Since then, Robertshaw Controls Company has been a world leader in the controls market, with more than 2,250 patented inventions in force.

thousands of other businesses, the company's marketing groups and manufacturing divisions are organized to custom tailor some of the world's most innovative electronic controls for their customers. Plus, Robertshaw's

CompAir Kellogg Manufacturing and Marketing Group, which offers reciprocating, rotary screw, and oil-free rotary compressors complements an already impressive array of organizations designed to better serve the engineering market.

With a new emphasis on consumer products, Robertshaw markets top burner and oven elements for ranges, timers, and thermostats to D-I-Y retail outlets. Since 1981 the firm has focused investment and effort on the expansion of its consumer products division, achieving a more direct, higher profile image with the public.

In 1986 Reynolds Metals Company sold its ownership of Robertshaw Controls, and the firm was purchased by Siebe PLC, headquartered in the United Kingdom. The Siebe Group is one of the world's largest engineering companies and is known for innovative developments in everything from controls to automotive equipment to safety and life support systems.

Now part of a worldwide engineering company, Robertshaw Controls continues to produce and market its inventions worldwide. With one or more of the firm's products in nearly every American home and sales in excess of $500 million and a projected one billion dollars by 1994, it is no wonder that as Robertshaw Controls Company enters its second century, the spirit of invention is alive and well.

Robertshaw continues to develop new innovative products such as the HS780I, which combines the functions of two controls in one by uniting hot surface ignition with blower control.

E.I. DU PONT DE NEMOURS AND COMPANY, INC.

HISTORY OF THE E.I. du Pont de Nemours and Company, Inc., is deeply embedded in the history of America itself. Founded in 1802 to manufacture high-quality black powder for America's armed forces, Du Pont has become a global leader in chemicals, fibers, energy, pharmaceuticals, and high-technology products. The Wilmington, Delaware, headquartered company prides itself in being a leader in safety and environmental matters.

Du Pont first established its presence in metropolitan Richmond in 1927, when the Du Pont Rayon Company broke ground for a plant in Chesterfield County. Once the home of cellophane and rayon, Du Pont/Spruance now manufactures such space-age fibers as Tyvek®, Kevlar®, and Nomex®, along with Teflon® and industrial nylon.

Along the way, the plant has be-come one of metropolitan Richmond's largest employers and is among the region's most active corporate citizens and supporters. Each year employees pledge record amounts to the dozens of UGF member agencies—more than $375,000 in 1989—and the plant itself contributes more than $300,000 each year to a variety of other Virginia charitable organizations.

Du Pont/Spruance is located on ground that was once the Ampthill Plantation, formerly owned by the historic Cary family. In an early demonstration of the company's dedication to history and to the Richmond com-

The Du Pont/Spruance plant manufactures such space-age fibers as Tyvek®, Kevlar®, and Nomex®, along with Teflon® and industrial nylon. Pictured here is the water-treatment holding pond that is a home for various wildlife.

munity, Du Pont had the early eighteenth-century plantation mansion dismantled piece by piece and moved to a bluff overlooking the James River, where it is used as a private residence today.

Du Pont's Chesterfield County plant is named in honor of Colonel William Corbit Spruance, a former chairman of Du Pont's board of directors.

The plant opened in 1929, just months before the beginning of the Great Depression. Despite hard times, the plant survived, providing jobs for more than 2,750 Richmond residents. Among its first products was a remarkable new transparent packaging material called cellophane. The Du Pont Cellophane Company discovered a ready market for its new material in the area's tobacco industry, which found it to be an ideal wrapping for cigarette packages.

With the outbreak of World War II, Du Pont/Spruance became a key component of the war effort. Its cellophane was used to wrap K rations, its Cordura® went into military vehicle tires, and its rayon was used for everything from parachutes to clothing.

New products were added in later years. First popularized in the form of women's stockings, Du Pont's 1938 discovery of nylon would be among the most important finds of the twentieth-century materials revolution. Du Pont/Spruance began producing the new fiber in 1957. By the mid-1960s Chesterfield County had become known as the nylon capital of the world.

Du Pont/Spruance has manufactured a fiber form of Teflon® since 1953. It is used in advanced surgical procedures (two Du Pont/Spruance employees were among the first recipients of Teflon® arteries), and America's lunar astronauts wore 21-layer suits topped with the material. But most of the Teflon® made in Richmond has more down-to-earth applications. It is widely used in products such as high-temperature filters and non-lubricated bearings.

Commercial production of Nomex® began at Du Pont/ Spruance in 1967. Nomex® is the primary component of the familiar orange space suits now worn by space-shuttle astronauts. Tough and inherently resistant to heat and flame, Nomex® is extensively used to make protective clothing for fire fighters, race-car drivers, and military pilots. The paper form of Nomex® insulates electrical motors and transformers as well as serving as a lightweight submaterial for airplanes and boats.

Begun in 1967, the Tyvek® manufacturing plant at Du Pont/Spruance was the first new building constructed on the site since the 1930s. The slick, tear-resistant material is used to protect items of all sizes and shapes, from house covering to overnight express envelopes to floppy computer disk jackets. Because it produces no lint or dust, Tyvek® is used to make garments worn in hospitals and electronics-manufacturing plants, also known as "clean rooms." Because they protect wearers against asbestos fibers and most acids, Tyvek® garments are also used by hazardous-waste disposal crews.

Kevlar®, the newest of the Du Pont/Spruance fibers, is known worldwide for its strength. Kevlar® is five times stronger than steel on a pound for pound basis, making it popular for fiber optics, rope, and cables. It is also widely used in protective bullet-resistant vests, helmets, gloves, and in chaps for chain-saw operators. On the road, it is used in automobile tires. On the sea, it is used in boat hulls.

Mylar® is made at other Du Pont plants, then shipped to Spruance for a coating that makes Mylar® moisture proof, heat sealable, and printable. Mylar® is used in boil-in-bag packages, lids for frozen and microwave food trays, snack-food wrappings, and long-lasting, shiny helium balloons.

Today Du Pont/Spruance employs more than 3,300 area residents. It is the largest manufacturing operation in the Du Pont fibers department.

As a result of the dedicated, safe work by the Du Pont/Spruance employees, the plant remains a strong, healthy, and productive operation more than 60 years after it first opened. The plant's safety record remains extraordinary, and Du Pont/Spruance prides itself on the fact that it works to exceed environmental standards.

Du Pont/Spruance has ambitious plans for the future. The renowned Du Pont focus on quality is being augmented through electronic and statistical quality-control systems. This new standard has several facets at Du Pont/Spruance, including the quality leadership and total quality programs.

Always a customer-focused operation, E.I. du Pont de Nemours and Company, Inc., expects its client businesses to grow with increasing ties both to global commerce and sister manufacturing operations within the worldwide Du Pont family.

The marquee at the entrance of the plant displays a daily safety message.

ETHYL CORPORATION

BACK IN THE days when every gas station routinely provided full service to all customers, an entire generation of Americans grew up knowing that "Ethyl" was another name for "high-test" or premium gasoline. Ethyl meant high performance. Things may have changed at the gas pump, but for the petroleum, chemical, plastics, and other industries, Ethyl Corporation still means high performance and high technology.

The original Ethyl Gasoline Corporation was chartered in 1924, a joint creation of General Motors and Standard Oil Company of New Jersey. At the time, General Motors held the basic patents on tetraethyl lead as a gasoline antiknock additive. Standard Oil was a giant of the American oil industry. It was a natural combination.

On November 30, 1962, a more modern style of corporate combination, a friendly takeover, was consummated when the Albemarle Paper Manufacturing Company of Richmond acquired Ethyl Corporation (Delaware), creating Ethyl Corporation of Virginia.

Founded in 1887, Albemarle Paper was a highly respected but relatively small corporation with less than $50 million in assets. Albemarle paid

Ethyl Corporation's picturesque headquarters complex, overlooking the James River from Gamble's Hill, is a landmark against the skyline of downtown Richmond. The recently completed Pavilion Wing (left) complements the original building's Great Georgian architecture.

$200 million for Ethyl. "Jonah swallows the whale," wrote one commentary at the time. To Albemarle president Floyd Dewey Gottwald, it was simply a case of Albemarle "enlarging and diversifying" the company's business.

Gottwald became president of Albemarle in 1941, just as World War II brought a drop in company earnings. Worse still, a 1943 explosion at one of the firm's Richmond paper mills killed nine people, injured a dozen more, and seriously damaged the plant.

At the time, Gottwald considered liquidating Albemarle. Instead, he and his handpicked team of executives consolidated control of the company, repaired and reopened the plant, and undertook an extensive refinancing and expansion. In the mid-1950s Albemarle began acquiring other paper and paper-product manufacturers. By 1960 it had become a dominant force in the folding-box manufacturing industry.

In 1969 Ethyl sold its Richmond-based paper facilities to a group of employees who formed James River Corporation, today one of the world's largest papermakers. In 1976 it sold the last of its paper operations, ending Albemarle's 89-year history as a papermaker and ushering in a new era for Ethyl.

Ethyl purchased VisQueen Film and formed its Plastics Group in 1963, created an Aluminum Group in 1966, and initiated European chemical operations in 1967. Other

The Floyd Dewey Gottwald Memorial Award is given each year to Ethyl employees selected for outstanding achievement in quality improvement.

acquisitions led Ethyl into coal leasing and processing in 1974, lubricant additives in 1975, and agricultural chemicals in 1978. Ethyl acquired First Colony Life Insurance Company in 1982 and the bromine chemicals operations of Dow Chemical in 1987.

Floyd D. Gottwald, Jr., became chairman of the board in 1968 and chief executive officer two years later. He still holds those positions. In 1989 Ethyl Corporation sales and insurance revenues exceeded $2.4 billion. Net income was some $231 million.

In mid-1989 Ethyl spun off its Aluminum, Plastics, and Energy groups, forming a new company, Tredegar Industries, Inc. The new venture is headed by John D. Gottwald, formerly Ethyl's vice president/aluminum, plastics, and energy.

Ethyl's business segments consist of the Chemicals Group and First Colony Life. Another subsidiary, Whitby Pharmaceuticals, Inc., is developing the company's interests in pharmaceutical research and ethical pharmaceutical marketing and sales.

Quality has become the key word in Ethyl's approach to designing, manufacturing, and marketing all of its products. The Chemicals Group's internal quality-control program, EQIP™ (Ethyl Quality Improvement Process), has resulted in widespread industry praise, sole-supplier status from several corporate customers, and more than one million dollars in annual cost savings.

Similar efforts at First Colony have resulted in widespread implementation of new approaches and improvements generated by the

The product that created Ethyl, tetraethyl lead, is no longer used in most North American gasoline products. However, the firm markets another product, HiTEC® 3000 performance additive. HiTEC 3000 has been used in unleaded gasoline in Canada for a number of years and offers promising opportunities in other markets worldwide. The environmental benefits of HiTEC 3000 include its ability to reduce emissions of nitrogen oxides, prime contributions to ozone-depletion problems.

Other Ethyl Corporation products with widespread applications include rust inhibitors, fuel detergents, and cold-flow improvers for diesel fuels and heating oils; a wide range of additives for lubricating oils; agricultural chemical products; polysilicon for use in the semiconductor and related computer product industries; flame retardants; and specialty chemical products with specialized, highly critical industrial applications.

Products offered by First Colony Life Insurance include a comprehensive range of annuity-style products, annual premium universal life and other interest-sensitive plans, several term life insurance programs, and employee benefit plans. With nearly $50 billion of insurance in force and almost $5 billion in assets, First Colony is rated "A+" (Superior) by the A.M. Best Company, the nation's leading insurance company rating firm.

The combined businesses of Ethyl Corporation employ some 5,500 people at plants, research facilities, and offices worldwide.

employees. Results include significant improvements in processing efficiency and cost control.

In recognition of this company-wide emphasis on quality, Ethyl established the Floyd Dewey Gottwald Memorial Award for Achievement in Quality Improvement. Employees at Ethyl's Houston, Texas, and Magnolia, Arkansas, chemical plants were the first recipients of this annual award.

TREDEGAR INDUSTRIES

IT IS NOT often that a newly created corporation starts life among the *Fortune* 500, but that is exactly what happened on July 10, 1989, when Richmond's Ethyl Corporation spun off its plastics, aluminum, and energy groups to form Tredegar Industries.

Tredegar is named for the Richmond-based Tredegar Iron Works, the antebellum South's premier industry and the former "arsenal of the Confederacy." Ethyl Corporation now owns the old Tredegar property. The late Floyd D. Gottwald, retired chairman and founder of modern-day Ethyl, directed the historically accurate restoration and reconstruction of Tredegar's main foundry building. Tredegar Iron Works is included in the Virginia Landmarks Register and the National Register of Historic Places.

The former Ethyl divisions now comprising Tredegar had 1989 gross sales totaling $638 million. Tredegar Industries' new headquarters is located on Boulders Parkway in Chesterfield County. Its stock is traded on the New York Stock Exchange.

Tredegar's Film Products division manufacturers polyethylene films

Tredegar Industries came into being on July 10, 1989, when Richmond's Ethyl Corporation spun off its plastics, aluminum, and energy groups.

for disposable personal products as well as industrial, agricultural, and packaging applications. The Molded Products division is a major manufacturer of injection-molded plastic components for packaging, business machines, and beverage closure products. It also has a tooling group that produces injection molds for internal use and for sale to other custom molders.

The William L. Bonnell Company, Inc., is a full-service manufacturer of high-quality aluminum extrusions used in residential and commercial construction, transportation, consumer durables, and other markets. Tredegar's Capitol Products Corporation subsidiary manufactures windows and doors for new and replacement construction markets. Fiberlux, Inc., another Tredegar subsidiary, is a leading manufacturer of vinyl extrusions and fabricated vinyl windows and doors for new and replacement markets.

Tredegar owns 97 percent of The Elk Horn Coal Corporation, which owns mineral and surface rights to mine coal on approximately 133,000 acres in eastern Kentucky. Tredegar also explores for and produces oil and gas in Western Canada.

Tredegar employs approximately 5,000 people at its 35 plants and offices in the United States and in the Netherlands. John D. Gottwald is president and chief executive officer; Richard W. Goodrum is executive vice president and chief operating officer; and Norman A. Scher is executive vice president, chief financial officer, and treasurer of Tredegar Industries.

ALFA-LAVAL THERMAL, INC.

MOST RICHMOND RESIDENTS may not know what a plate heat exchanger is or what a combination cross and spiral flow heat exchanger does, but they are starting to learn a lot about Alfa-Laval Thermal, Inc., the company that makes them. A manufacturing firm founded in 1883, Alfa-Laval supplies components and systems to dairy farmers, chemical processors, and other industries worldwide. Headquartered in Stockholm, Sweden, Alfa-Laval AB employs 16,000 people in 40 countries.

Alfa-Laval Thermal is the world's largest supplier of heat transfer equipment. It has an enviable international reputation for excellence in engineering and high-quality manufacturing. Its spiral and plate heat exchangers are the dominant products in the industry.

With its 1989 decision to relocate and consolidate its Fort Lee, New Jersey, Houston, Texas, and Poughkeepsie, New York, operations to Richmond, Alfa-Laval Thermal, Inc., became one of Virginia's leading industrial citizens. The company will base its headquarters at its new facility and will manufacture heat exchangers for the chemical, petrochemical, pulp and paper, HVAC (heating, ventilating, and air conditioning), oil and gas, wastewater treatment, and pharmaceutical industries.

The parent company has achieved an impressive record of commercial success. During the past five years its return on invested capital has averaged well over 20 percent, with sales increasing rapidly in the United States, Japan, and West Germany. Alfa-Laval holds a 10 percent share of the total world market for heat exchangers. With the help of the new Richmond facility, the firm plans to double its market penetration over the next few years.

Alfa-Laval's new 17-acre site is located in the International Business Park near Richmond International Airport. The office complex will be a two-story building designed to house 70 to 80 people. A one-story cafeteria building will connect the offices to the workshop. In all, the new thermal center will hold 90 to 100 employees, with ample room for building expansion on the premises.

Alfa-Laval Thermal, Inc., was attracted to Richmond by the "area's stable economy, proximity to major seaports for future exports and imports, efficient infrastructure, and charming and cultural heritage that will enable the company to attract and retain the best employees," says Kirk Spitzer, president of Alfa-Laval Thermal.

"Now we'll be able to produce the value-added portion of the plate heat exchanger product line domestically. This will translate into even better service and quicker delivery for our customers. We are quite confident that our long-term commitment to our customers is reinforced by this decision."

Construction of the Richmond facility is scheduled to be completed by mid-1990, with production start-up scheduled for the third quarter of 1990,

The world's leading companies for industrial applications in chemicals, pulp and paper, refining, pharmaceuticals, commercial heating, ventilating, air conditioning, and refrigeration use Alfa-Laval Thermal's heat exchangers. This photo shows a spiral heat exchanger (left) and a plate heat exchanger (right).

Alfa-Laval Thermal, Inc., employees.

WESTVACO

WHEN THE WILDLIFE Federation and Virginia Department of Game and Inland Fisheries needed a special box to assist with wild turkey relocation and stocking programs, they turned to Westvaco and its Container Division in Richmond. The plant is known nationwide for its ability to manufacture corrugated boxes and other forms of corrugated packaging that precisely fit customers' most demanding specifications.

Founded in 1888 as the West Virginia Pulp and Paper Company, Westvaco manufactures a broad range of high-quality papers used for graphic reproduction, communications, and packaging. The firm is also a major manufacturer of consumer and industrial packaging, and one of the largest producers of envelopes in the world.

Westvaco is a *Fortune* 200 company, with 15,000 employees and 1.5 million acres of forest. Westvaco's Bleached Board Division is among the world's major producers of quality solid bleached sulfate carton board. The division's primary product, Printkote®, is generally regarded as the standard of excellence in the packaging field.

With domestic operations in 25 states and Washington, D.C., Westvaco has a combined investment of $1.3 billion in its Virginia facilities. In 1989 Westvaco announced the investment of another $537 million for the construction of a large new paper machine and related equipment at its Covington, Virginia, mill.

Originally Westvaco was attracted to the Commonwealth by geographic factors such as its proximity to raw materials and prospective customers. Today the Commonwealth's favorable business climate and forward-looking relationship between state government and Virginia business foster the company's continued investment.

Westvaco facilities in Richmond include Folding Carton Division plants on Hull Street and on Cofer Road, the Flexpak Pre-printed Linerboard Facility on Cofer Road, the Liquid Packaging Division plant on

Cofer Road, and the Container Division plant on Jeff Davis Highway.

Bleached Board's Folding Carton Division operations produce high-quality printed cartons for many of the best known packaged products in America. The plants in Richmond are among the largest gravure carton printing operations in the world. High-speed gravure presses with up to eight-color capability efficiently produce cartons with a high degree of print and structural uniformity. Printed cartons made by Westvaco in Richmond are used to package cigarettes, pharmaceuticals, fast foods, detergents, cosmetics, frozen foods, and many other fine retail products.

In operation only since 1985, the Westvaco Flexpak facility was among the first packaging manufacturers in the United States to produce pre-printed linerboard with high-quality graphics. Flexography is a cost-effective, high-quality, high-speed, multicolor process used to print high-quality designs on flexible materials.

Westvaco Flexpak produces large-scale flexographic products that can be used in the manufacture of corrugated containers requiring high-quality printed graphics. Containers of this type are used for point-of- purchase displays; shipper displays; cartons for refrigerators, televisions, and other large appliances; and shipping containers for industries producing beverages, agricultural chemicals, personal care products, and a multitude

Westvaco's Folding Carton Division plants in Richmond produce high-quality printed paperboard packaging for a variety of fine retail products.

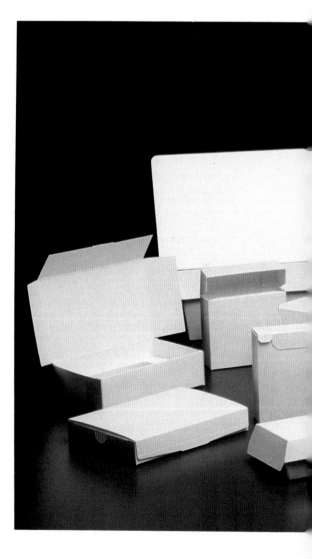

of other consumer products.

Westvaco's Richmond-based Liquid Packaging Division uses high-speed web offset and flexographic printing to produce cartons for milk and a variety of other products such as juice, cream, and similar consumables. Employing sophisticated barrier technology, unique carton configurations, and recloseable pour spouts with screw-on caps, the Liquid Packaging Division plant has expanded its conventional milk-carton business to encompass a wide range of enhanced liquid packaging applications in various national markets, spanning such diverse products as liquid detergents, salad oils, premium juices, liquid coffee, sports drinks, and wine.

The plant also makes flexographically printed custom-designed folding cartons for bakeries, fast-food operations, and institutional foods packagers.

One of Westvaco's Container Division's 10 corrugated box plants is located in Richmond. The Container Division manufactures corrugated boxes and related products. Originally built more than 40 years ago, the Richmond plant has been modernized and equipped with the latest generation of machinery.

In Richmond, the Container Division designs and produces corrugated packaging to transport thousands of consumer and industrial products. Westvaco's Richmond Container Plant and other printing and converting operations in Richmond offer packaging customers a wide range of innovative and differentiated products and services. It can even offer highly specialized custom modifications such as curtain coating and wax impregnating to make moisture-resistant, scuff-resistant, skid-proof, grease-resistant, and even fire-retardant boxes. Some of the products shipped in Westvaco corrugated containers include dynamite, powdered acid, live lobsters, and take-out pizza. Items packaged in Westvaco containers made in Richmond include food, beverages, paper, furniture, and large appliances.

All of the paperboard printed and converted by Westvaco's Folding Carton Division in Richmond is manufactured at the firm's Bleached Board Mill in Covington, Virginia. Located at the center of one of the largest hardwood forests in the world, Westvaco's Covington Mill has been in operation since 1899. The mill employs more than 1,400 people, working three shifts, 24 hours per day, seven days per week. More than 35 percent of the paperboard manufactured in Covington is printed and converted in Richmond.

PHILIP MORRIS U.S.A.

IN 1919, WHEN Philip Morris and Co. Ltd., Inc. incorporated in Virginia, few people took notice. Though the Philip Morris name was well-known in England, the company was still small in relation to the tobacco companies already firmly established in the United States. Nonetheless, in 1929, Philip Morris set up a production facility alongside the "big four" cigarette manufacturers on Richmond's Tobacco Row, a 20-square-block area along the James. Philip Morris' English Ovals, Oxford Blues, Cambridge, Players, and Marlboro brands held an almost insignificant share of the U.S. market at that time, but this was destined to change.

Philip Morris, quietly at first, began to compete in the U.S. tobacco industry. The company's emphasis on quality products and people, innovative marketing strategies, and sincere community involvement proved to be the right combination for them. Before long, the "big four" had become the "big five."

One significant event in Philip Morris' evolution was its 1933 introduction of Philip Morris cigarettes. To advertise this new product, the company hired a page boy named Johnny Roventini to "Call for Philip Morris." Soon, "Little Johnny" became the world's best-known living trademark, and the Philip Morris name became a household word.

Though still small in relation to its competitors, Philip Morris was gaining market share. To meet increased demand for its products, the company made plans for a second manufacturing facility in Richmond. In 1939, when production began in the new plant on Stockton Street, the competition was undoubtedly beginning to pay attention to this "little" cigarette manufacturer. They paid even more attention when, in the 1940s, Philip Morris moved up to

The Philip Morris U.S.A. Manufacturing Center is a showcase of state-of-the-art technology where employees take pride in producing top-quality cigarettes.

fourth place in the industry. Still, one of the company's most important changes was yet to come.

That change occurred in 1954, when a new Marlboro emerged. Made of the "Richmond recipe of fine tobaccos," Marlboro was introduced in a new hinged-lid, flip-top box. A year later, the rugged Marlboro cowboy made his debut. Things would never again be the same for the tobacco industry, for Philip Morris, or for Richmond, Virginia. Less than 20 years after its introduction, the new Marlboro became the world's best-selling cigarette; and to people around the globe, Richmond, Virginia, became known as "Marlboro Country."

Once the nation's smallest cigarette manufacturer, Philip Morris became the domestic industry leader in 1983. Six years later, the company celebrated its 70th anniversary as a Virginia corporation. Without a doubt, both the company and the community have a great deal to celebrate.

For Philip Morris, the past 70

years have been a time of tremendous change. Today Philip Morris Companies Inc. is the world's largest consumer packaged-goods company, with more than 150,000 employees worldwide. Philip Morris Companies Inc. has five principal operating companies: Philip Morris U.S.A., Philip Morris International, Miller Brewing Company, Philip Morris Capital Corporation, and Kraft General Foods, Inc.

Though Philip Morris is vastly larger than it was in 1919, it remains extremely proud of its Virginia heritage and deeply committed to its partnership with the city of Richmond. Even though corporate headquarters is today in New York, Richmond has been home to Philip Morris' largest cigarette manufacturing facility since 1974. As a matter of fact, Philip Morris is the only company still making cigarettes in Richmond. In addition, the company is the largest private employer, with more than 11,000 employees and 2,000 area retirees. Much of the average $37-million monthly payroll is spent back into the Richmond economy.

Philip Morris' impact on the area economy does not stop at its payroll. More than four of every 10 cigarettes sold in the Richmond area

The giant product tower in front of the Philip Morris U.S.A. Manufacturing Center has become a landmark to motorists on Interstate 95.

is a Philip Morris brand. Tax revenues from these sales have been critical in the building of new schools, new roads, and many other important public projects. As the largest purchaser of Virginia-grown bright leaf and the largest exporter of tobacco products, Philip Morris U.S.A makes a significant contribution to the

American side of the international balance of trade.

As in years past, Philip Morris continues to contribute to the overall welfare of the Richmond area. In 1989 alone, employees gave more than $1.7 million to the United Way, which was the largest employee contribution to the campaign. Philip Morris' two annual blood drives are the largest the Richmond Metropolitan Blood Service organizes each year. In addition, the company supports a variety of local cultural organizations and sponsors area education programs through scholarships and endowments. Philip Morris' Richmond employees volunteer time and contribute money to hundreds of community charities and activities.

The company welcomes visitors. Free tours offered in the manufacturing center attract more than 50,000 people annually. Philip Morris' huge identity tower off Interstate 95 has become a landmark to travelers. On it are the names of some of the world's favorite cigarettes: Virginia Slims, Merit, Benson & Hedges 100's, and of course Marlboro. The tower stands as proof that, without a doubt, Richmond, Virginia, is Marlboro Country.

WEIDMULLER INC.

WEIDMULLER INC. IS the United States subsidiary of C.A. Weidmuller GmbH, an international manufacturing firm based in West Germany. The Weidmuller Group is a worldwide leader in interface technology, with operating companies in 15 nations and qualified representatives in other markets. Weidmuller offers innovative solutions for electrical power and control applications through a product line which includes terminal blocks, terminal blocks and connectors for printed circuit boards, and electronic interface modules. Customers include manufacturers of industrial equipment and controls used in the manufacture of food process-

ing and packaging equipment, textiles, chemicals, and other industries.

Weidmuller's corporate offices, manufacturing plant, and distribution center are located in Chesterfield County's Southport Industrial Park. In August 1990 the company completed an expansion that more than doubled the size of its facility, which was originally built in 1979. This expansion was undertaken not only to support rapidly increasing sales, but also to enable Weidmuller to design and build products in response to the

Weidmuller's Richmond office.

needs of the American market.

"One of Weidmuller's most critical corporate distinctions is bringing innovation to the marketplace," says company president Wolfgang Schubl. "Innovation flows from creativity—where people have opportunities to make decisions. That is why our company is devoted to giving people the resources they need to do their best. Our new Richmond complex represents more than just added manufacturing capacity. Each area will have whatever is required to encourage thinking and communication. Better ideas are the key to bringing innovation to the market, and innovation results in market leadership."

9

BUSINESS AND FINANCE

RICHMOND'S SOLID FINANCIAL base has provided a dynamic environment for economic growth and opportunity for both individuals and businesses in the community.

Photo courtesy, Henley & Savage

METROPOLITAN RICHMOND CHAMBER OF COMMERCE

NO ONE CAN visit Richmond lately without immediately recognizing the dynamic vitality that infuses the entire surrounding region. While other regions trumpeted a "renaissance" or "boom," Richmond evolved from the capital city of Virginia to become the hub of a lively commercial region extending from Washington, D.C., to Atlanta, Georgia. New highways and strong railroads give the region a surface transportation network unparalleled in the country. Richmond International Airport and the Port of Richmond provide vital air and sea links with the world. Banks headquartered in the city, including the Federal Reserve Bank Fifth District, have made metropolitan Richmond a financial center. National retailers focus their operations in Richmond, and more than a dozen *Fortune* 500 companies have made metropolitan Richmond their home base.

The Metropolitan Richmond Chamber of Commerce deserves a good part of the credit for creating the commercial, political, and economic climate that has nourished the new Richmond. The chamber will celebrate 125 years of service in 1992. The mission of the founders was to re-

The Metropolitan Richmond Chamber of Commerce headquarters building at 201 East Franklin Street.

Gordon F. Rainey, Jr., chairman of the board for 1990-1991.

build an economy devastated by the Civil War and the fire that followed. Since its founding in 1867, the chamber's voice has become one of the most influential heard in the Executive Mansion, the halls of the state capitol, and in the chambers of local municipal governments.

If the spirits of the founders (and of the generations of chamber volunteers who followed them) could survey the new skyline at the falls of the James River and examine the membership rolls of the Metro Chamber, they could take great pride in a job well done.

The Metropolitan Richmond Chamber of Commerce is organized to provide business leadership in the enhancement of an economic and political climate favorable to all business and the free enterprise system in order to create a higher quality of life for all citizens of the counties of Chesterfield, Hanover, and Henrico and the City of Richmond.

To accomplish that mission, the chamber is organized into five policy groups: administration and finance, business and economic affairs, membership, metropolitan affairs, and public affairs. Within that structure, members work as part of task-

oriented committees.

The recently renovated and expanded headquarters of the Metro Chamber is located at 201 East Franklin Street. Wilson Flohr of Kings Dominion was 1989-1990 chairman of the board of the chamber. He succeeded E. Bryson Powell (1988-1989), John Hager (1987-1988), and George L. Yowell (1986-1987). Gordon F. Rainey, Jr., of Hunton & Williams is chairman for 1990-1991.

The fruits of the Metropolitan Richmond Chamber of Commerce's efforts can be seen by reading this book or by riding to the top of any of the new downtown skyscrapers and enjoying the view.

SIGNET BANKING CORPORATION

Signet Banking Corporation chairman and chief executive officer Robert M. Freeman.

SIGNET BANK PREDICTS in its advertisements that "one day we'll be your bank." It is a quiet, low-key, forceful message brought home by a distinguished and distinctive television commercial campaign. Featuring stars such as Jessica Tandy and Hume Cronyn and internationally known concert violinist Nadja Solerno-Sonnenberg, the advertisements speak of teamwork, accomplishment, and success.

"We selected these people," says Signet chairman Robert M. Freeman, "because they are doing the kind of job in their fields that we feel we are doing in banking. It's a solid image for us—a quality message delivered in a quality way." Freeman is a Richmond native, a former executive with North Carolina's Wachovia Bank and Trust, and a past president of the Virginia Bankers Association.

With assets exceeding $12 billion, the Signet Banking Corporation emerged from 1986 and 1987 mergers of the Union Trust of Maryland, Security National Bank of the District of Columbia, and the Bank of Virginia. It is among the 50 largest bank holding companies in the United States.

Signet provides investment services such as the sale and trading of federal, government agency, and municipal bonds; foreign exchange; and money market funds. It also operates a discount brokerage, provides a full-service international department, and offers specialized services for trust, leasing, asset-based lending, cash management, real estate, insurance, consumer financing, and investment banking.

Signet has branches throughout Virginia and the District of Columbia. It also has a strong presence in Maryland, especially from Washington to Baltimore and the Eastern Shore.

Tracing its roots to the Morris Plan Bank of Richmond, founded in 1922, Signet boasts a tradition rich in retail banking, consumer credit, and customer service. As the Bank of Virginia, it built an unparalleled reputation for innovation. Chief among its creations were its charge card program (now MasterCard), its commercial credit and checking program, and a statewide network of branches and affiliated institutions.

Now a major regional banking institution, Signet plans to develop a reputation as one of America's best banks in the 1990s. "We have successfully anticipated and adapted to changes in the 1980s," says Freeman. "Change is part of the natural progression. It is what keeps business moving forward and creates new opportunities.

"Right now, our primary commitment is to fully develop and serve our existing mid-Atlantic market of Maryland, the District of Columbia, and Virginia. This market offers the perfect environment for making Signet's vision for the 1990s a reality."

For Signet Banking Corporation shareholders, Freeman anticipates a decade of growing dividends and stock value. He says that the bank's customers can expect the products and services that represent excellent value. "In attracting customers, we seek to develop products and services in which we can be competitive and enjoy a good margin of profitability while delivering excellent value the customer can appreciate."

SOVRAN BANK

SOVRAN BANK, AMONG the most familiar companies in Virginia, is only seven years old. But tracing its origins goes back through 125 years of Richmond and Virginia history.

A subsidiary of Sovran Financial Corporation, Sovran Bank, N.A., was created by the 1983 merger of two of Virginia's oldest and most respected financial institutions: First & Merchants Corporation and Virginia National Bankshares, Inc.

Sovran traces its roots through that merger to the First National Bank of Richmond, which was chartered in April 1865, just a few days

Sovran Bank has deployed an extensive network of financial services offices through which it delivers a wide variety of top-quality financial products and services.

after the surrender of the Confederacy. The original capital for the bank, $100,000, came from a group of eight Virginians who had prudently managed to preserve some tangible resources through the war. Prudent management would remain a hallmark of the new institution.

The bank was located in the Custom House, the only financial district building left standing after the fires that followed the evacuation of Confederate troops. Among the first Richmond residents to open an account was General Robert E. Lee.

Other historic Richmond banks were also merged into the organization that later became Sovran. They included the National Exchange Bank, National Bank of Virginia, the Citizens Exchange Bank, the Southern Trust Company, the Richmond Trust and Safe Deposit Company, and Planters Savings Bank.

In June 1913 the bank moved into the newly completed 19-story First National Bank Building, a home it originally shared with the Chesapeake and Ohio Railroad and the Richmond, Fredericksburg & Potomac Railroad. The new building redefined the skyline of Richmond, just as the bank itself was helping to restructure and modernize the city's economy.

In recent years Sovran has pursued a strategy of garnering only the best resources available as a solid foundation for the future. Within its strong

and highly diversified markets, Sovran has deployed an extensive network of financial services offices through which it delivers a wide variety of top-quality financial products and services. Those services are backed by the most advanced automated information systems and technology.

Sovran Bank, N.A., is the keystone of Sovran Financial Corporation. Headquartered in the Sovran Center at 12th and Main streets in Richmond, it is the largest Virginia-based bank.

Sovran's 276 offices serve more than 80 percent of the state's population and hold 21 percent of the state's banking deposits. With assets totaling well over $12.5 billion and a work force of almost 7,000 Virginians, Sovran is one of the Commonwealth's most important corporations. The president and chief executive officer is Randolph W. McElroy.

Other subsidiaries of Sovran Financial Corporation are Sovran Bank/DC National in the District of Columbia; Sovran Bank/Delaware, a credit card subsidiary; Sovran Bank/Maryland; and Sovran Financial Corporation/Central South, a holding company operating banks in Tennessee and southern Kentucky.

COREAST SAVINGS BANK

FORMED IN 1988 by the merger of Richmond-based Colonial Savings and Loan Association and First Federal Savings and Loan Association of Roanoke (which had previously acquired American Federal Savings and Loan Association of Lynchburg), CorEast has assets of almost $1.2 billion. The 13th-largest financial institution in Virginia, CorEast has 33 branches in Virginia concentrated in the Richmond, Roanoke, and the Lynchburg metropolitan areas.

"CorEast has the capacity to be a superior performer in the business marketplace," says the thrift's recently appointed president and chief executive officer, W. Ronald Dietz. "We are working hard to demonstrate that performance."

Dietz, a veteran of Citibank, was head of a major division of one of the world's largest financial institutions. In 16 years at Citibank, Dietz had adapted well to the disciplined management style of the financial conglomerate and worked his way up to senior vice president in charge of Citibank's operations in 12 countries in Latin America and in the Caribbean.

After leaving Citibank Dietz applied those skills and concepts to a successful management consulting firm, which he founded with offices in Northern Virginia and New York.

Now as chief executive officer of CorEast, he has set out to give the thrift a new image and marketing presence. "We intend to be a player," says Dietz. "The foundation is here, and there is plenty of opportunity."

"We have two tracks for growth," says Dietz. "How we grow our business and how we grow our people." Just how to make CorEast grow in the right directions is what Dietz has been concentrating on since his arrival.

President and chief executive officer of CorEast Savings Bank, W. Ronald Dietz.

"We want our people to help us deliver relationship banking. We want out customers to know that we can do a lot of different things for them, that we are much more than just a place to buy a certificate of deposit or take out a mortgage. We are focusing on serving the marketplace as the quality-driven, service-oriented institution where customers want to do business."

One of the components to a bigger success story for CorEast will be its ability to increase its recognition in the marketplace. Dietz acknowledges that not enough people are familiar with what CorEast is and what it does. However, he views this as an opportunity to create the desired image instead of managing an institution that is burdened with preconceived notions.

Virginia residents reacted favorably to the new CorEast Savings Bank in 1989, when the thrift launched a major money market campaign. Today money market accounts comprise 62 percent more of CorEast's total deposits than before the program. Other revitalizing efforts are dedicated to accelerating the institution's response time on mortgage applications and developing value-added consumer products. Additional innovations are keyed to attracting more commercial customers.

As Ron Dietz continues to institute his management style and principles at CorEast, he believes customers and competitors will begin to see a difference. If he had one thought to tell them today, he would say, "Keep an eye on us."

FRANKLIN FEDERAL SAVINGS AND LOAN ASSOCIATION

DESPITE ALL THE recent news about the financial difficulties of savings and loans, there is one savings and loan association that is not in any trouble at all. Richmond's Franklin Federal Savings and Loan Association has always kept to the traditional, narrow financial role of locally investing savings in residential housing.

"We stuck with the tried and true," says J.B. Bourne, Jr., president of Franklin Federal. "That may seem simplistic, but the bottom line says that we were right." Franklin Federal had assets totaling $3 million in 1940. In 1990 total assets were well over $300 million.

That growth has come despite the fact that the thrift remains a mutual institution, completely owned by its depositors. "A mutual is judged by how well it fulfills its mission," says W.E.W. Frayser, chief operating officer. "A stock company is judged only by financial performance. This way, we're not pressured to take risks just to make money. We're still true to our New Deal mission."

Through their dedication to the original mission of savings and loan institutions, Bourne and Frayser have kept Franklin Federal a safe place for savings and a good place for home loans.

Franklin Federal was born in the midst of the Great Depression. Thousands of financial institutions nationwide had failed; unemployment was rampant. By March 1933 the Depression had also prompted the bank holiday—a week when people could not cash checks or withdraw savings.

The economic climate was bleak. Precious little money was available for capital investment, and J.B. Bourne, Sr., then a 42-year-old Sandston bookkeeper, recognized that desperate situations required bold action. Something had to be done to help area home owners satisfy notes held on the property.

On October 24, 1933, Bourne brought together a group of Sandston residents to discuss organizing a building and loan association that could raise funds through federal agencies and private investment. They agreed to apply for a federal charter and set out to acquire the necessary $2,500.

Despite a multitude of uncertainties, the requirement was oversubscribed by $209.50. On November 24, 1933, Federal Charter No. 30 was issued to the Federal Savings and Loan Association of Sandston, Virginia. There were 15 directors, 64 depositors (shareholders), and 3 elected officers: H.H. Fricke, president; C.B. Robinson, vice president; and Bourne, secretary, treasurer, and managing officer.

Cost of a full share was $100, and for those with less to invest (some of those first 64 depositors put in as little as 50 cents), installment thrift shares were available. Under this plan, monthly payments were made until the $100 was satisfied.

For every $100 in deposits the association received, the U.S. Treasury purchased two preferred shares, which enabled the new federal savings and loan to expedite capital funding. These shares later were repurchased by the association. The

Pictured here is the Franklin Federal Savings and Loan building on Franklin Street, circa 1941.

association was issued Certificate No. 7 by the Federal Savings and Loan Insurance Corporation. The tiny Sandston group had become one of the first such organizations in the nation to gain federal coverage.

In February 1937 the name was changed to the First Federal Savings and Loan Association of Sandston. Two years later Bourne became president. By 1941 the customer base of First Federal of Sandston had grown to include much of the surrounding area. Business expansion soon dictated the need for new quarters. The firm moved to 616 East Franklin Street, where it was renamed Franklin Federal Savings and Loan Association.

By the end of 1945 assets topped $7.8 million. Once more space became a consideration, and in 1952 the association purchased property at Seventh and Broad streets for a new home office. A branch was opened at Three Chopt Road and Patterson Avenue, in Richmond's west end, two years later.

Assets climbed to more than $21 million in 1955, there were 28 employees, and it was time to dedicate the new building. The new facility proudly featured both savings and loan departments in the main lobby, which boasted soft music, carpeted floors, and quiet surroundings, and a vault was located on the first floor with no steps to climb.

James B. Bourne, Jr., succeeded his father at the helm in 1959, and at 29 years of age became the youngest savings and loan president in Virginia. He proved a highly capable leader despite his youth and relative inexperience (he had been with the

firm only five years). But the influence of James B. Bourne, Sr., provided sound guidance: "Do the work. Don't look for glory."

In six years assets doubled from $38.1 million to $75.6 million, four additional branches were opened, and in 1963 Franklin Federal was the first savings and loan in the area to pay interest on savings accounts from day of deposit to day of withdrawal. The company moved into the electronic age with installation of a

punched card data system (1961), random-access computer (1965), and an IBM System 370 (1975), all to provide more efficient customer service.

By 1973 the main office was treated to a complete face-lift. Today the association maintains the downtown headquarters location as well as its five branches covering the city of Richmond and Henrico, Chesterfield, and Hanover counties.

More than 50 people are employed by Franklin Federal. The association's assets represent approximately 1,000 times the original expectation and 100,000 times the initial capitalization.

Size is an important yardstick for measuring success—as is philosophy. Franklin Federal's objectives are "to promote thrift by providing a convenient and safe method for people to save and invest money and to provide for the sound and economic financing of homes." No matter how it is measured, Franklin Federal Savings and Loan Association qualifies as one of the area's great success stories.

The downtown office of Franklin Federal Savings and Loan Association.

THE LIFE INSURANCE COMPANY OF VIRGINIA

THE LIFE INSURANCE Company of Virginia was formed in 1871 under a charter granted by the Virginia General Assembly. Its commitment to its policyholders was "to add to the prosperity of your community and pay your heirs, when you can no longer provide for them, without delay or quibble."

Although Life of Virginia has undergone many changes since those words were written and, in the process, has acquired a national reputation as an innovative and aggressive industry leader, the company still maintains an unswerving commitment to the welfare of its policyholders.

While the first policy issued by Life of Virginia forbade the insured (on penalty of policy nullification) "from working on railroad trains, handling explosives, fighting duels, imbibing too frequently of strong drink, or residing south of North Carolina," the company soon acquired more realistic policyholder expectations.

Life of Virginia remained a traditional life insurance company throughout much of its first century. Agents were assigned specific geographical areas in which to collect

Life of Virginia's annual gift to the community is a series of free summer concerts on the lawn at national headquarters.

weekly premiums on small policies marketed primarily to blue-collar workers. And during those years the firm acquired its reputation as a financially stable, highly reputable old-line Richmond institution.

In the early 1980s company management initiated a series of changes that signaled the beginning of a clearly defined transitional period. Maintaining the solid traditions of its first 100 years, the company prepared for its second century.

In 1981 Life of Virginia became the first major life insurance company to market a new kind of insurance called Universal Life. And with the introduction of Universal Life came a new, innovative, aggressive marketing posture that made the firm a recognized industry leader.

This new marketing posture, as well as changes within the life industry itself, highlighted a need for expanded, more efficiently positioned distribution capabilities. That need was met, in part, with the acquisition of an extensive network of brokerage agencies and, later, with the creation of the Forth Financial Network, an independent franchise distribution system positioned about midway between the company's tradtional career agency structure and its brokerage distribution system.

Since 1986 Life of Virginia has been a subsidiary of Chicago-based

Aon Corporation, an international holding company listed on the New York Stock Exchange with assets of more than $9 billion. Aon's operations include a wide range of insurance interests, together with extensive investment and management activities.

Richard T. Maurer, company president, sees many new opportunities for Life of Virginia as a member firm of Aon: "One of Aon's great strengths is bringing together multiple distribution and company assets. A lot of companies, frankly, don't have that available. It is one of our major advantages and one that I would like to utilize to the fullest.

"I see this exchange of product and marketing capabilities between distribution systems taking place in all those areas where it is appropriate. Frankly, that just plain makes sense to me."

One of Maurer's first concerns is that Life of Virginia deliver products of value to the consumer and to deliver them through a first-class distribution system. "While I know we can't be the best of everything, we have the best distribution system with the quality products consumers demand," he says. Over time, Maurer sees Life of Virginia as Aon's center for life insurance products worldwide.

Among the products that Life of Virginia has introduced recently are several of particular interest. These include variable life and annuity plans that allow the firm's clients to utilize the stock and bond investment skills of several major mutual fund managers in providing for their long-term savings and insurance needs. Other products recently introduced combine the current interest and cost of insurance features of Universal Life with

the guarantee of whole life. A third line of business that has gained widespread acceptance is single-premium deferred annuities, offering clients a way to provide for retirement and other life-style-related purposes by buying an annuity that accumulates at current, competitive rates, backed by Life of Virginia's long history of reliability and financial stability.

In the charter granted by the Virginia General Assembly, which created Life of Virginia in 1871, a commitment to both the company's policyholders and to the community was made. Since the beginning Life of Virgina has fully acknowledged that its first responsibility is to its policyholders. And it has met that obligation by continuing to provide those products and services that best meet its policyholders' needs. No responsibility is clearer; no promise more solid.

The second commitment "to add to the prosperity of the community" also falls into the category of promises kept. For many years Life of Virginia has been actively and prominently involved in the life of the community. As part of an ongoing effort toward being a responsible corporate citizen, the firm believes it has an obligation to "give something back to its headquarters' community and state."

Through its charitable corporate foundation, the company continues to support education, conservation, and philanthropic efforts, and to add to the cultural enrichment of its community through support of music, drama, and dance. Its series of free public summer concerts, a gift to the community, has become a Richmond tradition. The Christmas Village, a reproduction of an eighteenth-century village staffed entirely with employee volunteers, is enjoyed by more than 5,000 each holiday season.

As the Life Insurance Company of Virginia enters the 1990s, its commitment is unchanged—to retain its stewardship to its policyholders, employees, and community, and to grow and prosper through the fullest realization of its potential as a member of the Aon family.

Life of Virginia's national headquarters at Brookfield, a park-like complex located in Richmond's West End.

UNIVERSAL CORPORATION

UNIVERSAL CORPORATION DOES not manufacture tobacco products for the consumer, but this venerable Richmond company plays a vital role in the American tobacco industry. By consolidating and extending a tobacco business established in 1888, Jacqueline P. Taylor formed Universal Leaf Tobacco Co., now a wholly owned subsidiary of Universal Corporation.

Through operating subsidiaries such as the J.P. Taylor Company, Southwestern, K.R. Edwards, and Lancaster Leaf, Universal's corps of expert buyers purchases about 40 percent of all tobacco sold at auction in the United States and represents the company's interests in every major market in the free world. All around the globe, from the farmer to the customer, the tobacco industry is uniquely dependent on the skill and judgement of these experienced individuals.

Universal Corporation prides itself on its 100-year heritage built on the integrity and the competence of its people. An aggressive, modern corporation fully equipped with the latest technology, Universal executives always remember that their entire international organization is built on the extra care given customers.

From corporate headquarters in Richmond to regional offices in

The tobacco auction, a southern tradition, is the heart of the U.S. sales process. However, Universal Leaf Tobacco has expert buyers in every market throughout the world.

many foreign countries, Universal Leaf provides sales, financing, and administrative services to all of its customers. Its processing plants cover the globe and employ 20,000 people on average throughout the year.

Business is conducted in more than 22 countries, including Canada, the United States, Brazil, Argentina, Mexico, Guatemala, Italy, Greece, Zimbabwe, Malawi, India, Korea, Hong Kong, Turkey, and Spain.

In tobacco, Universal is synonomous with leadership. It is not only the largest, but also the most widely respected tobacco buyer and processor in the world. That leadership continues to produce impressive rewards. Universal Leaf alone generates annual sales in excess of one billion dollars.

Two additional subsidiaries of Universal Corporation are Deli Universal, Inc., an agri-products business acquired in 1986, and Lawyers Title Insurance Corporation, acquired in 1985.

Deli is engaged in the building products business in the Netherlands and Belgium, where it distributes and sells timber and related building products to the building and construction market. The majority of timber products is sourced outside the Netherlands, principally in North

Deli Universal's timber division supplies building products to the construction market worldwide. Here Asian hardwood arrives at port in Rotterdam.

America, Scandanavia, Eastern Europe, and the Far East.

The company's agri-products business also involves the selecting, buying, shipping, storing, and financing of a number of other products including tea, coffee, rubber, vegetable oils, cocoa, sunflower seeds, and peanuts. These commodities are supplied to large and small customers in the food and food-packaging industry and in the rubber and tire manufacturing industry.

Lawyers Title Insurance Corporation is engaged primarily in the business of issuing title insurance, which protects against loss due to encumbrances upon titles to real estate.

Richmond and Universal Corporation—for more than 100 years, its people have shared an admired, profitable heritage.

LAWYERS TITLE INSURANCE CORPORATION

IN REAL ESTATE circles, people still talk about the developer who built a high rise on land that he did not own. It seems that when he bought the land, the woman who signed the deed as the wife of the seller wasn't. When the real wife filed suit several years later, the title to a multimillion-dollar structure was at issue. That is why smart buyers and all financial institutions insist on the purchase of title insurance.

Title insurance provides elimination of risk. The insurer guarantees that the title to a piece of property is clear and assumes all risks not excepted to in the policy. Associated with title insurance is title search, the process of checking real estate records to make sure that all transactions have been properly recorded, and that ownership of the land and land rights is conveyed as stated in deeds, contracts, and covenants.

One of the largest title insurance companies in the world, Lawyers Title Insurance Corporation protects

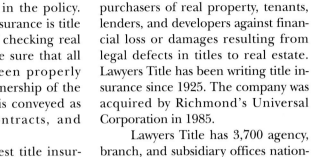

Lawyers Title Insurance Corporation's national headquarters facility in Richmond.

purchasers of real property, tenants, lenders, and developers against financial loss or damages resulting from legal defects in titles to real estate. Lawyers Title has been writing title insurance since 1925. The company was acquired by Richmond's Universal Corporation in 1985.

Lawyers Title has 3,700 agency, branch, and subsidiary offices nationwide. More than 26,000 approved attorneys are affiliated with the company.

Always in the forefront of electronic data-processing technology, Lawyers Title recently introduced its Genesis system, which is now in place throughout the company's branch and agency network. It ensures that the firm will continue to have the best automated title production system in the country. Furthermore, a new automated policy flow system, recently installed at the company's national headquarters, uses microfilming equipment and a computerized indexing system that allow instant access to policies, endorsements, and relevant financial information.

The National Division of Lawyers Title Insurance Corporation has played a significant role in commercial and industrial real estate for more than three decades. With 15 offices nationwide, the National Division provides title insurance orders and services on properties located anywhere in the United States and Canada.

Lawyers Title has enhanced its operations and marketing efforts on the West Coast through its largest subsidiary, Continental Lawyers Title Company. Based in Universal City, California, Continental Lawyers has branch offices and agency representation in its territory covering Alaska, Arizona, California, Hawaii, Nevada, Oregon, and Washington.

At Lawyers Title Insurance Corporation, as at all Universal Corporation operations, the firm continues to emphasize its unyielding commitment to client and customer service, technical and professional excellence, innovation, and leadership.

NELCO, LTD.

"THE DISTINCTIVE COMPETENCE of a computer-leasing company is its knowledge of the industry, its creativity, and its ability to manage the assets in its portfolio." That statement is one of the principles that have thrust NELCO, Ltd., into the forefront of the computer-leasing industry in Virginia as well as throughout the country.

Formed in 1979 by Richard A. Nelson and Judy D. Nelson, the firm is located in a modern office building at 10810 Trade Road. NELCO has grown as Richmond and the Commonwealth of Virginia have grown.

When Nelson started, he was the only full-time employee of NELCO. His firm now employs 21 people, six of whom are in sales exclusively. NELCO's senior management includes Thomas E. Shockley, senior vice president/marketing; R. McLean Duke, Jr., vice president/operations; and Kenneth E. Baker, vice president/finance and administration.

By 1981 NELCO's sales were $1.6 million. That figure had swelled to $5.5 million in 1984 and to $9.9 million the following year. By 1989 the firm's sales had grown to $31 million. In both 1984 and 1986 NELCO, Ltd., was named as one of the 500 fastest-growing, privately held companies in the United States by *INC.* magazine.

"NELCO purchases new computer equipment from IBM, Digital, Hewlett-Packard, AT&T, and other leading manufacturers," Duke says, "and also makes a market in used computer equipment." NELCO then leases this new and used equipment to customers ranging from small businesses to *Fortune* 500 companies."

"The four keys to successful computer leasing," Shockley says, "are equipment knowledge, structuring creative financing alternatives, defining and solving customer needs, and effectively procuring and selling used equipment."

"The computer business is very volatile," Baker says. "We have to stay on top of technological changes, used equipment market fluctuations, as well as tax law changes."

NELCO works with approximately 600 customers; about 50 percent of them are in Virginia. The firm is strong in Richmond with concentrations also in Tidewater and western Virginia. NELCO's customers include such Richmond companies as Philip Morris, Best Products, Reynolds Metals, Heilig-Meyers, James River Corporation, and Ethyl.

Nelson wants NELCO to be regarded as a good corporate citizen,

NELCO's senior management team of Thomas E. Shockley, senior vice president/marketing (left); Kenneth E. Baker, vice president/finance and administration (top); R. McLean Duke, Jr., vice president/operations (right); and Richard A. Nelson, president (seated) oversee the leasing, buying, and selling of computer and other high-tech equipment, including large mainframes, mid-range systems, and personal computers.

and his firm participates in and supports a variety of civic projects. As a graduate of Virginia Commonwealth University, Nelson has served on many committees at Virginia Commonwealth University and has created a NELCO merit scholarship in the School of Business.

Nelson is confident about the future of Richmond and about the future of NELCO, Ltd. "Richmond has faced the challenges of the past with success, and I'm sure it will meet the challenges of the 1990s with the same success," he says. "The smartest thing we did at the beginning was to crawl before we walked. We only committed to transactions that we could handle. We still employ that philosophy today." NELCO will continue to meet customer needs in the 1990s by utilizing its stability, adaptability, and experience.

CRESTAR BANK

DURING THE 1980s the Richmond metropolitan area emerged as a leading corporate headquarters city in the Southeast. The area's diversified economy, strong labor pool, and pro-business climate helped fuel the expansion of existing firms and convinced many other companies to relocate to the James River valley.

Crestar has been both a catalyst and beneficiary of this growth. With more than $11 billion in assets and approximately $8 billion in deposits, the bank and its people continue to play important roles in Richmond's progress.

The first half of the 1980s brought great changes to banking. At Crestar, formerly United Virginia Bank, the changes were seized as opportunities. The bank added insurance sales, discount brokerage, and investment banking activities. It began participating in regional and national automatic teller machine networks and selectively acquired several Virginia banking institutions.

In 1983 the bank moved into a new 26-story office tower in the heart of downtown Richmond. In 1985 United Virginia acquired the Washington-based billion-dollar NS&T Bankshares. Several months later it purchased Bethesda Bankcorp-

In 1983 Crestar Bank moved into this new 26-story office tower in the heart of downtown Richmond. Photo by Don Ikenberry

oration. The result was a bank with a firm footing in all three national capital area jurisdictions, and a market area with more than 4 million residents and tens of thousands of businesses.

In 1986 the bank decided to establish itself as the premier provider of high-quality customer service in its marketplace. It developed plans to place renewed emphasis on personalized attention to the customer, employee training, innovative products and services, and response to customer feedback.

Management felt the need to market the bank's products and services under one banner, free of any geographic connotation. In September 1987 United Virginia Bank became Crestar. The following year Crestar reached an agreement to acquire the $400-million Colonial American Bankshares of Roanoke, more than doubling its presence in Virginia's fourth-largest banking market.

Today Crestar operates 255 banking offices in the mid-Atlantic and southeastern United States. It also operates five subsidiaries providing mortgage, insurance, leasing, securities, and investment advisory services.

"As a service business and as a corporation that owes much of its success to the people and businesses in our local markets, we seek to improve the standard of living in the communities we serve," says Richard G. Tilghman, Crestar's chairman and chief executive officer.

Each year the bank contributes more than $500,000 to numerous social, cultural, and education activities, including Theatre Virginia, the Richmond Symphony, and the Special Olympics. Robert F. Norfleet, Jr., president of Crestar Bank/Richmond, served as chairman of the 1989 United Way campaign.

As Crestar Bank moves with Richmond into the last decade of the twentieth century, it will continue to look for innovative ways to serve its customers, its headquarters city, and the adjacent localities.

INVESTORS SAVINGS BANK

Robert G. Butcher, Jr., chairman and chief executive officer of Investors Savings Bank.

"WE SET OUT to build an important financial institution," says Robert G. Butcher, Jr., chairman of the board and chief executive officer of Investors Savings Bank, one of Virginia's leading savings and loan associations. "In our branches and in our practices, we have tried to position ourselves to be a full-service retail bank."

As a result of those efforts, Investors has 26 branches in the Richmond area alone and a strong presence throughout central Virginia, Tidewater, and in the Shenandoah Valley. With more than 50 branches statewide and an outstanding reputation for quality customer service, Investors has become a valuable retail banking franchise. Its steady growth of core deposits has continued despite the recent stresses on the national savings and loan industry.

Investors has come a very long way since its 1974 creation in a trailer on Richmond's West Broad Street. Its original mission was providing basic savings accounts and mortgage loans. It continues to provide those services, but now it is Virginia's eighth-largest banking institution.

"I thought a savings and loan institution would make a great client for my law firm," recalls Butcher, talking about his company's origins. "So we put together a board of directors, and we sold a bunch of stock. I don't think that it occurred to any of us that we would accomplish this much."

Butcher began devoting all of his time to Investors in 1981. By 1989 the firm boasted total assets of almost $2.5 billion and total deposits of almost $1.7 billion.

Throughout its history, Investors has maintained an outstanding record of access to local capital markets. Widely perceived as a young and rapidly growing company, it has proven attractive to young, successful investors. "We have a lot of friends in the investment community," says Butcher.

He does not say, as he well might, that many of those friends are attracted to Investors primarily by his own aggressive entrepreneurial style.

Instead he credits his hard-driving management team. "Our people were young, aggressive, and more willing to be different than some of the established S&Ls," he says. "We thought we should build a true banking network that would be viewed as valuable to both customers and investors."

At various times in the firm's history, its management has questioned the wisdom of its own growth policies. "In 1978 we faced major competition as a result of industry deregulation," says Butcher. "We looked at several strategies, including pulling back and cutting the business."

Instead of pulling back, Investors continued its aggressive marketing and expansion. The company even continued to hire staff and expand both its product lines and territory throughout the 1979 to 1981 recession, when high interest rates and soaring inflation produced a threatening climate for most savings and loan institutions. Once again its decisions proved correct.

Throughout the past decade's turbulent changes in the competitive and regulatory environment, Investors has continued to expand. In 1981 the company established Investors Home Mortgage Corporation (IHMC), a centralized division formed to centralize its mortgage loan activities and developed a high-volume operation. By 1985 IHMC was well on the way to becoming a dominant mortgage banking company in the Southeast and mid-Atlantic states.

In 1986 Investors purchased S.L. Nusbaum & Company, Inc., a Norfolk-based commercial real estate development firm specializing in shopping center properties. The same year Investors also acquired Citizens Savings and Loan of Richmond, which added 13 branches in Richmond and Tidewater, along with $340 million in core deposits.

In 1987 the company launched a commercial banking services program. It featured commercial checking accounts, merchant bank card services, and commercial loans.

Early in 1988 Investors sold IHMC, moving away from the high-volume, multistate mortgage lending business and back to a program of integrating residential mortgage lending into the full package of financial services available to its Virginia customers. As a result, Investors was able to concentrate its resources and reassert its high standards of quality control over services to borrowers and realtors in its home markets.

Later in 1988 the firm reorganized itself, forming Investors Financial Corporation as a holding company for Investors Savings Bank.

"We're continuing to focus on retail, consumer banking products," says Butcher. "Those products have been the key to our past successes. We expect them to carry us forward into the new decade." Recently added products include no-penalty certificates of deposit and transaction accounts designed especially to appeal to depositors in the over 50 age group.

Those programs have been successful, attracting substantial new deposits to the company, funds that are reinvested in Virginia in the form of

As one of Virginia's leading savings and loan associations, Investors Savings Bank has 26 branches in the Richmond area alone and more than 50 branches statewide, all with a reputation for quality customer service.

residential mortgage loans. Investors has always viewed its residential mortgage loan program as the cornerstone of all its lending efforts and a primary identification point with its customers.

In the future Investors Savings Bank will concentrate its lending on

residential mortgages, single-family construction loans, home equity lines, and other customer and small business bank credits.

"We've got to move more slowly now," Butcher says. "We're facing more competition for deposits, and we're operating in a tough regulatory environment. Our main concern remains the same. We want to protect and build the value of our franchise. We've already made Investors Savings Bank a great institution. Now the challenge is making it better than ever."

THE VIRGINIA INSURANCE RECIPROCAL

THE VIRGINIA INSURANCE Reciprocal was forged in the heat of the medical malpractice insurance crisis of the 1970s. Sponsored in 1977 by the Virginia Hospital Association because private professional liability providers had either withdrawn from the commonwealth or raised their rates to prohibitive levels, The Virginia Insurance Reciprocal has proven to be a successful and valuable adjunct to the association's program of members' services.

A cooperative-style insurance company (similar in nature to the "mutual plan" of insurance), The Virginia Insurance Reciprocal is owned by its policyholders. It was originally formed by the members of the Virginia Hospital Association. Virginia Professional Underwriters, Inc., is the management firm (the "Attorney in Fact") for The Virginia Insurance Reciprocal.

Over the years since it was founded, The Virginia Insurance Reciprocal has proven so successful that its programs are now sponsored by the state hospital associations of Tennessee and Mississippi, and its policies are widely held in 11 other states.

The concept behind the organization is simple. The members of the Virginia Hospital Association (and now the other policyholders as well) insure each other reciprocally—that is all of the members pool resources (pay premiums) to pay claims against each other individually.

Under this "mutual" or "cooperative" style of organization, there is no need to generate profits to benefit shareholders. All surplus revenues (premiums paid that were not needed immediately to pay member losses and to cover expenses) are retained by the company as surplus. Those retained monies earn additional income and eventually enable the Reciprocal to return savings to the policyholders in the form of dividends or lower premiums.

The key to successful operation of this form of insurance company is controlling losses by holding down claims. And the founders knew that the best way to reduce the number of claims was to find a way to eliminate incidents of malpractice.

"When we started," says Gordon D. McLean, the president of Virginia Professional Underwriters, "our underlying interest was to have an impact on the quality of health care in Virginia by offering an assertive risk-management program. The idea was that we would reduce claims by improving the quality of care."

The Hospital Association and The Virginia Insurance Reciprocal worked together to resolve the crisis. "We coordinated our efforts with quality-assurance programs in each of the hospitals," recalls McLean. "The key was assisting hospitals to meet

BELOW & FACING PAGE: The home office of The Virginia Insurance Reciprocal is located in suburban Henrico County, Virginia. The building was completed in 1983 and an addition doubling its size was added in 1988. The building is jointly owned by the Reciprocal and Virginia Hospital Association.

Joint Commission requirements so as to gain maximum accreditation."

The program succeeded far beyond its founders' hopes. The Virginia Insurance Reciprocal now insures 98 percent of the nonprofit hospitals in the state. In 1981 it began offering malpractice insurance to physicians in private and group practices. The Reciprocal has now attracted more than 25 percent of the medical doctors practicing in Virginia.

The company holds assets of more than $149 million. The home office is in Glen Allen; it has offices in

Fairfax County; Norfolk; Roanoke; Charlotte, North Carolina; Jackson, Mississippi; and Nashville, Tennessee. The headquarters building is jointly owned by the Virginia Hospital Association and the Reciprocal. Operating principally as a direct writer of insurance, Virginia Professional Underwriters and The Virginia Insurance Reciprocal have 180 employees.

"The real visionaries," says McLean, "were the leaders of the Virginia Hospital Association who showed great foresight in establishing and financing The Virginia

Insurance Reciprocal."

Those leaders include Stuart D. Ogren, the now retired president of the Virginia Hospital Association; John Simpson, then president of Richmond Memorial Hospital; and Carl S. Napps, then executive director of Winchester Memorial Hospital.

"Starting their own insurance company was a high-risk venture designed both to resolve a short-term crisis and meet the long-term needs of Virginia health care institutions," says McLean. "These men and the other members of the association took a big chance when they involved themselves and provided the initial one million dollars needed to start us off."

The rewards to the members include savings to date of more than $14 million returned to the hospitals and physicians. The 1989 surplus of the Virginia Insurance Reciprocal was almost $40 million.

"Our mission is to guarantee that the hospitals of Virginia will never again be subject to the vagaries of the commercial insurance industry," says McLean.

The board of directors is the governing body of the Virginia Insurance Reciprocal. Members of the board are elected by the policyholders. Felix Fraraccio, administrator of R.J. Reynolds-Patrick County Hospital, is chairman. Kenneth R. Patterson is senior vice president and chief financial officer. William R. Reid, president of the Community Hospital of Roanoke Valley, is chairman of the board of directors of Virginia Professional Underwriters, Inc.

MARKEL CORPORATION

THE MARKEL ORGANIZATION was begun by Samuel A. Markel shortly after World War I with the formation of a small mutual insurance company to provide insurance to the emerging public transportation industry. In 1930 Markel Service, Inc., was established to provide underwriting, loss control, and claims administration services for the insurance company.

In the early 1950s Markel Service changed its role from manager of a single affiliated insurance firm to a general agency representing several insurance companies. In 1951 the firm expanded into Canada with the creation of Markel Service Canada, Ltd., providing underwriting, safety engineering, and claims services for the Canadian trucking industry. This entity went public in 1972 as Markel Financial Holdings, Ltd. The organization then formed the Markel Insurance Company of Canada.

Significant changes in both the transportation and insurance industries in the early 1970s prompted fur-

In 1930 the trucking industry was starting to take off, and Markel Service, Inc., was formed. Since then Markel has been a vital part of the transportation industry and has diversified to meet the needs of other industries.

ther diversification. The firm developed products in the excess and surplus markets and developed marketing strategies that identified products and distribution systems representing maximum potential to the company.

In 1980 Essex Insurance Company was formed, and Markel Corporation was created as a holding company. After nearly 69 years as a family-owned business, Markel went public in December 1986, and it completed a second public stock offering in June 1988.

Today Markel is a diversified, customer-driven organization that operates as an insurer, an insurance broker, and a provider of claims administration services. Markel markets and administers diverse, highly specialized products and services to specific niche markets. This strategy allows the corporation to develop expertise and recognition in its markets, while insulating itself from the cyclical nature inherent in the insurance industry.

The corporation's brokerage and underwriting management company, Markel Service, Inc., markets uniquely specialized products through both wholesale and retail distribution channels. Among the company's leading products are equine

Today Markel Corporation is a multifaceted insurance organization that, through its subsidiaries, operates as an insurance broker and underwriting manager, an insurer, and a provider of claims administration services. Pictured is the Markel corporate headquarters, located in the Innsbrook Corporate Center.

mortality insurance and law enforcement liability insurance. With a recent acquisition, the operation has become a leader in providing insurance for summer camps and college student health coverage.

The underwriting entities, Essex Insurance Company and Markel American Insurance Company, provide specialty coverages for restaurants, contractors, taverns, and special events. These businesses also participate in the reinsurance of some programs marketed by Markel Service.

Lindsey & Newsom Claim Services is the independent claims administration operation of Markel. This division provides claims adjusting and administration services to insurance companies, agents, brokers, underwriters at Lloyds, and self-insured organizations.

Markel Corporation owns a minority interest in Fairfax Financial Holdings Limited. Subsidiaries of Fairfax include Markel Insurance Company of Canada, Chequers Insurance Company, and Morden & Helwig Group, Inc.

Fairfax and Markel are also partners in the Shand/Evanston Group, which specializes in errors and omissions coverage for various professionals and malpractice coverage for medical professionals and hospitals. The companies in the group include Shand, Morahan & Company, the Evanston Insurance Company, and The Insurance Company of Evanston.

Photo courtesy, Henley & Savage

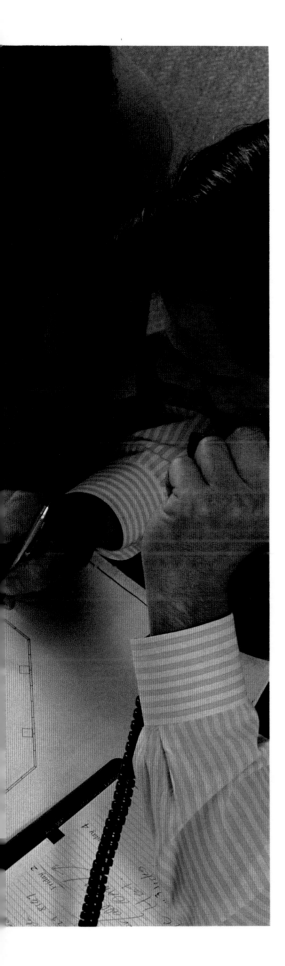

10

THE PROFESSIONS

GREATER RICHMOND'S PROFESSIONAL community brings a wealth of service, ability, and insight to the area.

Photo courtesy, Henley & Savage

MAYS & VALENTINE

MORE THAN TWO decades ago prominent Virginia attorneys John S. Davenport III and David J. Mays could foresee the pace of growth quickening and the legal environment becoming more specialized and complex. To respond to these challenges, Davenport and Mays proposed combining the skills and expertise of their firms—Denny Valentine & Davenport and Tucker, Mays, Moore & Reed—both well established in Richmond since the 1920s.

Charles S. Valentine and Collins Denny, Jr., had formed Denny & Valentine in the fall of 1926. Both were graduates of the University of Virginia School of Law (1924), and both had strong ties to the Richmond business community. Denny's experience as one of two assistant attorneys general of Virginia proved valuable to the new firm. So, too, did the firm's appointment as local (and later division) counsel for the Atlantic Coast Line Railroad, now a division of Richmond-based CSX Corporation.

The Depression exercised a direct influence on the young firm. Bankruptcies and business reorganizations were a law practice staple of the era; Denny & Valentine represented the Bondholders Protective Committee in the reorganization of Southern Bond & Mortgage Company and Standard Paper Company.

In March 1939, John Davenport, a partner in Edwards & Davenport, joined Denny & Valentine, bringing a change in the firm's name to Denny, Valentine & Davenport. Davenport would establish himself as a leading figure of the Virginia Bar, becoming one of the commonwealth's preeminent trial lawyers.

Two years before the firm of Denny & Valentine was organized, John Randolph Tucker resigned as general counsel for the State Corporation Commission to form a partnership with Sherlock Bronson. Tucker began his law practice in 1903 after graduation from Washington and Lee University and a postgraduate year at Harvard. Early in his career he was an adjunct professor at T.C. Williams

School of Law of the University of Richmond. There he taught both Bronson and David Mays, the first associate attorney of Tucker & Bronson.

Tucker became nationally known as the principal architect of the county manager form of government. Under his leadership, Henrico County became the first in the nation to adopt that system, which is now in widespread use nationwide.

Mays, in addition to a long and distinguished legal career, received the 1952 Pulitzer Prize for his two-volume biography of Virginia patriot Ed-

The reception area of Mays & Valentine's Sovran Center offices in downtown Richmond.

mund Pendleton. Publication of that work culminated more than a quarter-century of painstaking research and documentation.

The new firm became known as Tucker, Bronson & Mays. When David Satterfield became a partner, its name was changed to Tucker, Bronson, Satterfield & Mays. With the departure of Satterfield (following his election to the House of Representatives) and Bronson, the firm became known for some 10 years as Tucker, Mays, Cabell and Moore, incorporating the name of partner Robert Cabell. In 1956, with the addition of two new partners, Charles L. Reed and Richmond Moore, the firm took its final pre-merger name:

Tucker, Mays, Moore & Reed.

For many years the clients of the Tucker firm were almost exclusively business oriented. In addition to serving as counsel for the Virginia Bankers Association from 1933, the firm represented organizations such as Southern Bank and Trust Company, American Tobacco, the Virginia Highway Users Association, and Home Beneficial Life Insurance Company.

At the time of the merger, Mays, Valentine, Davenport and Moore had about 24 lawyers, a distinguished client base, and a firm foundation for subsequent growth.

Today Mays & Valentine is one of Virginia's largest law firms. From its traditional origins emphasizing litigation, real estate law, estate planning, and general business, the merger developed specialized fields necessitated by changing client needs. Mays & Valentine has earned respect throughout the region for its capabilities in municipal law, corporate finance, banking, taxation, labor/management relations, antitrust, environmental, and public utility regulation law.

The firm's headquarters is in the Sovran Center at 12th and Main streets in Richmond. By the end of 1989 Mays & Valentine had other office locations in Arlington, Norfolk, and Hanover.

Present and former Mays & Valentine lawyers have held positions as counsel to the president of the United States, secretary of the Army, secretary of the Navy, U.S. congressmen, attorneys general of Virginia, state court judges, commissioners of the State Corporation Commission and the State Alcoholic Beverage Control Board, and members of the Virginia General Assembly.

The firm's partners have included presidents of the Virginia Bar Association, the Virginia State Bar, the Richmond Bar Association, the National Association of Regulatory Commissioners, the Association of Life Insurance Counsel, the Legal Section of the American Council of Life Insurance, the Legal Services Corporation of Virginia, and the Metropolitan Richmond Legal Aid Society.

Partners in the firm are fellows or members of the American College of Trial Lawyers, the American College of Probate Counsel, the American College of Real Estate Lawyers, the American Board of Trial Advocates, the American Law Institute, the American Bar Foundation, and the Virginia Law Foundation.

Mays & Valentine lawyers are frequent lecturers at legal education programs sponsored by groups in Virginia and around the country, and at programs for laymen and business groups. Several have served as adjunct professors at the law and business schools of the University of Virginia, the University of Richmond, Virginia Commonwealth University, the College of William and Mary, and other institutions.

Mays & Valentine takes pride in its heritage of service to the people of Virginia and envisions a continuing and vital role as part of the commonwealth's business and legal communities.

John S. Davenport III, one of the founders of Mays & Valentine.

WILLIAM M. MERCER, INC.

THE HUMAN-RESOURCES consulting business is one of the nation's fastest growing and most dynamic industries. Over the past 50 years the business world has grown increasingly complex—and few areas have been as affected as the relationship between employers and employees.

Human-resources professionals today face challenges their predecessors never knew of: organizational change brought about by mergers, acquisitions, and divestitures; a work force whose values and priorities are in transition; burgeoning government regulations; and significant pressure to manage costs and contribute to the bottom line.

Each year more businesses and other organizations turn to independent outside advisers to help with the increasingly complicated aspects of the employment relationship. At the forefront of these independent advisers is William M. Mercer, Inc., the world's largest human-resources consulting firm.

Until 1990 the firm was known as William M. Mercer Meidinger Hansen, an amalgam of three merged firms, each with a respected name and long history in the field of employee-benefits and compensation consulting.

Bill Mercer founded William M. Mercer, Limited, in 1946 in Vancouver; Bernard Meidinger founded Meidinger, Inc., in 1936 in Louisville; and Arthur Hansen founded A.S. Hansen, Inc., in 1930 in Chicago.

Today William M. Mercer, Inc., headquartered in New York City, has a total of 6,700 employees, including 870 actuaries. The firm serves clients from offices in 102 cities in 20 countries and is the world's largest human-resources consulting firm with revenues for 1989 at $622 million. Mercer is a wholly owned subsidiary of Marsh & McLennan, the world's leading insurance broker. Marsh & McLennan was founded in 1871, and its stock is listed on the New York,

The headquarters building of William M. Mercer, Inc., at 6606 West Broad Street. The firm shares the building with other offices.

Midwest, Pacific, and London stock exchanges.

To meet the needs of its increasing number of international clients, Mercer has expanded to a network of 50 offices outside the United States. This global presence enables Mercer to help businesses coordinate their human resources needs worldwide by developing strategies based on the specific cultures of the countries involved.

Mercer's Richmond office has more than 125 professionals working together to serve organizations with headquarters or operations facilities in Virginia. "Although Mercer is the largest human-resources consulting firm, we are intentionally diversified," says Charles H. Metzgar, managing director of Mercer's Richmond office.

"We emphasize providing our clients with responsive, individualized advice through the professionals in full-service field offices. Our structure fosters independence and responsibility while supporting our consultants with the firm's worldwide professional and technical resources."

Paul Rehm in the computer room.

communications, personalized benefit statements, and human resources planning, training, and development.

Mercer's asset planning consultants provide investment consulting services relating to tax-exempt trust and endowment funds, including investment manager selection, performance evaluation and monitoring, development of investment policies, and the negotiation of guaranteed investment contracts (GICs) and annuities.

One of the key areas of focus for employers today is health care cost management. Mercer's consultants assist their clients in effecting greater management of health care costs through evaluating and negotiating managed-care delivery systems, evaluating utilization review organization, and conducting health benefit claim audits.

Recently Mercer's Richmond office has seen significant growth in the number of Virginia employers working with the firm to design, communicate, and administer flexible benefits programs. These programs are increasingly popular as they offer employees choices rather than a set package of benefits and compensation. The interest in these programs mirror what is happening nationwide as companies struggle to maintain and improve employee morale and efficiency while managing escalating benefit costs. With Mercer being a national leader in flexible benefits programs, the Richmond office will continue to be in the forefront of this trend.

William M. Mercer, Inc., is proud of its ability to help the full spectrum of employers, from *Fortune* 500 companies to family-owned businesses—and everything in between—as they advance their business goals. The Richmond office serves an expanding employer population in Virginia and, through working with the state's employers, continues to grow.

In both the domestic and international arenas, Mercer professionals play a significant role in helping clients clarify compensation and benefits objectives, meet those objectives in a cost-effective manner, and maximize returns on their human-resource investments.

In general, Mercer's consultants help clients find solutions to business problems through their expertise in the areas of design and administration of employee benefit programs, which include pension, group benefits, flexible benefits, and defined contribution plans.

Mercer's consultants further work with clients to ensure that their compensation systems support their business plans and strategies. Their work includes the design and administration of base salary and executive compensation programs, compensation surveys, and performance management systems.

The firm's communication and human resource management services include employee research surveys, compensation and benefits

A boardroom setting for a meeting with (from left) George Wagoner, Sandy Boardway, Larry Gibson, Chuck Metzgar, Herb Nichols, and Steve McElhaney.

WILLIAMS, MULLEN, CHRISTIAN & DOBBINS

SINCE ITS TURN-of-the-century origins, Williams, Mullen, Christian & Dobbins has evolved as one of Richmond's leading full service law firms.

The present firm is the product of a 1986 merger of two long-established leaders of the Richmond legal community. Williams, Mullen & Christian was founded by Lewis C. Williams and James Mullen in 1909. Williams and Mullen merged with the firm founded by Stuart Christian in 1961, creating what was then the second-largest law firm in Virginia.

Wallerstein, Goode & Dobbins was formed by Virgil R. Goode and Morton L. Wallerstein in 1919. This predominantly business-oriented firm emphasized banking and general business law. Howard W. Dobbins is now the senior statesman of Williams, Mullen, Christian & Dobbins.

From their beginnings these firms shared a vision of Richmond as a city with great commercial potential. They dedicated themselves to working with small to medium-size growth companies, and today a number of these companies have become some of the best-known names in Virginia business.

Similarly, Williams, Mullen, Christian & Dobbins has continued to grow in stature to become one of the most highly respected law firms in Virginia. With more than 85 attorneys, the firm has one of the state's major business-oriented law practices. "We are not so large that there is the tendency to over-staff on accounts, but we are large enough to cover a full complement of specialties," says Theodore L. Chandler, Jr., the firm's vice president/business development.

"We represent a lot of the area's high-growth businesses that have the potential to develop into large, thriving organizations. Historically that's been our strong suit. Because of that

focus, we also represent a number of large, publicly-owned corporations."

Never resting on its considerable laurels, the firm recognizes that today's legal environment is vastly different from doing business in turn-of-the-century Richmond. Williams, Mullen, Christian & Dobbins now offers a range of services that would have been far beyond the scope of their predecessors.

The firm's attorneys include specialists in business law, litigation, commercial banking and finance, real estate, labor and employment law, mergers and acquisitions, employee benefits, estate planning and administration, bankruptcy and creditors' rights, insurance, and taxation.

Traditional special strengths at Williams, Mullen, Christian & Dobbins are securities law, commercial litigation, insurance, and corporate law. The emerging high-growth areas of the firm's practice are environmental and energy law, several international

Julious P. Smith, Jr., Samuel W. Hixon III, and Howard W. Dobbins.

specialties, and regulatory and administrative law, including lobbying.

"In today's environment, you have to describe the firm in terms of areas of specialty," says Julious P. Smith, Jr., president of the firm, "but, in fact, the firm has always viewed each of our clients as individuals, and their legal needs as a call for individual service. Only with this understanding can highly specialized legal issues be properly analyzed and resolved."

Most clients of Williams, Mullen, Christian & Dobbins work with a team consisting of at least one partner, an associate, and, perhaps, a paralegal. In this way, the client has the assurance that experienced counsel is involved with the matter, while support work is being performed in the most cost-efficient manner.

Williams, Mullen, Christian & Dobbins is one of Virginia's major business-oriented law practices. Dating back to 1909, the firm maintains the integrity and traditions of its past while commiting itself to the legal complexities of the future.

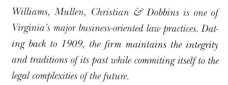

"We try never to lose sight of the fact that we are in the service business," says Chandler. "It is incumbent upon us to find cost-efficient ways to deliver quality products. Accordingly, we challenge everyone in our organization, lawyers and staff, to do the extra little things that enhance client relationships."

The firm often provides educational seminars for its clients on various subjects. It also produces regular newsletters such as *D.I.R.T. Law*, a newsletter published for real estate

The reception area of the offices of Williams, Mullen, Christian & Dobbins.

clients, and a new *Environmental Law Letter*. Similarly, *Laborbrief*, the firm's newsletter published for its employment law clients, was so popular that it has been reconstituted as the *Virginia Employment Law Letter* and is now available by subscription.

In order to maintain the high quality of its services and to expand its practice, Williams, Mullen, Christian & Dobbins recruits talented young men and women who are capable of engendering client confidence and satisfaction. In addition, the firm has formal in-house seminars for its attorneys that are designed to keep them up to date on emerging trends and changes in the law.

Associates come to Williams, Mullen, Christian & Dobbins with the expectation that they will remain and grow with the firm as their careers progress. Careful recruitment and that shared expectation have produced an enviably low turnover, with a resulting stability and continuity that is rare in the legal profession. That, in turn, allows the firm to cultivate the long-term client relationships that it has traditionally maintained and many other law firms have found to be elusive.

The firm has a similar dedication to the community. Williams, Mullen, Christian & Dobbins' attorneys participate in many leading civic and professional activities, including teaching at colleges and universities, serving on educational and cultural boards, raising funds for charitable organizations, participating in area churches and synagogues, and continuing the firm's long-standing tradition of leadership in the organized bar, particularly at the local and state levels. Among the firm's partners are former rectors of the University of Virginia, James Madison University, and the Hampton University, a former deputy attorney general of Virginia, and a former member of the House of Delagates of the Virginia General Assembly. Fred G. Pollard, who is of counsel to the firm, is a former lieutenant governor of Virginia.

Williams, Mullen continues to expand its specialties and geographical influence. "We're involved in an innovative network with other law firms, smaller firms, throughout Virginia," says Julious Smith. "We are also establishing legal networks in other areas, including internationally. But through the inevitable changes in the delivery of legal services, we will never outgrow our commitment to provide our clients with individualized, high-quality service."

ALLEN, ALLEN, ALLEN & ALLEN

GEORGE E. ALLEN ENTITLED his published memoirs *The Law as a Way of Life*. In fact, law has become a way of life for a large part of the Allen family. A dozen members of the Allen family have served as trial lawyers in the firm founded by George Allen. They include three sons of the founder, six grandsons, and two granddaughters.

Allen, Allen, Allen & Allen represents plaintiffs in personal injury cases. That is all they do. George E. Allen, Sr., began practicing law in Lunenburg County in 1910. He moved his family to Richmond in 1932. His firm has specialized in representing plaintiffs in personal injury cases since 1955.

Allen, Allen, Allen & Allen never divides its loyalties by representing insurance companies or corporations seeking defense counsel. Three generations of Allens have devoted their skills, experience, and expertise to plaintiffs' rights.

They have done so not just in the courtroom but also in the legislature. George E. Allen, Sr., was a Virginia state senator. His son, George E. Allen, Jr., served in the Virginia House of Delegates for 28 years.

The staff of Allen, Allen, Allen & Allen is comprised of more than 70 skilled personal injury experts, all dedicated to making certain that every case receives exacting attention. The firm's highly trained and experienced investigative department gathers all evidence needed to build successful cases. Allen, Allen, Allen & Allen is also highly regarded for its use of expert witnesses in the courtroom, including doctors, accident reconstruction experts, economists, engineers, and other professionals.

In its Staples Mill Road office, the firm has one of

the largest and most extensive personal injury libraries in the United States, with more than 6,000 volumes. The library includes not only law books but texts on medicine, engineering, chemistry, safety, and numerous other specialties related to personal injury. The firm's computers are linked to national data bases, providing its attorneys with instant access to the latest nationwide developments in personal injury law.

Allen, Allen, Allen & Allen has been an innovator among Virginia law firms using video and computer technology to enhance the value of personal injury cases. The firm was among the first in the state to take

The firm's ability to negotiate favorable settlements in the majority of cases is based on the Allens' proven abilities as trial lawyers.

depositions on videotape and to use videotape in the presentation of evidence.

In an era of full-service law firms that hire large numbers of lawyers, each with different specialties, the Allen firm stands out for its specialized approach to the practice of law. Allen, Allen, Allen & Allen was one of the first in the nation to limit its practice to personal injury cases. It remains among the largest of such firms in the country.

Its specialized experience enables the firm to fully assess the merits of each individual case prior to acceptance. As a result, the firm makes a strong commitment to take any case to trial if necessary. This willingness to go to court to fight for each client, backed by an impressive, winning track record, puts the Allens in the strongest-possible posi-

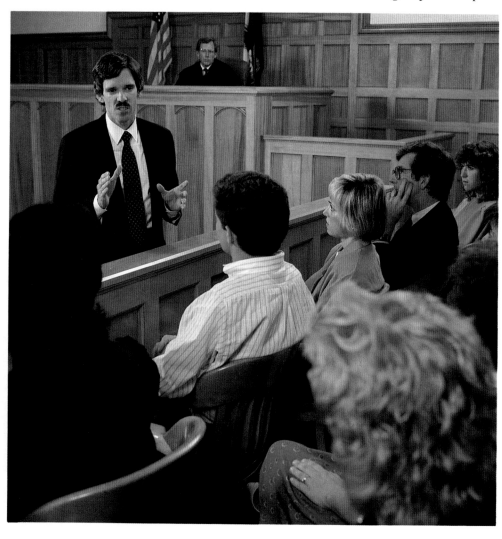

Three generations of Allens have devoted their skill, experience, and expertise to protecting the rights of injured victims. Pictured here are (from left) Ashby B., George E. Jr., and Wilbur C. Allen. The portrait in the background is George E. Allen, Sr., founder.

tion to negotiate a prompt, fair settlement. When necessary to defend the rights of injured clients, the Allen firm has taken cases all the way to the Supreme Court of the United States.

In 1965, when he was 60 years old, George Allen, Sr., became the first recipient of the Award for Courageous Advocacy by the American College of Trial Lawyers, in recognition of his successful pro bono defense of a black Harvard law student in a controversial civil rights case. He courageously accepted the case despite overwhelming popular sentiment in Prince Edward County against the defendant. "I have learned a lot about the decency of

other human beings through your example," the student later wrote in a letter to his lawyer.

George E. Allen, Sr., a native of Lunenburg County, was a graduate of Virginia Tech and the University of Virginia. George E. Allen, Jr., graduated from Virginia Tech and the T.C. Williams School of Law at the University of Richmond. His brothers, Ashby B. Allen and Wilbur C. Allen both

earned their law degrees at the University of Virginia.

Always devoted to community service, the Allen family has endowed the George E. Allen chair at the T.C. Williams School of Law. Allen, Allen, Allen & Allen also frequently sponsors high-impact public-service advertisements dedicated to reminding the public of the dangers of drinking and driving, the need for child safety laws and programs, and other related issues.

This public service safety campaign includes advertisements in print and on television. Readers and viewers would be well advised to pay very close attention. The Allens know what they are talking about.

HUNTON & WILLIAMS

"THE HALLMARK OF our firm and the reason for its success is quality," wrote the managing partner of Hunton & Williams in an internal memorandum some years ago. "That means superior professional expertise as well as those traits of character that inspire confidence and establish leadership. Quality of that kind does not come quickly." Hunton & Williams has been building its superior legal reputation for 90 years.

With more than 400 lawyers (and still growing), Hunton & Williams is not only Virginia's largest law firm, but it is also among the largest in the nation. The firm served early notice that it intended to play a dominant role in the state. Founded in 1901 by Beverley B. Munford, Eppa Hunton, Jr., Edmund Randolph Williams, and Henry W. Anderson, its four-lawyer staff instantly made it the most influential law firm in Richmond.

The founders deliberately modeled their partnership on the big legal firms of New York City, setting out to build a law firm in Richmond that could provide its clients with all necessary legal services. Their publicly expressed intention was to build a Richmond law firm that would be the equal of the profession's best, anywhere in the country.

Almost a century later Hunton & Williams is among the elite of the American legal establishment. Its client list includes some of the nation's leading corporations (and several smaller firms facing giant legal challenges). Its lawyers are equally at home in their Richmond headquarters, in New York, California, Florida, or anywhere else in America. As managing partner Taylor Reveley III says, "Our home office is in Richmond, but we've become a national organization. We can work wherever the client needs us."

The firm's first important client was John L. Williams & Sons, a leading investment banking firm in the South that just happened to be owned by founder Randolph Williams' family. Eppa Hunton, Jr., a delegate from Fauquier County, was a

When the Electric Building at Seventh and Franklin streets was completed in 1913, Hunton & Williams moved into the 10th floor and remained there until 1967, when a new office building at 707 East Main became home to the firm.

powerful voice at the Virginia Constitutional Convention of 1901-1902. Beverley Munford was a member of the Virginia General Assembly. Munford retired from the practice of law in 1906.

The fourth founder, Henry Anderson, established a reputation as one of the ablest lawyers in the country, particularly in the field of railroad reorganization. His activities helped the firm to expand its practice beyond the confines of Richmond and into the Southeast.

Within a few years the partners had built a powerful and distin-

guished clientele. It included the Virginia Railway & Power Company (later Vepco and now Virginia Power), the Seaboard Coast Line and Southern railroads (both now part of CSX), the Norfolk & Portsmouth Traction Company, the South Atlantic Life Insurance Company, and numerous other prestigious firms.

Thomas B. Gay became a partner in 1916 and stayed with the firm until he died in 1983. T. Justin Moore, the general counsel of Vepco, joined the firm in April 1932, and the firm name (changed in 1927 to Hunton, Williams, Anderson & Gay) became Hunton, Williams, Anderson, Gay & Moore. The firm adopted its current name in 1970.

Hunton & Williams became one of the first law firms in the nation to recognize that the increasing complexity of the legal system mandated the development of increasingly specialized counsel. Maintaining its traditional place as the largest law firm in Richmond, the firm had 17 attorneys on its rolls by 1939.

Through the middle of the century a third generation of lawyers, led by George D. Gibson and Lewis F. Powell, Jr. (now a retired justice of the United States Supreme Court), brought new luster to the firm's already well-polished image. As advances in transportation technology made geographic expansion possible, the firm began developing its regional practice.

In addition to its Richmond headquarters, Hunton & Williams has offices in Washington, D.C., Norfolk, Raleigh, Knoxville, New York, Fairfax, Atlanta, and Brussels, Belgium. Its influence extends even further. "Telephones and telemarketing, and the telecommunications revolution in general, make it possible to live where you want and practice law wherever you need," says Reveley.

Today the firm defines its primary marketing area as extending from New York to Atlanta, with Richmond and Washington as twin keystones, and Brussels as the gateway to the international marketplace. It is

partner in the extraordinary Riverfront Plaza complex, built along the James River in downtown Richmond. The firm will be among the building's first tenants.

Since its beginnings Hunton & Williams has encouraged its lawyers to be active in their profession and in service to their communities. Over the years its ranks have provided presidents of the Richmond Bar Association, the Virginia State Bar, the Virginia Bar Association, and the American Bar Association. In 1983 one of the firm's younger partners, John Charles Thomas, at age 32, was appointed to the Virginia Supreme Court.

Once all of Hunton & Williams' partners were Richmond natives. Today lawyers at the firm represent more than 60 different law schools and come from nearly every state and many foreign countries.

Hunton & Williams gains a commanding view of old and new Richmond with a move to new offices in the East Tower of Riverfront Plaza in 1991. The twin sunset-red granite towers form a dramatic addition to the skyline of Richmond's business and financial district and a fitting riverfront location for one of the top law firms in the nation.

aggressively seeking business nationwide and abroad. Hunton & Williams already provides representation in the United States for several foreign-based multinational corporations.

The firm has occupied several different locations in Richmond. Its original home was on the northeast corner of Ninth and Main streets, in what was then known as the Dispatch Building. It then shared office space in the Electric Building, owned by Virginia Railway & Power, the firm's leading client.

In 1967 Hunton & Williams moved to 700 Main Street. Nine years later it moved to 707 East Main, where it occupies 10 floors of offices. The firm's newewst home will be a dramatic addition to the skyline. Hunton & Williams is a joint-venture

Among the lawyers of Hunton & Williams are many distinguished alumni of educational and corporate administration and public service. They include the former president of Washington & Lee University, former executives of nearly a dozen major corporations, a former minority leader of the U.S. House of Representatives, and former Virginia governor and attorney general Gerald L. Baliles. Another former partner, former Virginia governor Charles S. Robb, now serves in the U.S. Senate.

CHRISTIAN, BARTON, EPPS, BRENT & CHAPPELL

THE WALNUT PANELING, subdued lighting, and gracious art collection of its headquarters reflects the heritage of Old Richmond. Its engraved letterhead on heavy, cream-colored bond is dignified and traditional. All of which belies the modernism and dynamic spirit that lie just below the surface of this Richmond law firm.

With more than 50 lawyers, Christian, Barton, Epps, Brent & Chappell ranks as a medium-size firm in Richmond. This gives members of the firm the luxury of specialization, yet allows clients to receive the kind of efficient, personal service that they have come to expect.

"Our size is one of our real advantages," says one partner. "We have both the capabilities of the giant firms and the personal touch of a small partnership."

The firm has built its practice on four basic tenets: the highest quality of legal services, the timeliness with which those services are rendered, the informed and practical nature of advice given, and the cost effectiveness of its legal services.

To maintain quality, the firm recruits its lawyers from among candidates possessing outstanding academic credentials earned at the nation's finest colleges and law schools. Many of the firm's lawyers are graduates of the University of Richmond, the University of Virginia, the College of William and Mary, and Washington and Lee University, but numerous outstanding out-of-state law schools are also well represented.

In 1987 the presidents of three prestigious professional organizations were all drawn from the firm's ranks. R. Harvey Chappell, Jr., was president of the American College of Trial Lawyers, Roderick B. Mathews (then a partner) was president of the Virginia State Bar, and Michael W. Smith was president of the Richmond Bar Association.

That tradition of community service has been part of the firm since its earliest days. Both founding partners—Andrew Christian and Robert Barton—volunteered for military service in World War I. The phe-

nomenon repeated itself in World War II, when all of the firm's lawyers physically able to do so again enlisted in the military.

Robert Barton retired from the military as a general, having previously served in the Virginia General Assembly. Andrew Christian died shortly after World War II and following his service in China. Alex W. Parker, who joined the firm soon

Pictured here (from left) are A.C. Epps, Andrew J. Brent, and R. Harvey Chappell, Jr.

after its founding, served with honor in the Navy.

While dedication to community, state, and nation remains a powerful tradition at Christian, Barton, it does not necessarily produce a common focus. "All of our people are different," says a partner. "There is no lock step."

There is, however, a common bond, notes that partner. "The lawyers who are here, and the way we operate, make something of this firm that both we and our clients enjoy and value."

The firm is generally organized into two practice areas: litigation and corporate, with these practice areas being further broken down into spe-

cialized departments. The litigation group generates a diverse practice, with a focus on tort defense in products liability, negligence, professional malpractice, insurance, environmental law, local government issues, and corporate, commercial, and contract disputes. Many of its cases originate with referrals from other attorneys.

The corporate group provides comprehensive legal services for its distinguished list of clients. Primarily medium- and large-size corporations, most of the corporate clients of Christian, Barton, Epps, Brent & Chappell have been with the firm for many years.

"There is a high degree of continuity between our lawyers and our clients," says one partner. "Most of us have known our clients personally for a long time. That personal chemistry is very important to us."

The firm is deeply rooted in Richmond and in the Commonwealth. Its clients include several governmental entities such as the Capital Region Airport Commission, the Richmond Metropolitan Authority, and the Virginia Housing and Development Authority.

A.C. Epps is a Richmond native, a graduate of the University of Virginia who has been with the firm since 1938. A former member of the Richmond School Board, he is a past president of the Virginia Bar Association, the Richmond Bar Association, and the Metropolitan Legal Aid Project, as well as a member of the board of directors and a past president of both Children's Hospital and the Friends of the Richmond Public Library. He has also been active with

Seated (from left) are Patricia M. Powis, Theodore F. Adams III, Alexander W. Wellford, Michael W. Smith, and Mary M. Grove. Standing are David C. Kohler, James L. Banks, Jr., and Orran L. Brown.

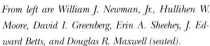

From left are William J. Newman, Jr., Hullihen W. Moore, David I. Greenberg, Erin A. Sheehey, J. Edward Betts, and Douglas R. Maxwell (seated).

the Carpenter Center for the Performing Arts, the Richmond Symphony, and numerous other community organizations.

Andrew Jackson Brent is also a Richmond-born graduate of the University of Virginia. A former member of the board of visitors of Virginia Commonwealth University, he has been chairman of the board of trustees of Mary Baldwin College and is a member of the board and former president of The Collegiate Schools. He has been an active leader of public broadcasting in Virginia, and he served as a director of numerous commercial communications firms.

R. Harvey Chappell, Jr., a graduate of William and Mary, has been a member of the board of visitors of his alma mater and its rector, a member of the board of visitors of Virginia State University, a member of the board of governors of the American Bar Association, and president of the American College of Trial Lawyers. A past president of the Bar Association of the City of Richmond and the Virginia State Bar, he has also served as president of Children's Hospital and as a trustee of Westminster Canterbury.

J. Edward Betts, the newly elected managing partner of Christian, Barton, Epps, Brent & Chappell, is a graduate of Colgate University, the University of Richmond Law School, and the Harvard Law School. He has served as a professor of antitrust law at the University of Richmond Law School, secretary of the board of trustees of Mary Baldwin College, vice president of the board of directors of The Steward School, president of the Friends of the Richmond Public Library, and president of the University of Richmond Law School Association.

BROWDER & RUSSELL

JOHN B. BROWDER BEGAN his law practice more than 50 years ago during a time when electric trolley cars rolled past the young attorney's office in the old Richmond Trust Building at 7th and Main streets. Today located in the heart of downtown Richmond, Browder and Russell is one of Virginia's most respected law firms.

In direct contrast to the traditional image of a venerable law firm, Browder and Russell is truly unique. The body of its lawyers are relatively young—only one partner is past 50 years of age—and the firm's style is aggressive and ambitious.

"This firm has a unique personality," says Jack B. Russell, chairman of the executive committee. "When we add attorneys, we look for highly trained, talented, capable people. But we also look for people who want to practice law in the environment that we have here."

When Jack Russell joined forces with Browder in 1952, he brought to the firm a new level of expertise in medical malpractice defense. As a re-

ABOVE: State-of-the-art data processing and traditional research join forces at Browder & Russell. Seated is H. Aubrey Ford III; standing is John M. Clayton.

LEFT: Pictured here (from left) are Michael L. Goodman, Michael E. Harman, Robert S. Brewbaker, Jr., and Richard K. Bennett.

sult, today Browder and Russell has a firmly established reputation throughout central Virginia as the law firm of the medical community. The region's leading medical malpractice insurer, the St. Paul Insurance Companies, has been a major client for more than 35 years. The firm has also played a vital role in several historic cases involving organ transplants and represents the national organ transplant network.

The firm continues to maintain its leadership role in litigation practice. From the youngest associate up, Browder & Russell strives to ensure that each lawyer has extensive in-court experience. It is this emphasis that results in the firm's maintaining its reputation as a top trial firm. "Lawyer for lawyer, we have more trial experience than any firm in town," says partner John D. Epps.

In addition to its extensive medical malpractice experience, the firm's litigation practice includes commercial real estate and construction litigation, products liability and personal injury, creditors' rights, employment matters, annexation, land use, domestic relations, and insurance defense and coverage.

The team approach has long been a part of Browder and Russell's environment of mutual support. "The attorneys here are willing to share solutions as well as problems," says executive committee member Richard K. Bennett.

Committed to their work, the attorneys at Browder and Russell also possess a strong sense of community. They are active supporters of a wide range of Richmond-area civic activities. Several of the firm's attorneys have participated in the Metropolitan Richmond Chamber of Commerce Metropolitan Leadership Program. Michael E. Harman and David P. Corrigan are champions of Elk Hill Farm. Thomas D. Stokes III is chairman of Camp Greenbriar for Boys.

The team approach has long been a part of Browder & Russell's environment of mutual support. Here, Thomas D. Stokes III reviews a file with P. Christopher Guedri.

The diversity of interests among the lawyers is broad-based. H. Aubrey Ford is on the board of The Richmond Ballet. Michael L. Goodman, a past president of the young lawyers section of the Richmond Bar Association, has been a syndicated cartoonist and his work is frequently featured in *Virginia Business* magazine and in legal publications throughout the region. W.F. Drewry Gallalee is a former tennis pro.

Professionally, the firm's lawyers are continually recognized for their outstanding achievement in the practice of law. Jack Russell is a Fellow of the American College of Trial Lawyers. John M. Clayton is vice president of the Virginia Association of Defense Attorneys. John Epps was one of only 10 lawyers to be selected as a Fellow of the Young Lawyers Section of the Virginia Bar Association for his contributions to that organization.

Browder & Russell's summer program is a major source of new attorneys for the firm. "It is designed to give each summer associated broad exposure to our various litigation specialties," says P. Christopher Guedri, chairman of the recruiting committee. Although legal research and writing are an important part of the summer program, each summer intern is also given the opportunity to participate in other aspects of cases, including direct client contact. Students eligible for third-year practice can obtain actual courtroom experience.

Above all, the lawyers at Browder and Russell value their clients and strive to provide excellent legal service at a reasonable price. Among the growing number of "mega-firms," Browder and Russell stands apart as a small, service-oriented firm. "We don't want to lose the personal touch," says Robert S. Brewbaker, Jr., a member of the executive committee. "Our clients expect personal service. They know us as individuals and expect us to take care of them personally. We all want and expect to keep it that way."

11

BUILDING GREATER RICHMOND

RICHMOND'S DEVELOPERS, PROPERTY management firms, and real estate professionals continually create and revitalize the urban landscapes of today and tomorrow.

Photo courtesy, Henley & Savage

THE WOOLFOLK COMPANIES

ONE OF THE Richmond area's largest developers and builders of commercial and residential real estate began when Douglass K. Woolfolk started constructing custom homes some 30 years ago. The quality workmanship that Woolfolk demanded in those finer homes in Salisbury, Cambridge, and River Oaks back in the 1960s and early 1970s can still be found in the major projects The Woolfolk Companies is developing today.

That reputation for quality construction and attention to detail has remained a Woolfolk trademark as the firm grew from a general contractor into a full real estate development corporation. In 1987 the family reorganized the business into The Woolfolk Companies: Woolfolk Properties, Inc., and Woolfolk Construction, with the capabilities of developing, building, leasing, and managing real estate properties.

Behind it all is a proud Richmond family. "If I can't drive by a project and look at it with pride, then we don't want to get involved in the first place," says Kyle Woolfolk, president of Woolfolk Construction and the oldest of the three Woolfolk brothers. Their father remains chief executive officer of The Woolfolk Companies. Neil Woolfolk is vice president/sales and leasing of Woolfolk Properties, and Alec Woolfolk is vice president/ project manager of Woolfolk Construction.

The men were not always company executives. "Dad insisted that we all start out in the field," remembers Alec. "It wasn't easy because you always expect more from your sons or brothers than from other employees.

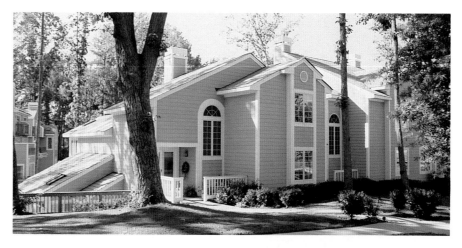

But Dad always respected our outlook, and we have always respected his vision."

The key to the Woolfolk concept, says Kyle, is loyalty. The brothers are loyal to each other, to the company, and to the clients. And most Woolfolk employees are made to feel a part of the family and see the firm as a lifetime career. "We hire good people," says Kyle, "and train them to be a part of the team so we can all be proud of the end results."

The Woolfolk Companies has grown into a diversified organization structured to provide services in all areas of real estate development. While the firm owns and manages many of its own properties, it also provides sales, leasing, and property management for speculative and joint-venture properties. In fact, Woolfolk can provide anything from a single service such as land planning,

This contemporary office building is part of a 150,000-square-foot office park built by Woolfolk Construction in its mixed-use development at Stony Point, in the prestigious Bon Air section of Richmond.

The Bluffs are comprised of 103 luxury condominium town homes, built by Woolfolk Construction. These award-winning residences are nestled in woodlands adjacent to Richmond's city park in Bon Air.

zoning assistance, or budgeting to complete turnkey service for an investor who wants to get involved with real estate development.

Woolfolk Construction continues to be the contractor of choice for many of the Richmond area's leading developers. Regardless of the contractual structure under which a project is developed, Woolfolk's work has continued to demonstrate the superlative quality that has always been its hallmark. And as Kyle points out, all of his supervisors are familiar with the entire development and property management process. No matter what their involvement with a given project, that knowledge and experience stands them in good stead. "We build everything," explains Neil, "as if we are going to own it for long-term value."

Woolfolk's diversity is also apparent in the many distinct styles and

Woolfolk Construction Company produces turnkey projects from steel framing to finished interiors as in this three-story contemporary office building. Centre-Court is a 135,000-square-foot office park in Chesterfield County being built for H.U. Development Corporation.

categories of its properties. Company projects include office parks, financial institutions, medical offices and clinics, industrial facilities, research and development centers, multiuse commercial space, shopping centers, and condominiums and mixed-use developments.

That diversity has allowed it to adjust to changing market conditions. The family first branched out in 1974, when the market for residential construction turned down, and it had a chance to develop the Sycamore Square shopping center. "It was a classic example of turning a problem into an exciting opportunity," remembers Douglass. Since then, the firm has continued to diversify.

As developers the Woolfolks receive high marks in their regard for the land and their community. Douglass is proud to say, "We like to feel we have been building community assets for some 30 years." A perfect case in point is the transformation of barren, unproductive fields at Stony Point into a highly successful shopping center, office and medical park, and residential development in the prestigious Bon Air section of Richmond.

The Stony Point offices near Huguenot Road, just off the Chippenham Parkway, is one of Richmond's newest class-A office buildings. The 100,000-square-foot modern complex is already among the city's more prestigious office locations.

The Woolfolk Companies received extensive publicity for its award-winning development of The Bluffs at Stony Point, condominium town homes surrounded by a heavily wooded city-owned park. "We didn't want to disturb existing trees, and we tried to follow the contours of the land and not move any more soil than necessary," recalls Douglass Woolfolk.

Westpark is a $5-million shopping center coordinated and built by Woolfolk Construction for S.L. Nusbaum Development Corporation. Including outparcels, the center totals more than 175,000 square feet of retail space built on 23 acres in Richmond's West End.

Huguenot Place offers another strategic business location between Chesterfield Town Center and the new Bellgrade development featuring a more traditional style of architecture. Designed for medical and professional offices as well as general business use, Huguenot Place provides easy highway access and ample parking.

A more recent project close to the heart of the senior Woolfolk is Bellgrade, just off the junction of Robious and Huguenot roads in Chesterfield County. Douglass remembers riding horses around this historic plantation as a young man. His plans today call for the restoration of the former Bellgrade manor house as the centerpiece for a 161-acre, mixed-use development.

It features a 70-acre, single-family-home residential community focusing on a central lake. The project also provides for luxury offices, a specialty retail arcade, and areas for multifamily housing and medium-density offices. The entire project is bordered and divided by a three-rail white fence with extensive landscaping to retain the equestrian theme of the old Bellgrade Plantation.

In the future, Woolfolk is planning development along Chippenham Parkway near the intersection with Route 10. Scheduled for construction

in 1990, the Winchester project will combine almost 150 acres of scenic Chesterfield County real estate with the convenience of nearly instant access to downtown Richmond.

"This kind of development provides us the opportunity to build in quality," says Kyle. "We can design projects to be timeless with classical design elements. And we can build with a balance between budget and aesthetics."

Until recently, The Woolfolk Companies has maintained a low profile in Richmond. It never advertised until 1986. "With our established customers, we knew that we could rely totally on our reputation," says Neil. "Now Richmond is changing. A lot of the newcomers don't know who we are, even though they see our work all around them. So now we're marketing our company to incoming prospects."

Those long-term clients include area banks such as Investors, Signet, Sovran, and Crestar. Woolfolk built the headquarters for Investors Savings

Monument Avenue Corporate Center is a highly successful office complex developed and constructed by The Woolfolk Company in 1980. The traditional colonial brick complex totals 11 buildings with more than 130,000 square feet of office space in the 5000 block of Monument Avenue.

Marble and mahogany entrance foyers provide Class A space in the Stony Point office managed by Woolfolk Properties.

Bank and the Virginia Association of Realtors, as well as medical office centers within the Johnson-Willis Hospital complex.

Kyle speculates that demand for medical, research, and mixed-use development will continue to expand. Plans are under way for building a complete medical complex with a major hospital, psychiatric clinic, and health and rehabilitation centers all in a campus setting with lakes and open parklands.

For many years Woolfolk confined its activities to the city of Rich-

mond and Chesterfield County. It now has projects under way statewide. "The turning point in our company history came when we started blending the new ideas of the second generation with Dad's established values," says Kyle. The firm has grown more than 500 percent in the past seven years. Gross sales are increasing by 15 to 20 percent each year.

Plans are to continue the firm's involvement in Richmond, Williamsburg, Fredericksburg, and Charlottesville. He is also considering expansion beyond the borders of the commonwealth.

As fast as The Woolfolk Companies is increasing, the family is able to maintain extensive outside interest. Douglass Woolfolk is an avid hunter and sailer. His sons play golf, scuba dive, ski, windsurf, and go deep-sea fishing.

They still find time to be active professionally. Both Kyle Woolfolk and his father are past presidents of the central Virginia chapter of the National Association of Industrial and Office Parks.

DANIEL CORPORATION

AS RICHMOND REVIVES its greatest natural resource, the James River, Riverfront Plaza has become a symbol of the city's entry into the next century. Scheduled for occupancy in the fall of 1990, the twin office towers faced in sunset-rose granite will provide 950,000 square feet of elegantly appointed luxury office space.

Riverfront Plaza is a joint venture of the developer Daniel Corporation and two of Richmond's leading businesses: the law firm of Hunton and Williams, and the brokerage house of Wheat, First Securities, Inc. The project is currently 68 percent pre-leased. Tenants who have already committed include Dominion Resources, Inc., Fluor-Daniel, Crestar Bank, and the Downtown Club of Richmond. The project was designed by HKS, Inc., of Dallas, Texas, and is being built by Fluor-Daniel.

"We're delighted to be a part of Richmond's emerging waterfront business district," says Nick Rossini, Daniel Corporation's director of marketing for Riverfront Plaza. "In fact, we're so excited by Richmond that we've selected this city as our base for mid-Atlantic regional operations," he says.

The offices, public park, landscaped plaza, shops, restaurant, and other amenities of Riverfront Plaza will renew the city's historic link with the James. The 3.79-acre site forms a gateway into Richmond's downtown commercial center. The development is bordered by Ninth, 10th, and Byrd streets and by the river.

The design of Riverfront Plaza is modern and uncomplicated. Daniel Corporation selected the neoclassical architecture to reflect the historic character of the riverfront district. Once a strategic location for Richmond's tobacco industry, Riverfront Plaza will remind future generations of Richmond's enduring riverfront heritage.

Amenities of the project include an impressively landscaped park framed between the building and the river's edge and consisting of gardens, walkways, and a magnificently landscaped design. Located in five underground levels are 2,300 on-site parking spaces. For even more tenant

convenience, the ground floors of both the East and West Towers will house an enticing selection of retail shops and boutiques.

Daniel Corporation is a full-service real estate development and investment firm. Headquartered in Birmingham, Alabama, Daniel Corporation currently manages or has ownership interest in approximately 3.2 million square feet of office and commercial space and approximately 5,500 apartment units in 10 states.

Riverfront Plaza is Daniel Corporation's largest single development. The company also has several other projects in the greater Richmond metropolitan area, including the Imperial Plaza Retirement Community and Park Central a 200-acre, master-planned business park in Henrico County.

The firm was originally established in 1964 as the Daniel Realty Corporation (DRC) to manage all properties owned by Daniel International Corporation (DIC). Created in 1934 and based in Greenville, South Carolina, DIC engages in large-scale engineering, construction, and industrial maintenance activities nationwide and in numerous foreign

This photograph portrays the future of downtown Richmond with Riverfront Plaza as its new central focus.

countries.

In 1977 Fluor Corporation acquired DIC and all of its subsidiaries. On August 26, 1986, a group of senior executive-management personnel joined with an outside investor and acquired DRC from Fluor. DRC changed its name to Daniel Corporation in October 1988.

Daniel Corporation currently focuses on key local markets in the Southeast and mid-Atlantic states.

BOWERS, NELMS AND FONVILLE

FEW FIRMS IN RICHMOND dominate their industry as convincingly as Bowers, Nelms and Fonville dominates the real estate market. As the number-one firm in the Richmond area Multiple Listing Service and throughout central Virginia, the firm's more than 500 sales associates operate from 13 office locations in the Richmond, Petersburg, Colonial Heights, and Northern Neck areas. Today Bowers, Nelms and Fonville commands about 30 percent of all the real estate business in the capital area, and nationally it ranks 43rd in size among independent real estate companies.

A firm doesn't get to be number one in any industry just by chance. Bowers, Nelms and Fonville's success is the result of a carefully planned program of growth.

Bowers, Nelms and Fonville was formed in 1967 by three close friends: Richard M. Nelms, Pace M. Fonville, and John Ros Bowers. "We all had been in the real estate business in Richmond for a number of years," says Nelms, now president and chief executive officer of the firm. "We liked each other and respected each others' ability. So we decided to go into business together."

In 1971 tragedy struck the young partnership when John Ros Bowers and a BNF sales associate, Bill Thomas, were killed in an automobile accident.

Not long after that, the firm, now some 20 sales associates strong, developed a mission statement, a copy of which hangs in every sales office. The first sentence reads: "The mission of Bowers, Nelms and Fonville is to provide the highest-quality real estate services to individuals and businesses." That commitment has fueled the impressive growth of the company over two decades.

Until the late 1970s the firm was, in the words of one Bowers, Nelms and Fonville executive, "content to be just another real estate firm." Then the senior partners decided to embark on a plan that would turn the company into Richmond's real estate leader.

In 1977 the firm implemented its first five-year plan and organized a recognition program for top producers. That year Nelms served as president of the Richmond Association of Realtors and was recognized as Realtor of the Year.

In 1979 the firm opened its first

The Bowers, Nelms and Fonville corporate headquarters is home to nearly 100 employees including a vigorous Commercial Real Estate Division and is located in Innsbrook Corporate Center, a trendsetting mixed-use community in western Henrico County.

"south of the James River" branch office on Huguenot Road. Over the 13 years since its formation, it had grown to 42 associates between its home location on Patterson Avenue and the new Huguenot branch. In 1981 the firm acquired the residential operation of a respected Richmond real estate competitor. Nelms was serving as president of the Virginia Association of Realtors at the time and counts this period as one of the crucial growth periods of the company.

Early in the 1980s high interest rates had almost put an end to the residential real estate market. Nelms and his partners sought new and creative financing solutions, secured a $50-million forward commitment of adjustable-rate mortgages (ARMs), and introduced this new financial product to its market.

"We went from selling houses to selling financing, and we beat the market and our competitors," Nelms recalls. From that point, momentum in the market helped fuel the growth of Bowers, Nelms and Fonville. Over the next eight years it acquired, by merger or buy out, a number of other smaller real estate firms that occupied strategic market positions.

Today Bowers, Nelms and Fonville's administrative operations are located in a strikingly designed, modern office building in

Richmond's impressive Innsbrook Corporate Center. In addition to leading the residential real estate market, with specialized divisions in new homes and relocation services, the company now includes a commercial sales and leasing division, operates a property management department, and has allied ventures in title insurance, a school of real estate, and a national realtor network, Real Estate Leaders of America.

And it continues to innovate. Most recently the company has helped develop a computerized loan origination program called ASSIST that allows buyers to apply for a loan and lock in a rate right in the BNF office, or even in the buyer's home. With ASSIST's mortgage brokerage license, the company has again expanded the services it offers to home sellers and home buyers.

"We go farther for a client, far beyond the service usually offered by the usual real estate company," Nelms

The partners of Bowers, Nelms and Fonville are (from left) Gayle Marlow, senior vice president for Residential Division; C. Lee Hilbert, senior vice president for Commercial Division; Pace M. Fonville, senior vice president for Joint Ventures and Development; and Richard M. Nelms, president and chief executive officer.

says. "For a relocating home buyer, for instance, we'll help with locating suitable schools for the client's children, help the client with financing, help in any way we can."

The firm's mission statement also affirms: "We believe that people are our most important asset and that it is our obligation to help every individual reach full potential." The company provides a nationally renowned sales training program for associates, and provides a full-fledged company marketing program to support the efforts of each sales associate and sales team.

The employees and sales associates at Bowers, Nelms and Fonville are encouraged to participate in a

broad range of community service projects, and more than 100 service organizations in central Virginia are supported by individuals, sales teams, and the company-wide projects of Bowers, Nelms and Fonville.

Nelms and his company remain enthusiastic about Richmond and the capital area's future. "The population of the Richmond metropolitan area is now 680,000," he notes. "By the year 2010, that total will be approximately one million. Those figures spell a bright future for the real estate business here. Bowers, Nelms and Fonville met the challenges of the 1980s head on, and we are confident we'll be able to meet the challenges of the 1990s head on and just as successfully."

Regardless of the changes ahead, Bowers, Nelms and Fonville believes that its commitment to providing the highest-quality real estate services to its clients will remain its true mission and the key to the company's success.

LINGERFELT DEVELOPMENT CORPORATION

HAROLD LINGERFELT RETIRED from his real estate development and construction business in 1979. By then the business he had started 25 years earlier had become one of Richmond's most successful real estate developers.

A graduate of Virginia Tech and a licensed professional engineer, Harold Lingerfelt started a utility construction business in 1954. The firm specialized in constructing and installing conduit systems for sanitary, storm, gas, and water lines. Five years later the company added a steel-rigging division and a manufacturing facility that made precast reinforced concrete panels. That experience enabled Lingerfelt to understand the inner workings of commercial structures and to subsequently create a development company that has earned an impressive region-wide reputation for quality work.

In 1968 Harold Lingerfelt undertook his first real estate development project, a warehouse facility built for lease to B.F. Goodrich. Then came a 205,000-square-foot project for Allen Industries. And the rest, as they say, is history.

Lingerfelt Development Corporation has become one of the leading mid-Atlantic development firms. Its sister companies include Lingerfelt & Associates, Inc., Consulting Engineers, and Lingerfelt Management Corporation, formed in 1980 to handle the growing management responsibilities relating to the company's increasingly complex real estate interests.

Harold and Alan Lingerfelt have not only worked years together on development projects, they have also developed a solid relationship bound by mutual admiration and re-

spect. "It may be hard to believe in this day and time," Alan says, "but I owe most of my business vision, ethics, and philosophy to my father. I learned that you should find your niche, become the best you possibly can be at it, and then maximize your potential in that area. Dad earned a reputation for being fair and honest and [taught me] how to build a company that could help build central Virginia."

Al Lingerfelt has followed his father's path. He too holds a bachelor's degree in civil engineering from Virginia Tech and attended the M.B.A. program at VCU. He has worked in

Harold Lingerfelt and his son, Alan T., have co-authored the Lingerfelt Development Corporation success story. Harold founded the firm in 1954; Alan is now its president.

the engineering and construction-related industries since 1964, specializing in the design, construction, and development of commercial facilities. He is now chairman and chief executive officer of Lingerfelt Development Corporation.

"Our company is built on Dad's spirit and vision. He's the one who taught me to attract top-quality employees and to rely on their judgment," states Alan. That vision has allowed Lingerfelt Development Corporation to stake a claim in the markets of low-rise office buildings, nursing home facilities, and light to medium industrial and office/warehouse complexes.

The company specializes in business developments with 30,000 to 300,000 square feet of space. Often these projects need to be constructed in record time. "It's difficult to shave

days off of the construction timetable without sacrificing quality, but we have found ways to achieve high standards within a short time frame. I wouldn't want to do it every time," Lingerfelt adds quickly, "but we have completed developments in just 45 days."

Not only does the firm construct buildings quickly, but Lingerfelt Development Corporation itself has matured in just six years. In 1984 it had only four employees and 900,000 square feet in the portfolio. Now it has more than 30 employees in Richmond, Norfolk, and Roanoke, and more than 4.2 million square feet of portfolio space.

The company's on-time, under-budget, and with-quality reputation has proven attractive to clients and investors. Most Lingerfelt projects have been 100-percent leased long be-

fore completion.

Lingerfelt Development's client list includes many of the region's *Fortune* 500 companies; federal, state, and municipal government agencies; and many other businesses and non-profit organizations. Tailoring design and structure to meet each client's specific development requirements, Lingerfelt specializes in build-to-suit projects, working with the client to meet specialized needs.

Major Richmond-area projects include the Fairgrounds Distribution Center and Hungary Spring Office Park in Henrico County and the Hermitage Business Park in Richmond. Lingerfelt also has 20 projects in 12 other cities currently in various stages

The Northridge office building in Charlottesville, Virginia, has 60,000 square feet of space.

Valleypointe in Roanoke, Virginia, is a 250-acre, mixed-use corporate park.

of development. Chief among them is Valleypointe, a 250-acre, mixed-use corporate park in Roanoke that will be phased in over a 10-year period.

Harold and Alan Lingerfelt have written the Lingerfelt Development Corporation success story together. Alan's father taught him mostly to never look to short-term profits, but to always plan with long-term goals. "I just hope I can do as good a job teaching my children," says Alan Lingerfelt. The third generation of the Lingerfelt family include four children: Ryan, Justin, Daniel, and Catherine. Ryan, the eldest, expects to begin helping out on Lingerfelt Development projects in the next few years.

FAISON ASSOCIATES

EXCAVATIONS FOR SKYSCRAPERS usually require massive construction equipment, so it was somewhat unusual when workers digging at the site of Richmond's James Center began using hand-held trowels and brushes. The change in technique was occasioned by construction workers' discovery of a part of Richmond's past. Embedded in the earth, 20 feet below the level of Cary Street, they discovered the remains of two canal boats, apparently abandoned in the canal boat basin more than 200 years ago.

Many contractors would have ignored the discovery. Faison Associates, the developer of the James Center, provided assistance in excavating the archaeological discovery. The decision was typical of the developer and of its president, Henry J. Faison, who delayed the construction schedule to allow full excavation to proceed properly.

"It would have been just stupid to ignore the boats or cover them up," says Faison. "It was a legitimate piece of history, and if we and CSX Realty [a joint-venture partner in the James Center] are going to be custodians of this site, we cannot stop exercising our responsibilities when we find some historical artifacts." Before the excavation was over, Faison donated thousands of dollars in cash and professional services. Workers eventually recorded the remains of 63 Kanawha Canal boats.

Faison Associates is based in Charlotte, North Carolina. Founded in 1966, the company originally gained its reputation as an outstanding developer of community shopping districts and regional malls. In the 1980s it diversified into office buildings, mixed-use complexes, and hotels. It currently has projects in nine states in the Midwest and the Southeast.

James Center was born in 1982, when Faison Associates and CSX Realty announced their joint-venture partnership and unveiled plans for the mixed-use complex of office buildings, hotel, and retail space. The partnership promised to include an

athletic club, lush landscaping, and prominent displays of artwork. James Center was to be a "people place."

"We wanted it to be a community place, not just a business place," says Faison. "We wanted an environment that is fun, where people can laugh. People spend over half their waking hours in the work place, and to create someplace where they feel good is the highest calling we can have."

Henry Faison is not really a hopeless romantic; he is quick to explain his approach to real estate development. "It's all business. I'm a pragmatist. Places that people like are much easier to rent." Whether altruism or pragmatism, his philosophy has produced dramatic changes in the Richmond skyline.

Covering 8.2 acres, James Center is the largest mixed-use development in the Southeast and the largest single development in the history of downtown Richmond. It houses the corporate headquarters for CSX, Chesapeake Corporation, Central Fidelity Bank, and Dominion Bank of Richmond. IBM has its regional headquarters in the James Center, as do two of the Big Six international accounting firms. Three of Virginia's largest law firms are housed in the James Center, and the Virginia Department of Economic Development now has its offices there as well.

"We work to make sure that our tenants are happy with their decision to move here," says Faison. "We want their employees to be productive. We want the James Center to have a concentration of talent and excitement. We want it to be a central, professional environment of Richmond."

The complex will total 2.5 million square feet of space when com-

The James Center.

plete. Exceeding the original promises to the community, the James Center includes retail stores, five restaurants, two private clubs, and the 365-room Omni Hotel, the new star of the Richmond hospitality industry. For lunch-hour or after-hours diversion, the attractions of Shockoe Slip are just a short stroll away.

A remarkable display of public artwork highlights the James Center. Its theme is the life along the banks of the James River. Its centerpiece is a 50-foot-high bronze sculpture on the plaza in front of James Center One. The Lloyd Lillie creation symbolizes the canal era.

The development includes the Clock Tower, a freestanding clock and bell tower that invites pedestrians into the James Center Plaza, the tree-lined park at the corner of 10th and Cary streets, which has become a gathering place for Richmonders.

The James Center has become a centerpiece of city life in other ways, as well. Each year the area is magically transformed into a Christmas fantasy featuring 100 white reindeer surrounded by 500,000 tiny lights. The lights are multiplied by the reflective glass of the office towers, and the dazzling display has already become a traditional highlight of Christmas in Richmond. Tens of thousands of people from throughout central Virginia

The Atrium at the James Center.

drive downtown to share this holiday vision.

Some of Faison Associates' other major real estate developments include Southpark Regional Shopping Center in Colonial Heights, Virginia; Interstate Tower in Charlotte, North Carolina; NCNB Plaza in Tampa, Florida; Enterprise Center in Jacksonville, Florida; 100 East in Milwaukee, Wisconsin; Valley View Regional Center in Roanoke; and Peachtree/Lenox Building and One Georgia Center in Atlanta. Other hotels developed by Faison include the Omni Jacksonville Hotel, the Charlotte Marriott City Center Hotel, and the Marriott Courtyard in Charlotte.

RICHMOND HOMES, INC.

ASKED TO DESCRIBE the operation of Richmond Homes, Inc., V. Earl Dickinson, Jr., replies, "We buy raw land, engineer and design it into subdivisions, and sell lots to our own divisions that build different styles of residential units to suit the market."

The firm has its own in-house real estate company to handle the sales and, if needed, Richmond Homes can even place the mortgage for a buyer through its own mortgage company. "Each house is built to order," says Dickinson, "but we have developed a system that gives us the benefits of large-scale, mass-market builders. Our homes are engineered to give the home buyer absolutely the best value for his or her dollar."

Houses constructed by Richmond Homes, located at several different subdivisions throughout the city and the counties surrounding Richmond, sell for prices starting at around $60,000 and topping out at around $200,000. The company antic-

ipates that it will build and sell more than 1,500 units in the first four years of the 1990s. In addition to its local developments, Richmond Homes has projects under way in South Fulton and Clayton counties in Georgia.

"It's just a common sense way of running a construction business," says Dickinson. "Our greatest strength is the motivation and dedication of our employees toward a single goal: to provide the best value in product and service to our customers. Management personnel have stock options, and we maintain a profit-sharing plan for all our employees."

Dickinson built and sold his first house during his college years. The profits from that first venture helped start the business. Founded in 1974 as Dickinson Homes & Development, the firm changed its name to Richmond Homes, Inc., in 1982. By 1990 the company was producing 300 homes in the Richmond and Atlanta

V. Earl Dickinson, Jr., president of Richmond Homes.

areas, with gross sales exceeding $25 million.

The firm's computerized inventory control and work-flow management system are the heart of Dickinson's common-sense approach to land development. Everything from lumber to carpets and doorbells is ordered on a just-in-time delivery basis. Construction is coordinated to maximize efficient use of equipment and specialized labor. All houses are built to order, but choices within models are somewhat limited to retain the advantages of large-scale buying.

It is an impressive system, and it works. "Our advertising budget is less than a half-percent of gross," says Dickinson. "More than 80 percent of our sales come through direct referrals."

Richmond Homes, Inc., has won several industry awards, including the 1986 Best in Show in the $60,000 to $79,999 category for the Richmond Parade of Homes. The company also won the Virginia Power/Commonwealth Gas Energy Award and the Builder's Trust Warranty recognition for quality workmanship and excellent service.

Richmond Homes develops and sells tracts of single-family, detached housing in the cities and counties surrounding Richmond and has projects under way in Georgia. The company also builds and sells town houses and condominiums.

TRI-EQUITY GROUP

IN JUST TWO short years Tri-Equity Group has accelerated development, with nine projects under way totaling 2 million square feet valued at more than $150 million—right in the Richmond marketplace. There is only one word to describe the Tri-Equity Group: successful.

Tri-Equity Group, with offices in Richmond and Vienna, Virginia, specializes in the development of community shopping centers of 15,000 to 550,000 square feet in the mid-Atlantic states.

Tri-Equity has developed and leased 18 shopping centers throughout its mid-Atlantic and southern-Atlantic regions. Through a series of affiliated partnerships, it owns or manages all those properties and several others as well. The firm has thirteen projects in Virginia, three in Florida, one in North Carolina, and one in West Virginia.

Tri-Equity has become an approved developer for the Wal-Mart chain—a name that is backed by more than $25 billion in annual sales. There are eight Wal-Mart anchored shopping center projects either currently under construction or planned in the mid-Atlantic area.

The Richmond area's first Wal Mart store will be located in the

One of eight Tri-Equity shopping centers currently under way in the metropolitan Richmond area, located at Courthouse Road and Route 360.

Hanover Square Shopping Center, near the intersection of I-295 and U.S. 360. The center will contain about 250,000 square feet of space, half of which will be used by Wal-Mart. The center will also contain a Ukrop's supermarket and a movie theater complex. The retail center should be ready for business during the first quarter of 1991. Eight other major centers are also currently under construction in the Richmond metropolitan area.

According to Russell B. Harper, vice president/director of development in Tri-Equity's Richmond office,

Tri-Equity has developed and leased 18 shopping centers throughout its mid-Atlantic and southern-Atlantic regions.

"Our aggressive approach, expertise, and ability to 'fast-track' project development is why Wal-Mart and other major retail chains are attracted to us."

"Tri-Equity's experience and versatility," Harper says, "is a must in today's development market, as we handle projects in scope from 20,000 square feet to major retail centers of nearly 550,000 square feet."

Much of Tri-Equity's success has come from the outstanding leadership and management of the firm's founders: Richard Weiser, Edward Highers, and Francis Jung.

Richard Weiser comments, "We have a good niche and a strong focus. Our typical center is a strong community-based operation in a high-growth corridor. We specialize in high-value merchants, such as Wal-Mart. And our centers include such amenities as theaters, restaurants, day-care facilities, and major health centers, as well as retailers."

"Richmond is an excellent market for retail development," Harper states, "especially near major interstate and beltway-type highways."

Currently, Tri-Equity Group is adding one million square feet each year to its inventory. "Our market region enjoys great living conditions, a good environment, and affordable land," Weiser says, "that a combination like that produces an unlimited growth potential."

RUFFIN & PAYNE, INC.

Designing and fabricating roof trusses is an important part of Ruffin & Payne's business.

RUFFIN & PAYNE IS a Richmond tradition. The firm has been supplying the Richmond area with lumber, millwork, and building supplies since 1892. It is one of the oldest firms of its kind in the area.

The company's history is wrapped inextricably to the history of Richmond. The firm has fared as the city fared, through good times and bad. It has grown to become the largest independent, privately owned lumber and building supplies dealer in the city of Richmond.

It has maintained the old-fashioned virtues of honesty, integrity, quality, and customer satisfaction. But, in may respects, Ruffin & Payne is as modern as tomorrow's headlines.

It maintains a staff of designers to support its custom millwork operation, the only one of its kind in central Virginia. The firm's designers work with architects to create millwork to meet the special requirements of residential and commercial building projects.

The firm has pioneered the use of several new products in the Richmond area. It introduced salt-treated lumber in 1932. In 1916 it was the first to stock Masonite hardboard products in the Richmond market. It became the first in Virginia to sell Anderson windows in 1939. Prebuilt roof trusses, a cost-saving construction development, were introduced by Ruffin & Payne in the early 1950s. In 1989 Ruffin & Payne completed construction of a new roof and floor truss manufacturing facility, making it the most modern facility of its kind in central Virginia.

The firm was founded in 1892 by Thomas C. Ruffin and Joseph P. Fourquean. They began business in a two-story building on Fifth Avenue. In the beginning the firm sold coal and firewood and stocked a little lumber as a sideline. In time, Ruffin & Payne built a lime and cement warehouse on the site, which was served by the Chesapeake & Ohio Railroad. The sale of coal and firewood declined, and the firm concentrated on lumber and lime.

In 1916 the firm was renamed Ruffin & Payne, when Albert Payne, who had many years of experience in the millwork industry, joined the company. At that time a small mill was erected. Craig Ruffin and Thomas L. Ruffin, both sons of the founder, joined the firm in 1923 and 1924. The firm was incorporated under the name of Ruffin & Payne in 1925.

In 1963 the firm was notified that it had to move to make way for Interstate 64. The business relocated to Laburnum Avenue where it currently operates a modern facility on 12 acres with 135 employees and a fleet of 16 trucks.

The company is very much a part of the Richmond community. In 1989 all of its employees contributed to the Richmond United Way campaign. Ruffin & Payne is also a significant contributor to the Virginia Foundation for Independent Colleges.

It is a member of the Architectural Woodwork Association, the Virginia Building Materials Association, and the Richmond Home Builders Association. At various times its executives have served the Richmond Better Business and the Richmond Chamber of Commerce.

George E. Haw III, a graduate of Washington & Lee University and president of the company, says the firm carefully guards its reputation for quality and service. "We feel that the people who work at Ruffin & Payne are the company's biggest asset. We try to be flexible and respond to the employees, with our success measured by the low turnover among the employees." Haw feels "very positive" about the future of Ruffin & Payne and the future of Richmond.

FLUOR DANIEL, INC.

FLUOR DANIEL, INC., an engineering, construction, and maintenance company, opened its Richmond office 35 years ago to serve the firm's growing client base throughout the Northeast. Since then, Fluor Daniel has established itself as one of the region's premier E&C service operations, completing more than 400 projects with a total value of more than $2.5 billion.

Recognized as the top engineering and construction company among contractors in the United States and around the world, Fluor Daniel provides a complete range of engineering, construction, maintenance, and related services to virtually all industries and government agencies. The company has as its mission to assist its clients in attaining a competitive advantage by delivering quality services of unmatched value.

Serving clients through more than 50 offices worldwide, Fluor Daniel globally links technology, experience, human resources, and a tremendous range of services to meet its clients' requirements.

Fluor Daniel offers a broader range of services to more industries in more geographic locations than any other company. A business-sector concept concentrates all of these resources on the specific needs of clients in their individual industries and markets.

All of these services and the professionals who deliver them have made Fluor Daniel the leader in the engineering/construction business, providing quality projects and the cost- and time-saving benefits that make significant contributions to clients' bottom-line profitability.

Fluor Daniel, Inc., is the principal subsidiary of the Fluor Corporation.

ABOVE: Two new towers will soon change the skyline of Richmond—joining other Fluor Daniel projects along the river. Courtesy, Lee Brauer Photography

A.T. MASSEY COAL COMPANY, INC.

THE A.T. MASSEY Company, a wholly owned subsidiary of Fluor Corporation, began in 1916 with an office in Richmond. The firm is now under the leadership of E. Morgan Massey, a grandson of the founder. Today it also owns and operates 11 major subsidiaries, located in West Virginia, Kentucky, Pennsylvania, and Tennessee.

Annually shipping more than 25 million tons of high-quality coal, Massey Coal is one of the world's 10 largest coal suppliers. It serves clients throughout the eastern United States, Canada, and more than 20 nations around the globe. It also holds one of the largest reserves of low-sulfur coal in the United States. This is a critically important asset as the world seeks solutions to the ecological challenges posed by acid rain.

The success of A.T. Massey Coal Company, Inc., is based on several important strengths. "It takes more than high-grade coal properties, modern mining machinery, and coal preparation plants to adequately serve the energy appetite of our electrical, industrial, and metallurgical customers," says E. Morgan Massey. "Coal is a people business. The experience and competence of our people are what make Massey a leader in coal production and distribution in North America and around the world."

LEADBETTER, INC.

TROY O. LEADBETTER WAS a developer with an instinctive sense for good business and, in the most constructive sense of the word, a dreamer.

In 1968 Leadbetter faced a skeptical world with his 332 acres of recently purchased land adjoining Interstate 95 in Hanover County north of Richmond. His controversial idea was to develop the land into something he called an airpark, an amalgam of a county-operated airport and a privately developed industrial complex.

Some of his friends and acquaintances were wary. They believed no one could succeed in developing an industrial complex in an essentially rural area. But Leadbetter did not consult with those fears.

Leadbetter was a native of Hanover County, a gifted businessman, and a hard worker. His dream for the airpark was founded on his belief that an industrial complex designed primarily for small businesses was needed. He was himself a licensed pilot and believed that an airstrip at the complex would help many small businesses that relied on light aircraft for transportation.

More than 120 acres of Leadbetter's original 332 acres were sold to Hanover County for use as a county airport. Originally it was believed that Federal Aviation Administration funds would be used to build the airfield facilities. When that proved impossible, state and county funds were used.

Long before he finished the first phase of development at the industrial complex, Leadbetter reached out to purchase 200 more acres of contiguous land. Now the Hanover Industrial Air Park houses approximately 280 businesses on 600 acres. There still is room for more development. By any yardstick imaginable, the Hanover Industrial Air Park must be rated a huge success.

Over the years the Leadbetter companies have supplied nearly total design and construction service for airpark tenants. One of the ideas

Troy O. Leadbetter, developer and founder of Leadbetter, Inc.

Leadbetter used in developing the airpark was the creation of what he called "the incubator concept." These are 1,500-square-foot spaces leased to operators of new small businesses. They are large enough to accommodate a desk, a telephone, a small truck, and some other equipment—enough for a small business to get started.

If a business succeeds, the business can move to larger space. If a business fails, the unsuccessful entrepreneur is not left with an expensive building to add to his or her woes. Leadbetter's incubator idea has worked well at the airpark.

On January 3, 1982, Troy Leadbetter died in a tragic crash while attempting to land at the airpark while returning from a trip to Florida. The crash also claimed the life of his wife and 14-year-old son. Leadbetter was 53 years old. His two adult daughters, Debbie and Donna, were not involved in the accident.

In 1983 Phillip W. Dean joined into the company as executive vice president. The company is called Leadbetter, Inc., since several subsidiary companies were either sold,

shut down, or absorbed into the parent organization. Leadbetter, Inc., is a closely held corporation, the Leadbetter sisters holding the shares.

Dean is in an unusual position for an executive in a firm such as Leadbetter, Inc. He is the chief executive officer of the corporation, but at the same time acts as an agent in a fiduciary capacity for the owners. In 1986, to take advantage of changes in the tax laws, Dean had the company reclassified for tax purposes as an "S-type" corporation.

Sometime in the future he wants to make equity positions available to himself and the two vice presidents who head the firm's construction activities. "That will assure more continuity of management," he says.

Leadbetter, Inc., still operates in the airpark and does industrial and commercial construction and development there and at other locations. Dean is a believer in the Richmond area. "The future here is very bright," he says.

And Leadbetter, Inc., continues to grow and prosper, guided by Dean's steady hand but still motivated to a great extent by the late Troy Leadbetter. He is still present in the minds of many people at the Hanover Industrial Air Park and his dream is today a reality.

NAPIER & COMPANY

THIS IS A thriving example of a classic success story: A father's vision sets the foundation, and his two sons fulfill the dream. Napier & Company is a family-owned business that was started 32 years ago by board chairman Oscar T. Napier. Early on he realized the importance of diversity and combined residential development with general real estate services.

Napier could also foresee the potential in relocation services and, more than 20 years ago, affiliated with Homequity, Inc. (now known as PHH Homequity, Inc.), the nation's oldest and largest corporate relocation network. "Homequity referrals quickly became our anchor," says president James T. Napier.

"As one of Richmond's first local realtors to offer national relocation services, we discovered that handling third-party properties (homes that companies buy from transferred employees) gave us a prominent position in the industry. Homequity's performance requirements are quite challenging, yet we've won their Circle of Excellence Award ever since its inception six years ago," he says.

As the new president of Napier & Company, Jim Napier is succeeding his older brother, C. Richard Napier, who had been president of the family business since 1980. In 1987 Richard Napier served as president of the Richmond Board of Realtors, now the Richmond Association of Realtors, and was named its 1989 Realtor of the Year.

Due to his board participation, the company gained more visibility in the industry and was asked to help form PRO, an association of professional realty organizations, in order to provide member agents with important educational programs. PRO members were among the first in the state to comply with the general assembly's new regulations requiring continuing education for real estate licenses.

Realty Service Group was created in 1989 to give Napier's home buyers and sellers the convenience of one-stop shopping for related services such as mortgages, home and auto insurance, pest control, and title insurance.

Pictured here are (seated, from left) James T. Napier, president of Napier & Company; C. Richard Napier, president of Napier Custom Homes; and Oscar T. Napier, chairman of the board, Napier & Company.

"After my brother's term as board president was over, we looked at ways to increase our opportunities through diversity, combining our strengths without duplicating our efforts. We have intensified our services in those areas which we see as natural extensions," Napier says.

Richard Napier now heads two wholly owned subsidiaries, BNB Properties (a development company) and Napier Custom Homes.

After 30 years of steady growth, the new plan has resulted in a jump in annual sales from $36 million in 1987 to $53 million in 1989, an increase of more than 47 percent in two years. During this same time the company doubled its office space and increased its staff by 50 percent, from 20 to 30 agents. Nearly half are million-dollar producers.

"We want to be considered as the top alternative to the megacompanies: large enough to compete head on with a full range of services yet small enough that we can stay in close personal contact with all of our people," says Napier. "Our family style of management in turn permeates how our agents treat our customers—delivering to them the kind of attention they deserve."

RICHMOND RELOCATION SERVICES/VIRGINIA PROPERTIES

THE KEY TO Richmond's dynamic growth and development has been the extraordinary success of its commercial community. The key to commercial success is attracting top-quality personnel. And as senior personnel executives at every major company in Richmond already know, the master key to bringing outstanding people to the area is Richmond Relocation Services.

"This company is involved in more than the transfer of employees. We assist in the transfer of lives," says Carolyn Meares, founder and owner of Richmond Relocation Services.

A few of the unique services provided by Richmond Relocation Services include full-day tours of the city and county neighborhoods, career counseling for spouses, academic advising for children, interior-design consultations, tax-planning advice, introductions and assistance with social orientation, and legal assistance. "We're selling life-style in Richmond as much as we're selling houses," says Meares.

A North Carolina native with extensive experience on Wall Street, Meares relocated to Richmond in 1974 and started Richmond Relocation Services seven years later. The success of Richmond Relocation led to the development of Virginia Properties, a full-service real estate company.

Virginia Properties is an affiliate of Sotheby's International Realty, the world's leading real estate firm specializing in prestige properties. The company has also been selected as a charter member of the National Trust for Historic Preservation Real Estate Program. Providing comprehensive real estate services for buyers and sellers, Virginia Properties deals with a full range of quality properties throughout greater Richmond, from "starter homes" to large estates.

"Prospective employees who are considering a move to the Richmond area are very interested in how the

Carolyn Meares, founder and owner of Richmond Relocation Services. The success of Richmond Relocation Services led to the development of the equally sucessful Virginia Properties, a full-service real estate company.

move will effect their personal lives as well as their careers," says Karen Berkness, director of marketing for Richmond Relocation Services. "Our staff talks with each customer, taking special care in assessing their specific needs in order to assist them on an individual basis in the transfer of their life-styles."

With more than 50 real estate agents, relocation associates, and support staff now working out of the company's Libbie Avenue headquarters, Richmond Relocation Services and Virginia Properties have become one of the city's outstanding entrepreneurial success stories. The secret to their success has been their ability to attract, develop, and retain a core group of highly competent employees and independent contractors who are accountable, supportive, dedicated, and committed to service excellence in a "team" environment. They have also proven to be a company with a vision for the future. By instituting a Buyer Brokerage program and its newest division, Career Access, a spousal career assistance program, the firm is well placed for success in the 1990s.

"We begin working with people when they are considering a move to Richmond," explains Anne Sullivan, director of relocation. "We assist them with the decision-making process and are a support system for them up to six months after they arrive. We and our corporate clients know that the sooner newcomers feel totally at home, the happier they will be and the more quickly they will be fully productive on the job."

Richmond Relocation Services has facilitated most of the major corporate relocations to the area. Clients include Alfa-Laval, American Tobacco, AMF, Figgie International, James River, Reynolds Metals, Virginia Power, Wella Corporation, all of the major banks, several hospitals and universities, and dozens more.

In the past nine years the company has helped well over 5,000 newcomers to Richmond. In the process, Richmond Relocation Services and Virginia Properties have contributed greatly to Richmond's reputation as one of the nation's most desirable communities.

Photo courtesy, Henley & Savage

12

METROPOLITAN MARKETPLACE

RICHMOND'S RETAIL ESTABLISHMENTS, service industries, and products are enjoyed by residents and visitors.

Photo courtesy, Henley & Savage

THE PEARSON COMPANIES, INC.

A SELF-RELIANT spirit, a gambler's self-confidence, and a single-minded dedication describes Max Pearson, president of The Pearson Companies, Inc. You won't come up with a carbon copy, of course. Pearson is strictly one of a kind.

The Pearson Companies, Inc., is a holding company that involves automobile dealerships in Virginia, Florida, and Texas. In Richmond, the dealerships are: Richmond Honda, Capitol Lincoln-Mercury, Chesterfield Dodge, Cavalier Hyundai, Capitol Chevrolet, Richmond Mitsubishi, and Richmond Subaru. Other dealerships in Virginia are Woodbridge Lincoln Mercury, Denbigh Toyota in Newport News, Danville Toyota, and Manassas Hyundai.

Pearson's other Richmond operations include Nationwide Leasing Corporation, Dollar Rent-A-Car, Old Colony Life Insurance Company, Radio Station WLEE-AM 1320, and Image Impact, Inc., the advertising agency that handles advertising for Pearson's widespread holdings.

Pearson says that loyal customers and loyal employees are the key to his career. "If you're going to ask someone for their loyalty, first you've got to offer them yours. I've always believed in that and always followed it.

Max Pearson's work force of more than 600 employees believe in him. His automobile stores and other operations show remarkably little staff turnover. Several of his salespeople and executives have been with him for more than two decades.

Pearson tries to always promote from within his own organization. "We have 14 general managers who started with us in sales. After all, I only have two children. Both are active in the business. With 21 different stores and only two kids, other people have great opportunity to advance."

Frank and Patti share their father's philosophy. Usually Pearson recruits new staff who have no previous automobile experience. "Most of our executives sold their first car working for us. That way, they learn our way of doing things."

That way is no big secret, says Pearson. "The way to long-term business success is to treat people the same way you want them to treat you. That goes for employees as well as for customers. It works. I've got a lot of customers who have bought more than a dozen cars from me over the past 20 years."

Each dealership operates independently. None of the stores carries the Pearson name. "I want the name of the store to tell people where it is and what it is, like Richmond Honda' or Woodbridge Lincoln Mercury.' That's all the people are concerned with. I don't need personal recognition. I'm selling cars and service. They don't care about me."

In 1988 Max Pearson was named Distinguished Retailer of the Year by the Retail Merchants Association of Greater Richmond. In 1989 he received the *Sports Illustrated* and AIADA Imported Automobile Dealer of Distinction Award and the *Time* magazine Quality Dealer Award.

A native of Mena, Arkansas, and onetime professional baseball player, it has taken Max Pearson more than 40 years to build his organization. He started after his discharge from the U.S. Navy, working as a taxi driver in Washington, D.C. "I practically lived in the cab so I could save enough to buy my own," he recalls. "By the time I was 24 I owned 13 cabs." He later sold that operation, which is now the Arlington Yellow Taxicab Company.

His business has grown by building new dealerships from the ground up. The Pearson Companies, Inc., has been remarkably successful in winning new franchises when they are offered by manufacturers. "I guess I'm known for being aggressive. We sell a lot of product. But we're also known to be stores with an outstanding record of customer loyalty and customer satisfaction. That's very important in today's automobile business."

To Pearson, each new location is one more chance to show what he can do. He acts as his own real estate broker for the purchase of land and as the general contractor for design and construction of the new facilities. As a result, each is something of a showcase, featuring not only spacious showrooms, but extraordinary service facilities.

The newest Pearson Companies, Inc., automobile store in Richmond is the Capitol Lincoln Mercury facility at Broad Street and Parham Road, completed in 1989.

Pearson is a licensed multi-engine aircraft pilot and a not-too-serious golfer. "I really don't have any hobbies that I enjoy doing more than what I'm doing. I like building companies and helping people. I love watching some guy start out as a rookie salesman and develop into a general manager."

What kind of car does a man with 21 dealerships drive? "It varies—whatever the guys bring out for me." And what is his favorite make? "My favorite car is whatever the public is buying."

Max Pearson, president of The Pearson Companies, Inc.

THALHIMERS

SELDOM HAS AN enterprise become so much a part of a community as Thalhimers department store has become a part of Richmond. Since 1842 Thalhimers has played an important, sometimes vital, role in a long list of events that have helped shape the city's cultural, historic, and economic foundations.

The encouragement and support that have flowed over the years from the big store at Sixth and Broad streets have been instrumental in bringing colorful splashes of art, music, literature, history, and drama to the everyday life of the capital city. Thalhimers' six suburban Richmond stores and its stores in Petersburg and Colonial Heights represent a major economic investment in the greater Richmond community. The company is among the city's larger employers.

The role Thalhimers plays in the Southeast is comparable to the role it plays in Richmond. Thalhimers now operates 26 stores in Virginia, North Carolina, South Carolina, and Tennessee. The firm employs approximately 6,000 people, making it a major economic factor in the region.

Thalhimers' mission statement, posted in every store, states, "The business of Thalhimers is to provide merchandising and other related services as are appropriate and practical to meet the demand of the people in trading areas in which Thalhimers operates. The business is dynamic and is not restricted by traditional concepts of merchandising. The keystone of our business is the highest degree of integrity." For 148 years Thalhimers has lived up to that statement. It has done so with the unique flair that is the hallmark of a major, well-managed, creative department store.

It began in 1842, when a young German immigrant, a scholar and a teacher named William Thalhimer, opened a one-room dry-goods store on 17th Street in Richmond. At the outset the store employed six people. The business prospered. The store moved to a larger facility on 17th Street. There it weathered the Panic of 1857 and the Civil War. The store was damaged during the fire that devastated Richmond at the end of that war. It was rebuilt and continued to prosper.

In 1870 Thalhimers relocated to East Broad Street and, in 1875, to a three-story building at Fifth and Broad streets. During this period two of William Thalhimer's sons, Isaac and Moses, joined their father's store. Both were veterans of the Confederate Army. In the 1900s William B. Thalhimer, son of Isaac, joined the firm. The store was incorporated in 1922. That same year the business moved into a five-story building at its present location on Broad Street.

The fourth generation of the Thalhimer family became involved in the business when William B. Thalhimer, Jr., joined the firm in the 1930s, and his brother Charles G. Thalhimer followed in the 1940s. In the early 1930s Thalhimers pioneered in the use of escalators and air conditioning. In 1947 a new wing was added, and each of the six floors in the store was remodeled to create the impression of six separate stores. Two years later Thalhimers opened its first out-of-town store, in Winston-Salem, North Carolina.

In 1955 the downtown Richmond store was renovated again, and an aluminum facade—the first aluminum facade installed anywhere in America—was added. In 1959 and 1960 Thalhimers joined the move to the suburbs with branch stores in the metropolitan area.

Thalhimers remained independently owned until 1978, when it

Thalhimers expanded to a three-story building, located at Fifth and Broad streets, in the late 1870s. Ready-made clothes were added to the store stock at that time.

The newest Thalhimers store opened in August 1989 in Colonial Heights Southpark Mall.

merged with Carter Hawley Hale Stores, Inc., a Los Angeles-based corporation that operates a number of fine department stores nationwide. William B. Thalhimer, Jr., is chairman of Thalhimers, and Robert Rieland is president and chief executive officer. The fifth generation of the family is actively represented by William B. Thalhimer III, executive vice president.

Another sentence in the Thalhimers' mission statement says, "Thalhimers closely identifies with the communities it serves and recognizes its responsibility to play an active role to improve the quality of life." The store has lived up to that principle, too.

The store's director of special events recently was asked to list all of the community-based affairs in which the store had participated in the preceding year. The list included fashion shows, celebrations of the year's new crop of Beaujolais wine, fashion awards for student designers in local universities, the Children's Book Festival, the Virginia Historical Society Lecture Series, the Fourth of July celebration at Maymont, and dozens of other events.

In any year the store is a strong supporter of the Richmond Symphony. It maintains a lively interest in a children's zoo in Maymont Park, the annual Richmond music festival, the Valentine Museum, the Virginia Museum, The Science Museum, the Richmond Craft Fair, the Richmond Public Schools' Art in Action exhibition, and dozens of other causes and events.

Another principle expressed in the store's mission statement is "the business should provide a fair return on investment to the shareholders, which will encourage further investment and continued growth. Only through profitable growth will the company be able to meet its obligations to customers, associates, the community, and shareholders."

"Thalhimers will go forward with the same merchandising philosophy that has sustained it in the past," says president Robert Rieland. "The focus will always be on quality at whatever the price, but the emphasis will be on upper moderate to better price ranges.

"Customer satisfaction will continue to be the major concern of everyone in the company. Prompt and caring service, a satisfaction-guaranteed return policy, and alertness to the changing needs of the community have helped Thalhimers maintain its warm relationship with its customers. That will not change."

"The desire to grow will not change, either. Thalhimers will open another store in Winston-Salem, North Carolina, in the fall of 1990 and one in the Cary Mall, in a suburb of Raleigh, North Carolina, in 1991," he says. "Plans are to open one or two stores a year in existing or new markets in the stable and fast-growing southeast area of the country."

THE RETAIL MERCHANTS ASSOCIATION
OF GREATER RICHMOND

The Retail Merchants Association of Greater Richmond board members are (seated, from left) Zoe H. Green, director; Joseph M. Kelleher, Jr., director; Jeff D. Smith, president; Jack M. Kreuter, chairman; Jo Anne C. Cole, senior vice president; Kenneth P. Scott, Jr., director; Vern W. Henley, director; (standing, from left) Arnold Lowenstein, director; Russell L. Rabb, director; Hugh D. Lipscombe, director; William D. Selden IV, director; Donald E. Gugelman, director; William J. Gouldin, Jr., director; and Dorothy J. Hall, director.

"RICHMOND IS THE retailing hub of the Southeast," says Jeff Smith, president of the Retail Merchants Association of Greater Richmond (RMA). "It is the destination marketplace for the entire region extending south from Washington, D.C., to northern North Carolina, and west to western Virginia."

The Retail Merchants Association of Greater Richmond is an 85-year-old trade association, headed by a board of directors, that has addressed the concerns of retailing through nine decades. Current chairman Jack Kreuter is president of Schwarzschild Jewelers, Inc., an established Richmond quality retailer. In fact, W.H. Schwarzschild, Sr., was one of the 12 founders of the Retail Merchants Association.

RMA membership varies from landmark Richmond retailers, to regional and national firms, to smaller neighborhood shops and specialty boutiques, financial institutions, and service-oriented companies. "The association's job is to create support for Richmond's retail community and, by supporting retailers, to create support of all of the greater Richmond community," says Jeff Smith.

Founded in 1906 in rented offices at Third and Broad streets, the association has grown to become a respected influence in the marketplace and one of Richmond's leading community advocates.

The association purchased its own property in the spring of 1987. Located on a full-block frontage on historic Monument Avenue, the building was renovated to meet the needs of the association and its members. The spacious, graciously appointed offices and meeting rooms make it among the most beautiful in Richmond and an appropriate setting for a collection of original art by local artists. The use of the facility by many members for meetings and entertainment has become one of the intangible benefits that has evolved from the association's growth.

In December 1988 RMA sold its Credit Bureau operation to CBI/Equifax for $23 million, thus presenting the association with exciting opportunities to move in new directions for the benefit of its 2,500 members. The Credit Bureau was organized in 1907 and separately incorporated in 1952 to address specific needs of the retailing community in the areas of credit approval, check acceptance, and debt collection.

As these problems are now being addressed on a national level, the association determined to liquidate this asset and direct its attention to new needs of the local retailing

The Retail Merchants Association of Greater Richmond headquarters building, located on Monument Avenue in Richmond.

community. A task force of prominent retailers was appointed by the board of directors to study new benefits for members that are not being otherwise addressed. Many ideas on cost savings and sales promotion are being considered, or have been initiated, by the board.

RMA is established as a legislative and political voice on behalf of its members and is active in local governmental affairs.

The association's educational programs cover a series of topics that assist members in doing a better job in their businesses and are presented on a monthly basis. Two popular seminars are "Striving for Excellence in Retail Selling" and "Quality Customer Service," which are presented on a quarterly basis to assist retailers in training their sales associates. An extensive video library and printed materials on a number of topics important to retailers is also available for members' use. A "First Friday Forum" is held each month for breakfast, networking with peers, and listening to a topical speaker address current problems and solutions in the business environment.

Another educational benefit to members is the Tuition Assistance Partnership, whereby the association shares 50/50 in the tuition cost with members who send their employees to take courses at one of the five local colleges. An annual scholarship is also offered to students preparing for a career in retailing.

The association also offers a group health and life insurance plan, group travel abroad, electronically transmitted Alert Service, management of special trade groups within the association, and major

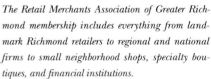

The Retail Merchants Association of Greater Richmond membership includes everything from landmark Richmond retailers to regional and national firms to small neighborhood shops, specialty boutiques, and financial institutions.

investments in community cultural, civic, and educational programs.

RMA has been providing major financial support for the Richmond Forum and the Richmond International Festival of Music since its inception. In 1989 the association funded a $50,000 grant to the Virginia Council on Economic Education to implement a program called Choices and Changes in Richmond City Schools, which is designed to motivate at-risk students to stay in school, and an additional $10,000 to help promote a twofold program for at-risk students at the middle and high schools. These are just a few of the many cultural/educational programs in which the association invests each year on behalf of its members.

The association is especially active in the area of local law enforcement. It is particularly proud of its role in starting, and its continued support of, the local Crime Stoppers program and of its 100 Club, which benefits local public safety officers.

Proud of the past—not content with the present—the Retail Merchants Association of Greater Richmond is dedicated to its one single objective: service to its members.

RENT-A-CAR COMPANY, INC.

THE COMPANY DOES business under the name of "Avis Rent-A-Car," but the operation and all the cars are owned by Rent-A-Car Company, Inc., a Richmond-based corporation. C. Kenneth Wright is chairman of the organization he founded in 1954. "Even in Richmond, Rent-A-Car Company is somewhat anonymous," says Wright.

Rent-A-Car Company, Inc., operates Avis franchises in Richmond, Newport News, Charlottesville, Lynchburg, Hampton, Williamsburg, Harrisonburg, Waynesboro, Weyers Cave, and Petersburg, Virginia; Salisbury, Easton, and Ocean City, Maryland; and Dover, Delaware. It has a fleet of cars and trucks totaling more than 2,000 vehicles and 150 employees.

In addition to the daily and short-term car rental business that primarily serves airline passengers, Rent-A-Car Company, Inc., leases automobiles and trucks on a long-term basis, both to individuals and to businesses.

As an Avis franchisee, Rent-A-Car uses the Avis identity, logo, and advertising program. Wright is still a member of the committee that originally adopted the "We're No. 2—We Try Harder" Avis campaign, an advertising classic that has become part of American popular culture.

As an independent operator, Rent-A-Car sets its own rates, buys and sells its own cars, buys its own real estate, and hires its own staff. That includes not only the uniformed rental sales agents behind the counter at the airport but also its own mechanics, insurance experts, used car salesmen, office and clerical staff, executives, and others.

Rent-A-Car Company purchases more than 1,500 cars and 175 trucks every year, a fleet ranging in size from subcompacts to 18-wheelers. All of its vehicles are purchased locally.

The company typically holds its cars for six to 18 months, then sells them either to other dealers or at Rent-A-Car's retail used car sales lot on West Broad Street. "Resale value is the most important consideration in

C. Kenneth Wright, chairman of the board, Rent-A-Car Company, Inc.

our selection of new cars," says Wright, "but we also want them to be the kind of cars that people want to rent and drive."

Wright was born and raised on a dairy farm. He started working in the car rental business when he was 16 years old. His first job was parking and washing cars for a firm known as U-Drive-It Co. After World War II service in the U.S. Air Force, he re-

turned to U-Drive-It Co., working extra long hours and saving his money.

Wright was assistant manager of U-Drive-It Co. in 1954, when he purchased the Richmond Avis franchise. At the time, the operation had four employees and a fleet of 20 cars. Now Wright sits in his company's graciously appointed boardroom overlooking Franklin Street and remembers how it all happened.

"I started with nothing and now Rent-A-Car Company is a viable part of Virginia's economic community.

Marc Hallberg, president of Rent-A-Car Company, and Audrey L. Pape, vice president/office manager.

We've been at this location for more than 30 years, so I guess you can say that we're pretty well established. We did it with honesty and hard work. This is what America is all about."

Marc Hallberg, a former vice president with Central Fidelity Bank, has been president of Rent-A-Car since 1983. He came to Richmond after graduating from the University of Georgia in 1977, and earned his M.B.A. at the University of Richmond.

Vice president and office manager Audrey L. Pape has been with Rent-A-Car for 25 years. "Mr. Wright is one of the smartest men in Richmond," says Pape. "He's always planning ahead, always has good ideas, and knows what has to be done. Even a few years ago when we faced those extremely high interest rates, Mr. Wright kept the company sound and growing. That took good planning."

"We've grown with the city of Richmond," says Wright, a native of Amelia County, "and we've helped the city grow." Rent-A-Car Company, Inc., is the only major automobile renting and leasing firm with a downtown location.

Wright attributes much of the success of Rent-A-Car to the favorable business climate in Richmond, including the cooperation of hotels and financial help from the banks and suppliers. He also recognizes the importance of the growth of the facilities and activity at Richmond International Airport.

"Airline deregulation was a positive factor for the car rental industry," says Wright. "When the airlines get new customers, there are more customers to rent cars."

Rent-A-Car Company, Inc., is a complex, sophisticated operation. It is authorized by all of the major manufacturers to perform its own warranty repairs. It also takes care of its own initial servicing of new cars, repairs them as necessary, and prepares them for resale. The firm manages its own insurance program and most of its own advertising.

Wright also owns several other Richmond businesses, including Basic Rent-A-Car Company, Inc. He is vice president and part owner of Ambassador Travel & Tours, the general partner with Franklin Leasing Associates, and the owner of Wright Investments, a real estate operation.

He is also active in his professional associations. A past president of the American Car Rental Association, an organization responsible for lobbying and monitoring legislation and regulations affecting the car rental industry, Wright has been vice president of the Car and Truck Rental and Leasing Association of Virginia since 1970.

The sign says "Avis," but the operation is owned by Rent-A-Car Company, Inc., of Richmond. The facility shown here is located at Richmond International Airport.

CIRCUIT CITY STORES, INC.

PROBABLY NO AMERICAN specialty retailer is more closely identified with high-technology, new-era consumer electronics and major appliances than Circuit City. So it may come as something of a shock to learn that the Richmond-based company is more than 35 years old, with roots that go back to the era of "The Lone Ranger," "Howdy Doody," and black-and-white television.

Richmond only had one TV station that broadcasted for only a few hours each day when Samuel S. Wurtzel set out to sell television sets in a former Broad Street tire store. A skeptical public needed to be convinced that the new gadgets were really here to stay, so Wurtzel provided free home demonstrations. That started a company tradition. More than 35 years later Circuit City still stands out from the crowd because of the high quality of customer assistance provided by its salespeople.

In 1975 Circuit City (then known as Wards) closed its small neighborhood stores in Richmond and opened a giant new retail facility named Wards' Loading Dock. Its 3 million cubic feet of space housed a merchandise showroom, a service and repair section, and a gigantic warehouse. Later dubbed the "Superstore," the Richmond facility brought a new vocabulary, style, and approach to American electronics and appliance retailing.

Four years later the firm began opening Superstores outside of Richmond. By 1983 Wards' had expanded its Circuit City Superstores and smaller electronics stores to 16 states in the Northeast, South, and West. The following year the company changed its name to Circuit City Stores, Inc.

The Superstore is the key component to Circuit City's rapid-growth strategy. By firmly establishing itself within a market and meeting consumer demands for value, service, and convenience, Circuit City has made itself a major national force in

retailing consumer electronics and major appliances.

Over the past five years the firm has rapidly expanded its base, opening 111 Superstores. The company has a strong presence in Los Angeles, Washington, San Francisco, Atlanta, Louisville, and throughout Virginia, the Carolinas, Georgia, Florida, Alabama, and Tennessee. The newest Superstores are in Miami, Tampa, Bal-

timore, Charlotte, Knoxville, Philadelphia, San Diego, Santa Barbara, and Phoenix.

Circuit City Stores, Inc., plans to build aggressively on its current base. During fiscal 1990 it opened 29 Superstores. The company plans to open 30 more Superstores in the next year.

The growth of Circuit City's sales averaged more than 35 percent per year during the 1980s. In 1989 total sales were $2.1 billion. Company plans call for doubling Circuit City sales over the next three to five years. Richard L. Sharp is president and chief executive officer of Circuit City Stores, Inc. Alan L. Wurtzel, the son of the founder, is chairman of the board.

LEGGETT OF CHESTERFIELD TOWNE CENTER

THREE GENERATIONS OF Virginians have shopped at Leggett department stores. Now the fourth generation can shop this traditional southern department store chain without leaving Richmond.

The five sons of Alexander L. Leggett founded the Leggett organization with the help of North Carolina's Belk family. Fred B. Leggett, Sr., opened the first Belk Leggett store in 1920, in Danville, Virginia. His partners were William Henry Belk and Dr. John Belk, founders of the Belk organization. The Belk Stores organization has remained closely linked with the Leggett group ever since.

William A. Leggett later became manager of the Belk department store in Durham. Robert, George, and Harold Leggett soon followed the new family tradition. In 1927, in Lynchburg, Virginia, Harold opened the first Leggett store.

Today there are nearly 350 Belk and Leggett stores in 16 states from Delaware to Florida and from the Carolinas to Texas. Leggett and Belk stores are the largest family- and management-owned department store organization in the country.

While their merchandise, interior design, and retailing management technology are strictly state of the art, Leggett stores continue to reflect many old-fashioned values. Despite new locations in regional malls, all Leggett stores remain closed on Sundays. Leggett remains devoted to people. "My boss is not the Leggett family," says Russell Miller, manager of Leggett of Chesterfield Towne Center. "My boss is the Leggett customer."

Leggett of Chesterfield Towne Center, opened in late 1988, is the company's first store in Richmond. "We stock a range of merchandise for every customer in the Richmond market, from top designer fashions

such as Anne Klein II and Liz Claiborne to more price-sensitive lines," says Miller. "We combine the volume clout of all Belk and Leggett stores with the purchasing selection of our in-store buyers, but it's our associates who will make the difference."

At the ribbon-cutting ceremonies for Leggett of Chesterfield Towne Center, T.C. Leggett commented that the opening was "as important to the organization as the opening of our first store," and challenged the associates to give the best

The cosmetics area of Leggett of Chesterfield Towne Center combines attractive surroundings with the finest merchandise and outstanding service.

customer service in Richmond. Less than a year later *Richmond Surroundings* magazine recognized Leggett as having the best sales associates in the region.

Not bad for the new kid on the block—a "new" kid that brings Richmond a century-old southern retailing tradition.

With its main entrance inside the mall, Leggett of Chesterfield Towne Center invites Richmond shoppers to join its family.

MAZDA MOTOR OF AMERICA, INC.

THE RICHMOND PARTS Distribution Center for Mazda Motor of America, Inc., ushered in a new era for Mazda when it opened in February 1989. It also established a new standard for warehouse technology.

The building is centered on a neatly maintained 16-acre site at 5700 Audubon Way in Sandston, Virginia, just across the fence from the Richmond International Airport. It provides 317,400 square feet of working space, enough room for four football fields. The exterior walls of the building are made of massive, precast concrete panels that are 31 feet high and 22 feet wide.

The center shipped its first part on February 28, 1989. It was then staffed by a crew of 11 people. By the start of 1990 that number had increased to 21 workers. The crew is expected to continue to increase to 36 people, 28 of whom will work in the warehouse.

The high productivity of this parts distribution center is support

through the use of an automated guided vehicle system designed and installed by the Warres Corp. of Rockville, Maryland. Six computer-controlled, wire-guided robotic carts deliver freshly received parts for stocking. They also collect and bring to the shipping department parts ordered by the 106 Mazda dealers in six states served by the Richmond Parts Distribution Center.

The carts are guided by electronic signals sent to the carts from cables buried in the warehouse floor. Use of the guided vehicles reduces the number of personnel needed to operate the facility. Employees can concentrate on stocking and picking parts instead of transporting them

Located on a 16-acre site at 5700 Audubon Drive in Sandston, Virigina, The Richmond Parts Distribution Center for Mazda Motors has 317,400 square feet of working space (four football fields) and serves as the master distribution center for the entire East Coast.

around the warehouse. The wire-guided steering system also controls 16 Raymond order pickers.

Another feature of the warehouse is the narrow-aisle, high-cube storage layout that maximizes space. Clear space in the warehouse is 25 feet high, and access aisles are 76 inches wide.

Small parts are stored in 30,000 rack-mounted plastic bins. Up to 18,000 medium-size parts are stored in slightly larger bins. Storage crates provide a capacity for an additional 4,500 items. The facility also provides for wire basket/pallet, standard pallet, and large bulk crane items. The automatic guided vehicles have a capacity of 13,000 pounds each. They are programmed by a console in the shipping department.

Orders for replacement parts come to the Richmond Parts Distribution Center through Mazda's national computer network. Each Mazda dealer gains access to the system through individual computer terminals. The

The Richmond Parts Distribution Center has set an industry standard for warehouse technology. Its high productivity is a result of the automated guided vehicle system. Six computer-controlled, wire-guided robotic cars deliver, collect, and bring parts received and ordered within the plant.

orders are processed through the main computer center at the Mazda Motor of America corporate offices in Irvine, California. The appropriate orders then are relayed to the Richmond center, where they are processed in an efficient and professional manner to satisfy the Mazda dealer and the ultimate user.

When the Richmond facility first opened it was processing approximately 1,000 spare parts lines per day. By 1990 it was processing 3,900 per day.

All ordered spare parts are shipped daily using several modes of transportation such as: Dedicated Trucking, UPS, Federal Express, and Common Carrier.

The Spare Parts Distribution Center itself is replenished through parts orders prepared by an inventory management system. The spare parts are ordered from the Mazda Motor Corp. in Japan. The parts are delivered by sea containers at Norfolk, Virginia, and the containers are then delivered to the distribution center by truck. There are also domestic accessories and air conditioners purchased within the United States.

The Richmond Parts Distribution Center is one of eight such centers operated in the United States by Mazda. Because of its central position it has been designated the master distribution center for the entire East Coast. It stocks both slow- and fast-moving parts and also provides a master parts stock designed to be able to supply any item stocked by Mazda Motor of America to any location in the country.

Parts handled by the Richmond Center range in size from a tiny washer to an entire automobile quarter-panel. The parts inventory stocked at Richmond averages about $22.5 million in value.

"This multimillion-dollar facility is one more concrete expression of what we called the 'Mazda Way,'" a Mazda executive says. "That means that Mazda Motor of America and its employees will do whatever is necessary to assure total customer satisfaction for the hundreds of thousands of Mazda owners in North America. The Richmond Parts Distribution Center is one more way in which Mazda is striving to ensure that its customers' needs—in this case, to obtain delivery of parts in a timely fashion—are met as quickly and as completely as possible."

Danny Ryder, a native of Jacksonville, Florida, is the Parts Distribution Center manager at Richmond. Ryder has had 14 years of experience in the auto-parts field. He worked in the Mazda Parts Distribution Center in Jacksonville before being assigned to open and run the Richmond center.

"Mazda is an employee-oriented company," Ryder says. "Our employees frequently are consulted by management. Employee input in the problem-solving process is solicited and used. This facility has frequent meetings at which employees are invited to comment on operations. And that same rule applies to other Mazda facilities."

Mazda has not been in Richmond long, but it already is working its way into the fabric of the Richmond community. It is deeply involved in activities of the Metropolitan Richmond Chamber of Commerce. It already has made a significant contribution to the annual United Gifts campaigns.

"Richmond has a lot to offer, and Mazda Motor of America, Inc., plans to be in Richmond for a long time," Ryder says. And that is partly because it is good business and perhaps just because, as Mazda's slogan says, "It just feels right."

MARRIOTT HOTEL

THE THREE MARRIOTT Lodging facilities in Richmond offer the city a new horizon in hotel comfort, quality, and convenience.

Marriott entered the Richmond market in September 1984, when the Richmond Marriott opened its doors at Broad and Fifth streets. Since then, Marriott has become a major player in the Richmond community, known for community service and warm, friendly accommodations for the traveling public.

The Richmond Marriott, the city's largest hotel, is a full-service hotel offering 401 guest rooms, two fine restaurants, recreation facilities, and outstanding meeting and banquet facilities.

In the years since the opening of the Richmond Marriott, two other Marriott facilities have opened their doors in Richmond. They are the Courtyard by Marriott at 6400 West Broad Street and the Marriott Residence Inn at 2121 Dickens Road. The Courtyard offers 145 guest rooms, and The Residence Inn offers 80 suites and efficiencies. All three lodging products serve specific niches in the hospitality market.

The Richmond Marriott was built to appeal to a broad spectrum of guests. Business travelers, vacationers, and conventioneers alike all find facilities designed for their convenience.

The Courtyard is aimed primarily at business travelers. It includes a 100-seat restaurant and lounge, limited meeting facilities, and other amenities such as a pool and exercise room. Marriott now has more than 150 Courtyards in operation.

Marriott Residence Inn is a moderately priced residential-style motel that features beauty with homelike comfort. It was designed to accommodate guests who plan to stay for more than a few days. Marriott's Residence Inn provides a swimming pool, a heated spa, and a sports court.

In addition to the Lodging Division, Marriott also is represented in Richmond by their Health Care Services, Business Food Services, Educational Food Services, and Facilities

Management Divisions.

The Marriott Corporation, based in Bethesda, Maryland, operates more than 500 lodging facilities world-wide. Of those, more than 200 are luxury hotels and 21 are world-class resorts. Marriott hotels abroad are located all the way from Warsaw to Toronto and from Puerto Vallarta to Hong Kong. In addition to Marriott Hotels, Courtyards, and Residence Inns, Marriott also operates Fairfield Inns, a number of fully equipped, economy hotels.

The Marriott Corporation is the leading operator of hotel rooms in

ABOVE AND LEFT: The Richmond Marriott appeals to a broad spectrum of guests, with fine accommodations and excellent service.

the United States and offers the broadest array of services. It also is one of the largest international hotel chains. The firm maintains one of the most sophisticated research and development operations of any hotel chain.

"When Marriott comes into a market," a Marriott executive says, "it is the result of long-term and careful study. Everything about that market's potential is fully understood." That careful appraisal of a market is backed up by Marriott's operational philosophy. "Simply stated, we take better care of our customers."

The Marriott Corporation is also noted for its executive career development program. "In general, Marriott requires that entry-level executives hold four-year degrees," the executive says. "Then those people are trained carefully in the various aspects of the business. The program is one of high expectations; Marriott

expects a lot from its young executives and, in return, they expect a lot from Marriott."

The result is a corps of motivated, well-trained people in the various career fields. The customer enjoys both better service and a very consistent product.

The Richmond Marriott, under the supervision of general manager Frits Huntjens, bears the unmistakable stamp of a first-class, well-managed hotel. From its spacious, comfortable lobby to its handsome, well-planned public meeting spaces, the hotel shows the sparkle, the movement, and the gloss of sheer class.

Due to its reputation for service excellence and its abundance of meeting space, the Richmond Mar-

riott is the unquestioned leader in public meetings in Richmond. It headquarters more city-wide conventions and, likewise, small conferences than any other hotel in the city. It offers the largest banquet facilities in the city and the second largest in the state of Virginia. Overall, the hotel provides 30,000 square feet of flexible meeting space.

The hotel's unparalleled facilities are reinforced by the fact that it is connected by a skywalk to the huge Downtown Richmond Centre for Conventions and Exhibitions.

The hotel is close to such downtown points of interest as the Sixth Street Market, the Virginia State Capitol, and downtown's noteworthy museums and historic buildings. It is

only 20 minutes from the Richmond International Airport.

The hotel's bright and attractive Court Plaza Cafe seats 150 people for breakfast, lunch, and dinner. Its upscale restaurant, Chardonnay's, serves a gourmet cuisine in an elegant, candlelit setting. The specialties are the crab soup, seafood, and chateaubriand. Triplett's, the lobby lounge and cocktail bar, features music, dancing, snacks, and a bar.

All of the Marriott's lodging products are deeply involved in the community in which they do business. In the course of a year they contribute meals, guest rooms, meeting spaces, and supporting services to dozens of civic and philanthropic causes.

"This year, for example, the hotel provided more than $25,000 worth of support to Heartstrings, a program to raise money for AIDS victims," says Rick Southard, the hotel's director of marketing. "We pride ourselves in being not only good businesspersons but also good neighbors."

Marriott executives are delighted with their connection with Richmond. "Richmond residents are the nicest, most congenial people I have ever met," says one executive. "The city has so much to offer as a convention destination and business center. And the metropolitan area is attractive and successful.

"The emergence of downtown Richmond as one of the leading financial centers on the Atlantic Seaboard has been vastly encouraging. All of these are positive things. We're happy to be a part of Richmond."

BUSINESSLAND

CHANCES ARE THAT Richmond businesses that use computer systems are already familiar with the Richmond branch of Businessland. Part of the vast Businessland network—the nation's largest integrator of microcomputer systems—the firm has helped hundreds of Richmond-area businesses with every aspect of buying and using personal computers.

Founded in 1982 in California, the international Businessland corporation employs 2,300 people in more than 110 locations in North America and the United Kingdom. The company represents all the major PC manufacturers, including IBM, Apple, Compaq, Hewlett-Packard, and NCR, and is the exclusive retailer of Next Computers, the firm started by former Apple president Steven Jobs.

But guidance on purchasing a computer is only one of a wide array of services that Businessland offers its customers. The firm also provides installation, on-site customer training, on-line telephone support, and hardware maintenance. For every Businessland salesperson, there is one Businessland service person supporting the technical side of the product.

The Richmond service operation, now centralized and separate from the office and retail outlet, has 15 technicians on the road at all times in 15 trucks.

"We don't just sell computers," emphasizes Burl Wingold, head of the Richmond Businessland. "We sell solutions." Companies struggling to integrate PCs or local area networks (LANS) into a mainframe environment, for example, find that Businessland is an ideal partner with whom to work. In fact, the firm has an advanced systems group whose primary responsibility is to consult with businesses on any high-end problem.

The Richmond Businessland, located at 3900 Gaskins Road near Interstate 64, was originally Dardick Computer, a microcomputer sales and service outlet started in 1981 by Glenn Dardick. By the time Businessland acquired Dardick's in 1989, the small company had two locations, including the facility on Gaskins Road, and had become the largest reseller of microcomputer hardware and software in central Virginia.

With the merger, Burl Wingold, Dardick's executive vice president, was named to head up the Gaskins Road facility and was also selected as

Businessland's district manager. As a longtime Virginia resident and graduate of Virginia Commonwealth University, Wingold has led the company to an active role in local service organizations, charities, and chamber of commerce work. "Richmond has been loyal to Dardick Computer and Businessland," he says. "We hope to repay that loyalty by being an active member of the community."

Businessland's future plans call for expansion to other locations throughout the state as well as expanding services in Richmond. "The economic future of the Richmond area is extremely promising," says Wingold. "We've been the dominant business-computer player in Richmond to this point, and we intend to keep it that way."

Businessland, located at 3900 Gaskins Road, has become the largest reseller of microcomputer hardware and software in central Virginia.

13

QUALITY OF LIFE

MEDICAL AND EDUCATIONAL institutions contribute to the quality of life of Richmond-area residents.

Photo courtesy, Henley & Savage

VIRGINIA COMMONWEALTH UNIVERSITY

RICHMOND IS THE home of Virginia Commonwealth University, the commonwealth's largest public urban university. VCU, today a major research doctoral-granting institution, has shared the city's heritage since the Medical College of Virginia was founded in 1838 as the medical department of Hampden-Sydney College. By an act of the Virginia General Assembly, Richmond Professional Institute and the Medical College of Virginia merged in 1968, tightening the ties between the city and the university.

In addition to traditional educational settings on the campuses, VCU offers its 21,000 students the entire city and the region as their classrooms and laboratories. VCU's 141 degree programs in 11 schools and one college support students in programs as diverse as urban studies and theater, dentistry and business administration,

Undergraduate and graduate students on the Academic Campus complete degrees through the Schools of the Arts, Business, Community and Public Affairs, Education, and Social Work, or the College of Humanities and Sciences, which includes the School of Mass Communications. VCU also offers one of the largest and most comprehensive evening programs in the country with 65 degree programs that can be completed after business hours.

and medicine and political science. They offer one associate, 60 baccalaureate, 59 master's, 2 first-professional, and 19 doctoral degrees.

Forty of VCU's educational programs are not offered anywhere else in the state. The university's School of Social Work is the oldest in the South, and its School of the Arts is the nation's largest art school.

VCU's diversity also means that working students can continue their professional lives as they learn. The university's evening studies program, offering students the opportunity to complete 65 degree programs after business hours, makes it one of the largest and most comprehensive in the country.

As a leading Richmond employer, the university is second in size only to state government. Through faculty consultation and survey research centers such as those on consumer behavior and infectious diseases, VCU research links the university with government and private

VCU graduates more than 3,000 students each year in degrees ranging from the associate's to the M.D. and the Ph.D. that are offered through 141 programs.

industry. With more than $60 million in research and scholarship funds annually, VCU is among the top 70 institutions in the country in terms of sponsored support.

ABOVE: Students on the Medical College of Virginia campus study in the Schools of Allied Health, Basic Health Sciences, Dentistry, Medicine, Nursing, and Pharmacy. VCU offers the only dentistry and pharmacy schools in the state.

VCU traces its founding date to 1838, when the Medical College of Virginia opened as the medical department of Hampden-Sydney College in the old Union Hotel in downtown Richmond. In 1845 MCV completed the Egyptian Building, one of the finest examples of Egyptian Revival architecture in the country and the oldest medical education building in the South. Today VCU boasts 33 historic preservation sites on its Academic and MCV campuses.

a Level I Trauma Center.

The university contributes to the cultural and multicultural life of the city through its Terrace Concert Series in cooperation with the John F. Kennedy Center for the Performing Arts, exhibitions in the Anderson Gallery and performances and master classes through the Department of Dance and Choreography, its theater program, and through the Community School for the Performing Arts. Students and staff also affect people's lives in community programs that deal with health and social needs from alcoholism to education to prisons.

VCU's two campuses in the state capital support the university's comprehensive educational, research, and public service mission. The Medical College of Virginia Campus is part of a vital urban hospital complex in the heart of a revitalized downtown. Two miles west lies the Academic Campus situated in the Fan District, a restored section of turn-of-the-century town houses. As a leader in the adaptive preservation of its buildings, VCU boasts 33 national historic preservation sites.

Building on VCU's traditions, its partnership with the community, and its enlightened approach to its mission, the Campaign for VCU, the university's first comprehensive fundraising campaign, sought $52 million in private support for endowment, facilities renovation and equipment, new programs, and current support. The campaign exceeded its minimum goal eight months ahead of schedule, and at the campaign's conclusion in June 1990, more than $62 million had been raised. More than 150 business and community leaders served as volunteer leadership, and more than 60 percent of VCU's faculty and staff participated in the campus campaign.

With its wealth of resources and its 13,000 faculty and staff members, Virginia Commonwealth University continues to excel in the quality of education for its students and to make a difference in the city, the state, the nation, and the world.

Research meshes with professional training and patient care in the Medical College of Virginia Hospitals through its departments and 92 outpatient clinics. Treating 32,400 patients each year, MCV Hospitals is the largest acute care center in the state. The Massey Cancer Center is one of 20 cancer centers in the country specially designated by the National Institutes of Health.

MCV Hospitals' neuroscience specialists work in one of the top 20 head trauma units in the country, linking research with an international scope to innovative treatment and rehabilitation. A neonatal intensive care unit with a national reputation supports newborns at risk. MCV Hospitals, home of the oldest burn unit in the country, also is designated

THE MEDICAL COLLEGE OF VIRGINIA HOSPITALS

LEFT: Main Hospital.

FACING PAGE: North Hospital.

THE MEDICAL COLLEGE of Virginia Hospitals is an academic hospital—part of Virginia Commonwealth University's Health Sciences complex—and a training center for physicians, nurses, and other health care professionals. MCVH is consistently ranked as one of the country's best hospitals.

The consumer guide, *The Best Hospitals in America,* published by Henry Holt & Company, listed MCV Hospitals among the 64 best in the country (in the top one percent). Its editors found that MCVH provides virtually every contemporary medical service, including "one of the world's largest organ-transplantation programs, a first-rate cardiac surgery de-

partment, a major burn unit, a regional head-trauma center, and a nationally famous neonatal intensive care unit." The book also cites MCVH for its status as a Level I Trauma Center and for its quality nursing care.

As an academic hospital, MCVH offers a tremendous concentration of medical expertise in one setting. At MCVH there are experts in *every* specialty, from anesthesiology to urology. More than 700 specialists are full-time attending physicians at MCVH.

MCVH's neurological center receives referrals from across the country and is visited by physicians and researchers from around the world. MCVH doctors developed methods to control pressure on the brain in the first crucial hours after a head injury.

In both the adult and pediatric intensive care units, computer monitoring devices developed at MCVH—unique in the world—provide contin-

uous monitoring of the brain and bodily functions of comatose patients.

MCVH's Massey Cancer Center treats all forms of cancer and is noted for its development of anticancer drugs. Breast cancer and childhood cancer are two of many areas in which MCVH physicians and researchers are setting an international standard.

The MCVH Children's Medical Center is the only comprehensive medical/surgical center for infants, children, and adolescents in the Richmond metropolitan area. It admits more than 8,000 patients per year from throughout the United States and the world. New techniques developed by MCVH surgeons are correcting heart defects in newborns who only a few years ago could not have been saved.

The first successful non-twin heart transplant was performed by MCVH surgeons in the early 1950s. Today MCVH is an internationally prominent heart transplant center and is one of about 25 centers in the nation performing heart/lung transplants. Other transplant programs at MCVH include bone marrow, pancreas, kidney, liver, and cornea.

Virtually all patient beds at MCV Hospitals are housed in buildings less than 10 years old. Yet MCVH, located in Richmond's historic Court End near the White House of the Confederacy and the Valentine Museum, preserves several buildings of historic and architectural significance. The Egyptian Building was built in 1845 to house the classrooms and patients of The Medical College of Virginia. A rare surviving example of Egyptian revival architecture, it has been adapted for teaching and office space. West Hospital is part of Richmond's history. As a vital center for teaching, research, and patient care, The Medical College of Virginia Hospitals is shaping the future of health care for Richmond and for the world.

BELOW: An aerial view of The Medical College of Virginia Hospitals campus.

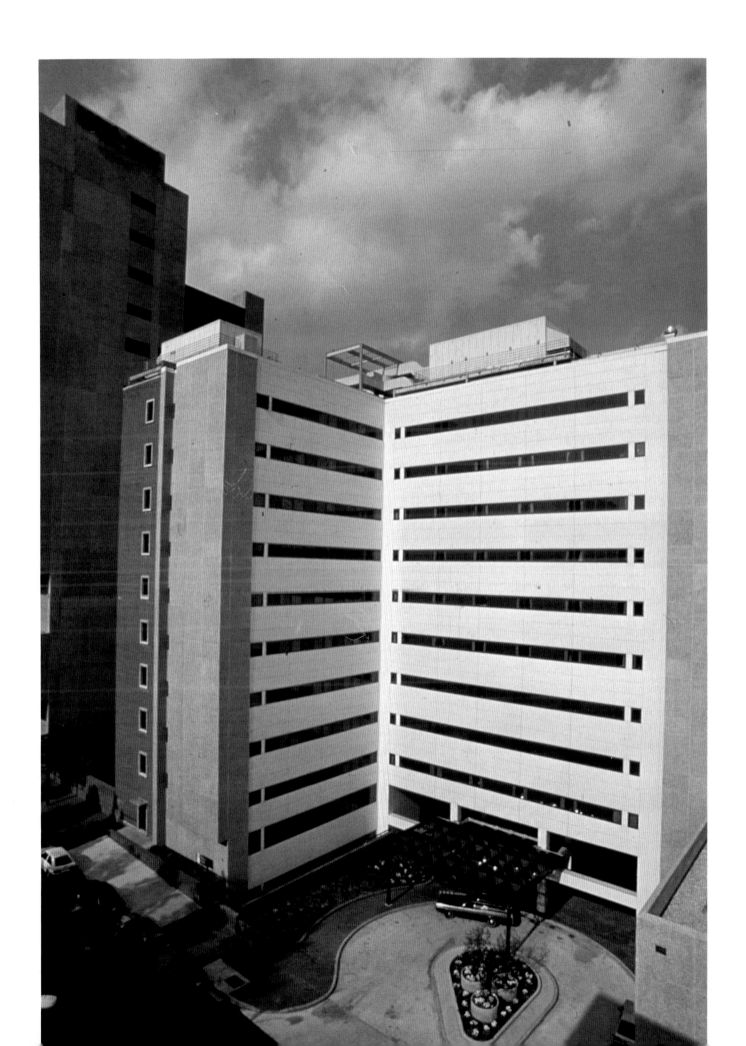

CHIPPENHAM MEDICAL CENTER

PREDICTING STEADY POPULA-TION growth for the beautiful South-side area, Richmonders saw the need for a high-quality, critical care facility as early as the 1960s. That dream became reality when Chippenham Hospital opened in 1972. Since that time, Chippenham and its parent company, the Hospital Corporation of America (HCA), has served the wide-ranging health care needs of 2 million patients in the Richmond region.

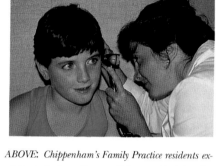

ABOVE: Chippenham's Family Practice residents examine patients as they would in a medical practice. Each year six new residents train at the hospital.

ABOVE RIGHT: The Children's Center is the only pediatric unit south of the James. Nurses are trained specifically to care for infants, children, and young adults.

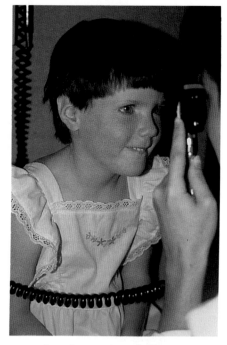

While serving patients in the last 18 years, Chippenham evolved into a regional medical center with several centers of excellence. On July 23, 1990, the hospital was renamed Chippenham Medical Center, and hospital officials broke ground for a $20-million expansion. The aggressive construction project will include a new Outpatient Center with a four-story parking deck and medical office building. Walkways will link it to the main hospital.

The Laser Center was added in the fall of 1990. It provides patients with the most technologically advanced techniques in surgical services. More than 130 physicians, nurses, and technicians have been specially trained for laser surgery. With laser surgery there is less pain and blood loss and a faster recovery time.

Chippenham is a well-respected and heavily used full-service health care facility. The emergency room is the second busiest in the Richmond metropolitan area, serving the critical care needs of 40,000 people annually. Each year 20,000 people use Chippenham's out-patient diagnostic and rehabilitative services. While high-quality critical care is the core of Chippenham's reputation, the hospital also offers a wide variety of special services: wellness programs, mental health services, and special women's and childbirth programs.

Tucker Pavilion, the largest psychiatric facility in the region, provides psychiatric treatment for patients with mental and emotional illnesses. Its chemical-dependency unit for patients addicted to alcohol and other drugs is one of the most influential in the country, and its inpatient eating disorders program was the first of its kind in Richmond.

Formerly Tucker Psychiatric Hospital, the Pavilion became an integral part of Chippenham in 1976, and was substantially expanded five years later to include an intensive care unit. In 1989 Tucker acquired a Brain Atlas—a high-technology medical instrument for diagnosing psychiatric and neurological disorders. Only 100 hospitals in the country have this kind of brain-mapping equipment.

"The Brain Atlas allows us to read the responses of the brain to stimuli," explains Dr. Stan W. Jennings, a psychiatrist affiliated with Tucker. "The mapping techniques analyze the brain's responses and measure differences between EEGs, that the physician can't see with the naked eye. Many psychiatric and other illnesses can be differentiated with greater accuracy."

In 1989 Chippenham opened a new Diabetes Treatment Center. Located on the sixth floor of the hospital, the center is the only one of its kind in Virginia.

The Virginia Heart Center, the hospital's comprehensive cardiac care facility, is among the region's finest. In operation since 1979, the center includes a cardiac stress laboratory, two-dimensional echocardiography, Holter monitoring, and an advanced cardiac catheterization program. New

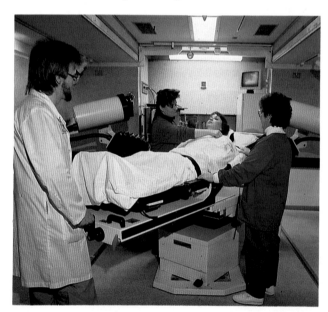

Here a patient is being positioned for lithotripsy, which is a form of treatment for those who suffer from kidney stones. This nonsurgical procedure disintegrates kidney stones with a special high-pressure shock wave treatment called ESWL (extracorporeal shock wave lithotripsy). Richmond's first mobile lithotripter is being provided through a partnership between Chippenham and other HCA hospitals.

coronary care and intensive surgical care units complete the comprehensive coronary facilities. In 1990 the Virginia Heart Center opened an Electrophysiology Laboratory, a state-of-the-art clinical treatment for patients suffering from heart arrhythmias.

Chippenham's Women's Medical Center provides a wide range of women's programs, from childbirth to mammography, as well as seminars about women's health issues. The center offers classes and tours to expectant parents and siblings, prenatal aerobics for new moms, membership in the Silver Pin Club, and parenting classes.

The Sports Medicine Center offers counseling on injury prevention and wellness; diagnosis, treatment, and rehabilitation of athletic injuries; exercise, diet, and conditioning programs; and several other services.

To help cut back on skyrocketing health care costs, Chippenham

has placed special emphasis on outpatient services. In 1989 Chippenham expanded its Same Day Surgery Center, which opened in 1983, and experienced a sharp jump in patients over its first five years.

The hospital also shares a mobile unit to provide lithotripsy (a painless treatment for kidney stones), and magnetic resonance imaging (MRI) (a high-technology form of X ray).

Perhaps the biggest factor in the hospital's success is its people. Chippenham Medical Center's talented medical staff includes more than 600 physicians representing every major medical specialty, along with 1,800 other full- and part-time employees.

Chippenham Medical Center's helipad receives an incoming patient. The hospital treats 40,000 emergency cases and performs more than 400 open-heart surgeries each year.

Many of the hospital's professional personnel are housed in the 40 medical office suites adjacent to the hospital, property that was originally purchased as part of the hospital site.

In addition, Chippenham's board members are active in the Richmond community, leading philanthropic and service organizations and working with the state legislature to improve medical care throughout Virginia. Numerous Chippenham physicians, administrative staff, and board members hold key positions in medical professional associations.

No hospital can prosper without a dedicated group of community volunteers, and Chippenham is no exception. Area residents have donated more than 500,000 hours of volunteer service since the hospital opened.

With the Southside population still growing, Chippenham Medical Center will continue to be a major health care provider in Richmond and all central Virginia.

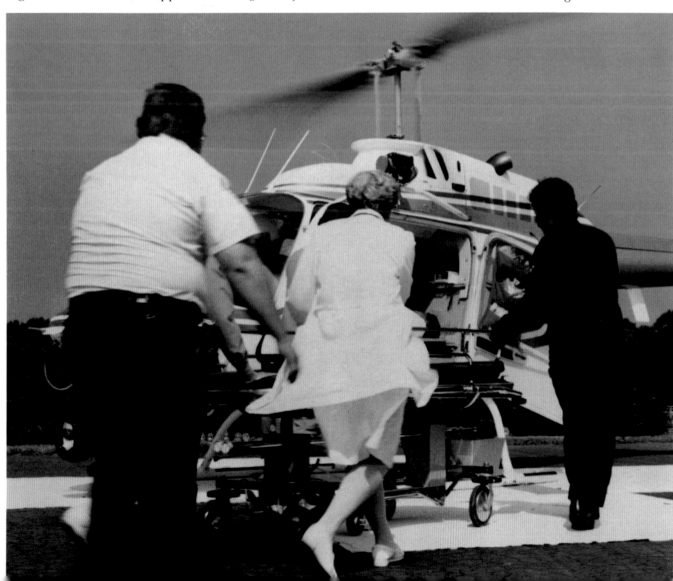

METROPOLITAN HOSPITAL

METROPOLITAN HOSPITAL STANDS at a focal point in the rapidly changing Richmond urban area. The hospital is positioned on the edge of the city's storied Fan District, an area of tree-shaded streets and gracious, historic Victorian mansions.

In another direction, Metropolitan borders on the Virginia Commonwealth University campus, an area of dynamic growth and change. The hospital also is only a few blocks from burgeoning downtown Richmond.

The hospital's location, its skilled and dedicated staff, and its progressive management endow it with tremendous potential for growth, change, and increasingly higher levels of service to the community. The people in charge at Metropolitan Hospital fully intend to realize all of that potential.

Metropolitan Hospital is a seven-story, 180-bed, all private room, acute care general hospital at 701 West Grace Street. It operates with a staff of approximately 500 people. Metropolitan is the only general hospital in the Richmond area that offers all private rooms. This arrangement,

Metropolitan Hospital, a seven-story, 180-bed, all private room, acute care general hospital, is positioned on the edge of the city's storied Fan District at 701 West Grace Street.

Metropolitan executives say, offers superior infection control, optimum flexibility, and a more spacious environment for patients. It also enhances the personalized, specialized care that is a hallmark of the hospital's approach to its patients.

The hospital has a fully staffed and equipped emergency room, medical/surgical floors, a psychiatric service, same-day surgery, outpatient surgery, and complete laboratory and diagnostic procedures. Metropolitan's Occupational Medicine Program helps local employers and employees confronted with injuries in the work place. The program is set up on a team basis, which provides for cost containment and case management.

The hospital's Sports Medicine Center is operated in conjunction with the Medical College of Virginia and Virginia Commonwealth University. Metropolitan's chemical depen-

dency program offers a wide variety of inpatient and outpatient services to meet the individual needs of patients. The treatment process is managed by clinicians skilled in thorough assessment and evaluation, so that patients receive the level of care indicated by the severity of their illness.

Metropolitan Hospital was organized as the outcome of a merger between two earlier hospitals, both of which were located in the same general area. One was Grace Hospital, built in 1913 at 401 West Grace Street. The other was St. Elizabeth's Hospital, built in 1912 on a site next to the present Metropolitan Hospital.

Ground breaking for the new hospital was held on September 14, 1977. Speaker for the occasion was James J. Kilpatrick, the well-known syndicated newspaper columnist. The hospital was completed, ahead of schedule, in December 1978. It was funded in part through tax-exempt bonds issued by the Industrial Development Authority of Richmond.

While not technically regarded as a teaching hospital, Metropolitan does provide hands-on training for nursing students at the J. Sargeant Reynolds Community College, the John Tyler Community College, the Career Training Center of Richmond, and the Richmond Technical

LEFT & RIGHT: Personalized, specialized care is the hallmark of the hospital's approach to its patients.

Center. It also cooperates in the training of degree nurses and occupational therapists at the Medical College of Virginia.

In 1989 Metropolitan Hospital was acquired by AmeriHealth, Inc., a hospital holding/management company. AmeriHealth had been managing the hospital since 1984. AmeriHealth now owns and operates hospitals in Richmond and in Prattville, Alabama. It also manages hospitals for other owners in Jeannette, Pennsylvania; Coral Gables, Florida; Folkston and Clayton, Georgia; and Newport News, Virginia. AmeriHealth was organized in March 1983 and became a public company in January 1984. Its stock is traded on the American Stock Exchange.

The firm's management team is headed by William G. White, a former senior executive at Hospital Corporation of America. White also serves as chief executive officer for Metropolitan Hospital. White and other Metropolitan spokespeople are optimistic about the future—the future of Richmond and the future of Metropolitan Hospital.

"We are looking at a reversal," says a hospital spokesman. "In the

past four decades hospitals once located downtown or close to downtown have gravitated toward the suburbs in an effort to stay close to their middle-class clients.

"But we believe we are seeing the start of a different trend. We believe that the time spent in traveling

Metropolitan Hospital is the only general hospital in the Richmond area that offers all private rooms.

daily between jobs downtown and homes in the suburbs is beginning to have an impact," he says. "Some middle-class patients, particularly those whose children have grown up and left home, are starting to shift to housing closer to their jobs downtown. The gentrification of older residential structures in the Empire and Fan districts is increasing rapidly."

That trend will mean an expanding patient base for Metropolitan Hospital, the hospital's managers believe. "The Richmond community in general will continue to grow at a steady, positive pace—probably free of the obstacles that temporarily beset many other cities," administrator White says.

"The question of the future growth of the hospital is an interesting one. We are now in the process of analyzing the results of a strategic study we recently conducted," White says. "It seems likely that the hospital will expand—perhaps in the field of geriatric medicine."

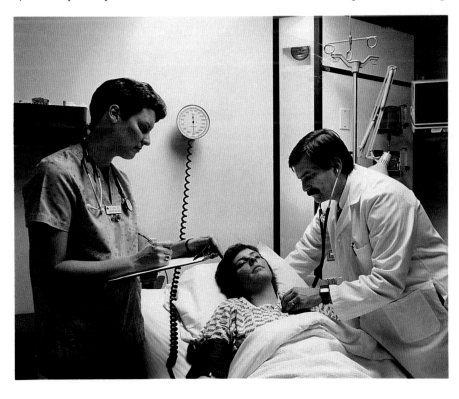

RICHMOND MEMORIAL HOSPITAL

A FIVE-STORY GREEN marble plaque fills one wall of the Chapel of Richmond Memorial Hospital. It bears the names of 984 natives of the city of Richmond and Henrico and Chesterfield counties who gave up their lives in World War II to preserve and protect democracy. Richmond Memorial Hospital is a living memorial to these valorous sons and daughters of Virginia.

"Richmond must have a new 500-bed hospital," said Dr. Robert Buerki, a local expert in hospital administration, as he presented the results of survey and analysis of the city's medical needs to the Richmond Community Council in 1945. Only with a new hospital, said Buerki, could the area stop the exodus of young physicians and alleviate the chronic shortage of hospital space.

The Reverend Dr. Theodore F. Adams of the First Baptist Church was host for the council meeting. He and D. Tennant Bryan, James Galleher, Buford Scott, and Harry Augustine became members of a newly formed hospital study committee.

A fund-raising campaign led by Overton Dennis and Morton Thalhimer produced $3.8 million in donations from 33,000 businesses and individuals. The site for the hospital, a 14-acre estate on Westwood Avenue in the fashionable and charming Ginter Park neighborhood, was donated by Bryan. The generous gift included Laburnum House, widely recognized as among the most beautiful residential structures in Richmond and the Bryan family home for three generations.

Dedication ceremonies for the seven-story hospital were held January 13, 1957. In its lead editorial that day, the Richmond *Times-Dispatch* heralded the 411-bed, 66-bassinet hospital as a "milestone in southern medicine," with facilities "unsurpassed in any hospital anywhere."

Richmond Memorial Hospital welcomed a new neighbor when Sheltering Arms Hospital moved next door from a downtown location in the 1960s. The 50-bed, physical rehabilitation hospital operates under a separate board of directors.

Richmond Memorial Hospital is a 420-bed, not-for-profit community hospital.

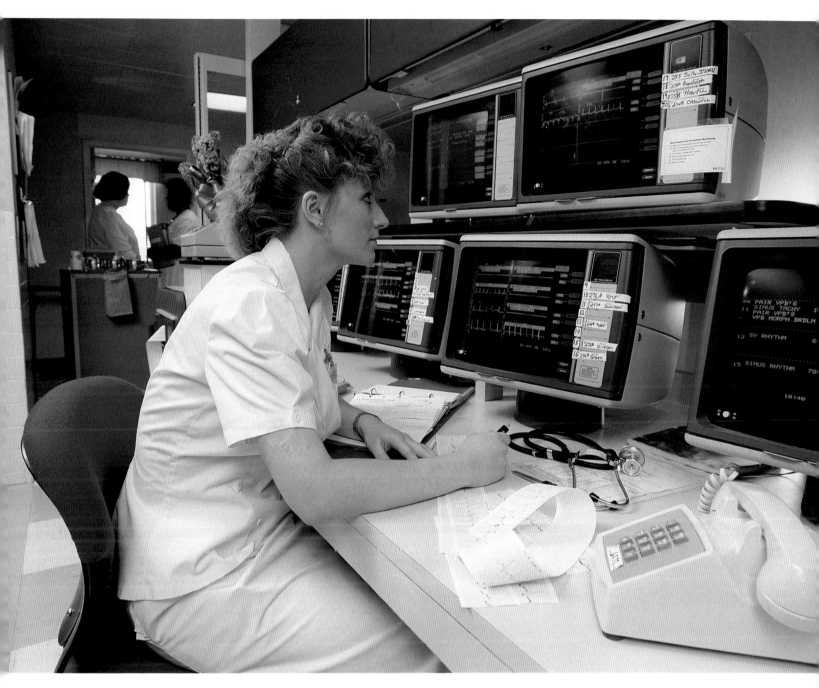

When the hospital commemorated its silver anniversary in 1982, it chose "Celebration through Service" as the theme. Now nearing its 35th birthday, Richmond Memorial Hospital and its corporate parent, Health Corporation of Virginia, have become one of the main pillars of the Richmond medical community.

"Outstanding health care, understanding people" is the motto of Health Corporation of Virginia, which has evolved into a sophisticated health-care and health-delivery sys-

Richmond Memorial Hospital and its parent corporation, Health Corporation of Virginia, employ more than 1,800 people in the Richmond area.

tem. A nonsectarian, community-owned company headed by a private board of trustees, HCV's system and its related institutions provide a comprehensive range of services meeting the health care needs of the Richmond area.

In addition, Richmond Memorial's accredited diploma School of Nursing, one of the few schools of its type in Virginia, helps meet the needs of the medical community for professionally trained nursing staff. The hospital also offers an administrative residency program in affiliation with the School of Health Administration of the Medical College of Virginia.

The hospital's emergency room is among the busiest in the city, with approximately 30,000 patient visits annually. Staffed around the clock, its state-of-the-art equipment includes specialized equipment for cardiac patients, two fully equipped trauma rooms for multiple injuries, and a private gynecological examination room.

The hospital, in a joint venture with The Medical College of Virginia, now offers open-heart surgery in its new state-of-the-art Heart Operating Suite.

The miracle of birth occurs at Richmond Memorial Hospital nearly 1,000 times each year. The hospital is extensively remodeling its obstetrics and gynecology facilities, and provides a homelike physical and psychological atmosphere for childbirth.

Richmond Memorial has an oncology program dedicated to the special needs of cancer patients and their families. The multidisciplinary format of the program involves several departments working together to provide the best quality of life for the patient, and to facilitate the transition from hospital to home.

Richmond Memorial Hospital's Pediatric Urgent Care Center is a new concept in the care of children. The center is a separate facility from the regular Richmond Memorial Hospital Emergency Room. An autonomous center offering after-hours urgent pediatric care, it is unique in the nation. The Pediatric Urgent Care Center's personnel, equipment, and physical surroundings are totally oriented to meeting the medical needs of children.

Richmond Memorial's psychiatric services use occupational therapy and therapeutic recreation to help patients once again become involved in life activities and explore and develop new skills. Patients are taught methods of developing better relationships with others, gaining self confidence, and expressing themselves constructively.

A multidisciplinary Cardiac Rehabilitation Program is another unusual service provided by Richmond Memorial Hospital. The program, staffed by an experienced registered nurse specializing in cardiac rehabilitation, provides progressive ambulation with cardiac monitoring, dietary consultation, and individualized instruction as needed.

Sensing the need for expanded outpatient treatment, Richmond Memorial Hospital opened the first of five satellite medical centers in 1975. These satellites provide not only doctors, but all of the expert services available through the hospital to Mechanicsville, eastern Henrico County, and the city itself. In addition, Richmond Memorial Hospital and HCV are affiliated with the Brook Run Family Practice Center (Richmond), Kentwood Square Family Practice Center, and Aylett Family Medical Center.

Richmond Memorial is committed to the senior citizens of Richmond, and provides a wide range of services designed to meet the special medical needs of elderly residents. Services include care ranging from inpatient treatment to independent living.

Home Care Alternatives, a subsidiary of HCV, offers a program of service designed to assist individuals in remaining at home and independent for as long as possible. In-home care, including medical monitoring and the full range of personal hygienic and nutritional needs, is provided by a staff of certified nursing assistants under the direction and supervision of a registered nurse. Patients needing highly skilled at-home nursing care (registered nurses) are serviced by Westwood Home Health, another subsidiary.

Older community residents living independently may also wish to subscribe to Richmond Memorial Hospital's Lifeline service. Subscribers have a Lifeline Communicator at home and a portable button that can be worn on clothing or carried in a pocket. The system provides

instant communication with the Emergency Response Center at the hospital.

HCV operates a community for retired residents (aged 55 and older), Summerhill at Stony Point. Summerhill's 90 beautiful, traditionally styled condominium cluster homes are located within walking distance of a major shopping center and medical office complex. The Lodge at Summerhill, the activities center for the community, includes a gracious dining room.

Westwood Hospice Care hospice provides support and comfort to terminally ill patients in their last months of life. Hospice assists patients and their families to enhance the quality of life of each remaining day. It also assists the family in coping with loss.

Richmond Memorial Hospital is the main operating subsidiary of Health Corporation of Virginia. Other affiliates include Laburnum Properties (the real estate holding company of HCV), and HCV Service Corporation, which provides data-processing and other management services, and oversees the operations of HCV subsidiaries. The philanthropic subsidiary is the Memorial Foundation.

The for-profit business activities of the Hospital Corporation of Virginia are organized under HCV Enterprises. They include HCV Management Corporation, Memorial Pharmacy, and The Collection Agency, which serves Richmond Memorial Hospital and other health providers in the metropolitan Richmond area.

"There are many guideposts with which the public can measure a hospital," observes John Simpson, president and chief executive officer of Health Corporation of Virginia. "The true guidepost should be whether a specific health care facility operates with a social conscience. It has been our aim in the past to manifest this social conscience. Our challenge for the next 25 years is to continue to build on this goal."

UNIVERSITY OF RICHMOND

FOR MORE THAN 150 years the University of Richmond has been committed to cultivating in students the interest and desire to learn through critical and questioning thought. Throughout its history, the university has emphasized a classically inspired liberal arts and sciences education.

Founded in 1830 as Dunlora Academy, the university soon developed into a men's liberal arts institution known as Richmond College. Westhampton College, the women's liberal arts college, was established in 1914.

In addition, four other divisions comprise the university: The E. Claiborne Robins School of Business and its graduate division; The T.C. Williams School of Law; the Graduate School; and University College (summer school, evening school, and continuing education).

The 1987 gift of $20 million by Mr. and Mrs. Robert S. Jepson, Jr., will enable the university to create a seventh division, the Jepson School of Leadership Studies. Anticipated to open in the fall of 1992, the school will be the first of its kind in the nation.

Approximately 2,800 full-time students from 36 states and 18 foreign countries attend the University of Richmond. The student/faculty ratio is 14 to one. The university maintains a comparatively small enrollment by choice, not wanting to sacrifice quality for size.

The University of Richmond consistently is mentioned among the nation's finest small private universities in *U.S. News and World Report*'s annual survey. Over the past five years the average total SAT score of incoming freshmen has risen from 1,116 to 1,215. *USA Today* recently named the University of Richmond one of the 53 most selective colleges in America.

The university's 350-acre campus, considered one of the country's most beautiful, features a 10-acre lake, rolling hills, tall pines, and collegiate Gothic-style buildings, all located six miles west of the heart of Richmond.

The quality of the University of Richmond and its students also can be seen through community involvement. The University of Richmond invites public attendance at numerous sporting events, plays, concerts, films, lectures, and exhibitions. More than one-third of the university community

The tower of Boatwright Library is a widely recognized symbol of the University of Richmond.

is involved in local volunteer efforts, and more than one-quarter of recent graduates choose to remain in the Richmond area.

The university is also sound financially; its endowment ranks among the top 2 percent of all colleges and universities. And with innovative programs such as the Jepson School of Leadership Studies, the University of Richmond remains committed to preparing itself and its students for the future.

HUMANA HOSPITAL-ST. LUKES

THE ST. LUKES tradition is part of the fabric of Richmond and the South. It dates back to 1863 and the battlefield near Chancellorsville, where Confederate General Stonewall Jackson was wounded. A surgeon in Jackson's medical corps, Dr. Hunter Holmes McGuire, tried valiantly to save Jackson's life. McGuire went on to become the most famous physician in Richmond and a president of the American Medical Association.

In 1882 McGuire founded St. Luke's Home for the Sick, a predecessor institution of today's Humana Hospital-St. Lukes. Four years later he started the first professional training program for nurses. That program continued for more than 80 years. The nursing school graduated its last class in 1986.

In 1899 Dr. Stuart McGuire, son of Hunter McGuire, took over St. Lukes. "Dr. Stuart" ran the hospital until he left to volunteer his services with the U.S. Army during World War I. In 1923 he created the McGuire Clinic, a private medical practice that pioneered the team approach to medicine. A neighboring institution, the McGuire Clinic, has shared much of the hospital's history and tradition. While not part of the hospital, it is a member of the Humana-St. Lukes family.

Humana is a publicly owned corporation based in Louisville, Kentucky. Founded by David A. Jones, chairman of the board and chief executive officer, and Wendell Cherry, president and chief operating officer, Humana owns more than 80 hospitals in 23 states, as well as in London, England, and Lucerne, Switzerland. Humana acquired St. Lukes Hospital in 1971. Humana Hospital-St. Lukes is one of two Virginia hospitals owned by the corporation.

The mission of Humana is to achieve an unequaled level of measurable quality and productivity in the delivery of health services that

In 1882 Dr. Hunter Holmes McGuire founded St. Luke's Home for the Sick in Richmond, the predecessor institution for today's Humana Hospital-St. Lukes.

are responsive to the needs and values of patients, physicians, employers, and consumers.

Nowhere is this more evident than in Humana's dedication to providing the finest program of care for senior citizens. The Humana Seniors Association, a nonprofit hospital-based service organization, provides assistance with access to health care, educa-tion, and social activities with a wellness focus. Association membership includes help with insurance forms and health screenings on a monthly basis. Humana Hospital-St. Lukes serves more than 3,900 members of the Humana Seniors Association.

The laser-assisted peripheral angioplasty program at Humana Hospital-St. Lukes offers patients with atherosclerotic blockage of arteries in the lower half of the body an alternative surgical option over bypass graft surgery. Using lasers to partially vaporize or burn a path through blocked arteries, the procedure can

St. Lukes Hospital as it looked when it was located on Grace Street.

bring an instantaneous return to normal or near normal blood flow through the previously blocked vessels, eliminating symptoms and allowing the patient to return to an active life-style.

The Center for Orthopedics is internationally recognized for its sports medicine care of world-class athletes. The center provides diagnosis, treatment, and rehabilitation for a wide range of connective tissue, bone, and joint disorders.

The St. Lukes Cancer Center is a patient and family care program designed to meet the many needs of patients and their families who are living with cancer. Services include inpatient, outpatient, and home care; cancer rehabilitation; and patient-family support programs.

The Emergency Department offers 24-hour, seven-days-per-week emergency care services by special-

Humana Hospital-St. Lukes provides specialized care and a wide range of services with its highly-trained and dedicated staff.

Humana Hospital-St. Lukes is a 200-bed, full-service, medical/surgical facility located on Parham Road in Henrico County.

ized independent emergency medicine physicians. The Comprehensive Occupational Medicine Program is designed to provide health

care services to business and industry based on individual assessment and consultation.

Humana Hospital-St. Lukes, a 200-bed, full-service, medical/surgical facility, is located on Parham Road in Henrico County. Nancy R. Hofheimer is the executive director of the hospital.

MEMORIAL SURGERY CENTER

Memorial Surgical Center provides each of its patients with the best medical care incorporating the personal touch of a private practice and the specialized knowledge associated with a much larger organization.

MEMORIAL SURGICAL CENTER consists of five surgeons from several different specialties, supported by a skilled nursing staff and outstanding facilities. The organization has the personal touch of a private practice and the specialized knowledge associated with a much larger organization. With locations throughout metropolitan Richmond, Memorial Surgical Center restores the concept of neighborhood care.

The group is committed to providing its patients with full medical and surgical care, including comprehensive education about their medical problems and available procedures. Memorial Surgical Center continues to be a leader in introducing new procedures and techniques to the Richmond area.

Maintaining this trend, the group is now in the forefront of the diagnosis and treatment of vascular diseases. The facility is one of the first in the area to acquire and utilize an angiodynography vascular imaging system, which provides a merger of the latest in

aerospace computer technology and medical science. Led by the center's two vascular surgeons, Dr. Paul McTamaney and Dr. William Snoddy, its patients now have available to them the most precise, painless, and noninvasive evaluation of vascular problems.

Dr. Manikoth Kurup, founder of the center, is a general surgeon who also specializes in gynecological surgery. He was born in India and completed his medical education there before coming to the United States in 1964 for advanced surgical training at Richmond Memorial Hospital and the Medical College of Virginia. Dr. Kurup served as chief of surgery at Richmond Memorial Hospital from 1977 through 1985. He is a member of Richmond Memorial's board of trustees and also serves on the board of the Health Corporation of Virginia. Dr. Kurup is currently chief of staff at Richmond Memorial Hospital. Dr. John William Snoddy, a general and vascular surgeon with Memorial Surgical Center, also serves as chief of surgery at Richmond

Memorial Hospital. A graduate of the University of Virginia and the Medical College of Virginia, he has been with the practice since 1979.

Dr. James Paul McTamaney also specializes in general and vascular surgery. A graduate of Manhattan College and John Hopkins University School of Medicine, he completed his internship and residency at the Medical College of Virginia, where he also was a fellow in transplantation surgery.

Dr. William R. Timmerman specializes in colon and rectal surgery. He graduated from South Dakota State University, the University of South Dakota School of Medicine, and the University of Minnesota School of Medicine. He completed his internship and residency in general surgery at Hennepin County Medical Center in Minneapolis. A fellowship in colon and rectal surgery at Presbyterian Parkland Hospital in Dallas followed.

Dr. Malcolm Magovern, an ophthalmologist, completed his undergraduate studies at the College of Holy Cross and was awarded a medical degree from Georgetown University Medical School in Washington, D.C. He completed postgraduate training at Emory University's Grady Memorial Hospital in Atlanta and D.C. General Hospital. Dr. Magovern served with the U.S. Army in Vietnam, including one year as chief of ophthalmology at the 91st Evacuation Hospital.

Memorial Surgical Center has offices in the professional building at Richmond Memorial Hospital in Northside, an office in eastern Henrico County, an office in Mechanicsville, and a West End office, as well as plans to expand to other geographic areas in the community. A proud component of the Richmond medical community, Memorial Surgical Center is dedicated to providing each patient with the best medical care.

STUART CIRCLE HOSPITAL

IN A CITY rich with history, Richmond's Stuart Circle Hospital proudly upholds an equally rich history of service to that city and its surrounding counties. For 77 years the institutions has brought hospitality to hospital care, providing personal service, medical excellence, and health education.

Stuart Circle Hospital is located at Monument Avenue and Lombardy Street in the heart of the Fan District, one of Richmond's most beautiful residential areas, famed for its period architecture, large mansions, Civil War monuments, and tree-shaded avenues.

When the hospital was established in 1913, its founders set out to provide superior services and high-quality patient care. That dedication to medical excellence has not diminished. Every member of the staff is concerned about making the hospital's patients feel at home.

Stuart Circle Hospital, with 153 licensed beds, offers some of the most advanced medical services and equip-

ment in Virginia. State-of-the-art technology is routinely used in the hospital's cardiology and cardiac catheterization laboratories. The hospital's Cardiology Diagnostic Department was one of the first in the community to offer a full cardiac rehabilitation program. Stuart Circle also maintains one of the most sophisticated medical laboratories in the city. And the hospital's Immediate Care Center can handle most medical emergencies promptly and efficiently.

Other specialized services include the hospital's Chemical Dependency Program, which offers safe, short-term medical detoxification and referrals for continued counseling. And a variety of diagnostic and therapeutic services are available from Women's Services. These services include mammography for early detection of breast cancer and plastic and reconstructive surgery to improve physical function and appearance.

The therapists in Stuart Circle's Rehabilitation Services Department help patients achieve recovery goals after an illness or injury, including treatment for lower-back injuries. Stuart Circle also offers comprehensive facilities for health promotion and injury management through special programs geared for industry

Stuart Circle Hospital has brought hospitality to hospital care for more than 77 years.

Occupational Medicine and Return to Work. Other medical and diagnostic services provided at Stuart Circle Hospital range from nuclear medicine to magnetic resonance imaging to outpatient surgery. And patients who need care but don't require hospitalization can take advantage of the hospital's professionally supervised Home Health Care Service.

At Stuart Circle, physicians, nurses, and the entire staff work together to ensure that patients and their families are fully informed about their condition and care so patients can make educated decisions. The hospital also sponsors free seminars open to the public on health topics.

Stuart Circle Hospital's unique Call for Health line provides members of the community with access to health information over the telephone. The hospital's staff of registered nurses provides answers to health questions and refers callers, when appropriate, to a physician, community health organization or support group. It's a way for the nurses to lend a personal touch to the caller's health concerns and a way for Stuart Circle Hospital to demonstrate its commitment to health education and medical excellence.

Stuart Circle's Call For Health nurses have answered thousands of questions since this unique service began.

SOUTHERN HEALTH SERVICES

WHEN 43 RICHMOND-area physicians began studying the future of local health care delivery in the early 1980s, "they thought HMO meant cable television," says Emerson D. Farley, M.D., chairman of the board of Southern Health Services.

With the influx of outside insurance companies and managed care organizations in the area, this group banded together to explore forming a Health Maintenance Organization (HMO). Thus the inception of Southern Health Services.

Southern Health's mission is to provide quality health care coverage in a cost-effective manner. As a locally owned and operated HMO, Southern Health's physician providers represent an overwhelming majority of the private practicing physicians in central Virginia. "Because we were familiar with the local problems," Dr. Farley says, "we could better address the need to control skyrocketing costs and maintain quality care than a large, out-of-state insurance company devoid of input from local doctors."

Southern Health is an Independent Practice Association (IPA). The physicians maintain their private practices and see Southern Health members as they would any other patient. Southern Health is uniquely qualified to achieve the goals of access, cost, and quality, because who knows more about the delivery of thoughtful medical care than a physician?

Southern Health is a system of checks and balances—procedures and standards that foster accountability. Four committees serve as arms to the board of directors: utilization review, quality assurance, pharmacy and therapeutics, and network management. These committees function as a

Southern Health Services was formed in the early 1980s when 43 Richmond-area physicians began studying the future of local health care delivery. Pictured here is the Southern Health Services headquarters building.

complement to Southern Health's commitment that managed care is the way to control health care costs.

As a Richmond-based company, Southern Health has a vested interest in the community. The organization supports the Richmond Chapter of the American Red Cross and the Arts Council, as well as sponsors events for local schools. Southern Health is also an active member of the Metropolitan Richmond Chamber of Commerce.

The existence of Southern Health injects more competition into the health insurance market, thus helping to keep premium costs down. Area businesses have a local health care option to offer their employees. And Richmond-area doctors have the only HMO that pays them a fee for each service rendered.

"Our goal," Dr. Farley explains, "is to continue to develop a locally owned health care delivery system that benefits employers, citizens, and those providing health care services."

ST. MARY'S HOSPITAL OF RICHMOND

ST. MARY'S HOSPITAL of Richmond is a comprehensive, not-for-profit community hospital. Opened in 1966, St. Mary's offers a full range of health care services, including medical, surgical, obstetrical, and pediatric care. The hospital is owned by Bon Secours Health System, Inc., a Maryland corporation. The Sisters of Bon Secours were invited by the Most Reverend John J. Russell, the Bishop of Richmond, to be the sponsors of the city's only Catholic hospital.

Throughout the central Virginia region, St. Mary's is recognized as a special hospital. The entire staff understands that St. Mary's is not just a business but a commitment to caring. The hospital acts out the French name "Bon Secours," meaning "kindly care."

St. Mary's regards itself as a value-driven organization. Eight core values are central to the mission of Bon Secours: respect, justice, integrity, stewardship, innovation, compassion, quality, and growth continue to play a central role at St. Mary's Hospital. A low-cost health care provider, St. Mary's never turns away a patient from its doors. All patients are admitted regardless of race, religion, or ability to pay.

"We combine the latest high technology medical equipment with

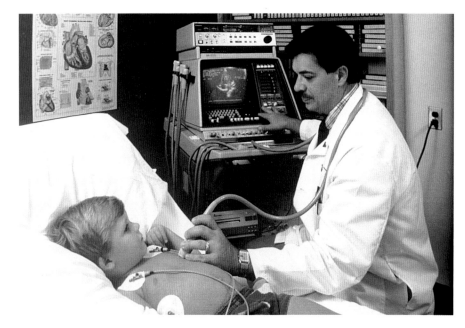

a skilled, dedicated staff and a commitment to community," says a St. Mary's spokesperson. "Pastoral care is part of who we are and what we do. So are support groups, including our cancer care program and our hospice. The philosophy of the Congregation of Bon Secours is good help to those in need."

That combination has made St. Mary's the hospital of choice for many physicians and patients in the greater Richmond area. The 401-bed hospital is the market-share leader among Richmond's community hospitals.

St. Mary's sophisticated capabilities include lithotripsy and laser-supported surgery. The hospital also is home to an advanced open-heart sur-

Fully equipped with the latest in medical technology and staffed with the finest nurses and doctors, St. Mary's is a low-cost health care provider—all patients are admitted regardless of race, religion, or ability to pay. Pictured here is a cardiac graphics technician performing an echocardiogram (a visual record of the heart made by a noninvasive and painless diagnostic procedure) on a young patient.

gical unit, the largest community pediatrics service in central Virginia (including pediatric intensive care), and clinical teaching affiliations in internal medicine, pediatrics, and orthopedic, oral, and plastic surgery.

St. Mary's has recently acquired a new Siemens linear accelerator in radiation therapy, a new laboratory computer system, and an on-site Magnetic Resonance Imaging (MRI) Center. The Nurses First Choice Program is St. Mary's innovative approach to the challenge of recruiting and retaining skilled, dedicated nurses.

During the past two decades more than 20 Sisters of Bon Secours have contributed to the health and spiritual well-being of patients at St. Mary's Hospital of Richmond. Sister Nancy Glynn serves as Sister president and director of Mission Effectiveness for the Bon Secours-St. Mary's Health Corporation. Christopher M. Carney is the chief executive officer of the organization.

An exterior view of St. Mary's Hospital of Richmond as seen from Monument Avenue.

PATRONS

The following individuals, companies, and organizations have made a valuable commitment to the quality of this publication. Windsor Publications and the Metropolitan Richmond Chamber of Commerce gratefully acknowledge their participation in *Richmond: A River City Reborn*.

Alfa-Laval Thermal, Inc.*
Allen, Allen, Allen & Allen*
AT&T
Bowers, Nelms and Fonville*
Browder & Russell*
Businessland*
Chippenham Medical Center*
Christian, Barton, Epps, Brent & Chappell*
Circuit City Stores, Inc.*
Columbia Gas Transmission Corporation*
Commonwealth Gas Services, Inc.*
Continental Cablevision of Virginia*
Coopers & Lybrand*
CorEast Savings Bank*
Crestar Bank*
Daniel Corporation*
Draper Aden Associates*
E.I. du Pont de Nemours and Company, Inc.*
Ethyl Corporation*
Faison Associates*
Fluor Daniel, Inc.*
Franklin Federal Savings and Loan Association*
Humana Hospital-St. Lukes*
Hunton & Williams*
Investors Savings Bank*
Lawyers Title Insurance Corporation*
Leadbetter, Inc.*
Leggett of Chesterfield Towne Center*
The Life Insurance Company of Virginia*
Lingerfelt Development Corporation*
McSweeney, Burtch & Crump, P.C.*
Markel Corporation*
Marriott Hotel*
Martin, Dolan & Holton, Ltd.*
A.T. Massey Coal Company, Inc.
Mays & Valentine*
Mazda Motor of America, Inc.*
The Medical College of Virginia Hospitals*

Memorial Surgery Center*
William M. Mercer, Inc.*
Metropolitan Hospital*
Napier & Company*
NELCO, Ltd.*
The Pearson Companies, Inc.*
Philip Morris U.S.A.*
Port of Richmond*
Rent-A-Car Company, Inc.*
The Retail Merchants Association of Greater Richmond*
Richmond Homes, Inc.*
Richmond Memorial Hospital*
Richmond Relocation Services/Virginia Properties*
Robertshaw Controls Company*
Ruffin & Payne, Inc.*
St. Mary's Hospital of Richmond*
Signet Banking Corporation*
Southern Health Services*
Sovran Bank*
Stuart Circle Hospital*
Thalhimers*
Tredegar Industries*
Tri-Equity Group*
Universal Corporation*
University of Richmond*
Virginia Commonwealth University*
The Virginia Insurance Reciprocal*
Virginia Power*
Weidmuller Inc.*
Westvaco*
Williams, Mullen, Christian & Dobbins*
The Woolfolk Companies*
WRIC-TV
WRVA Radio*

*Participants in Part Two: "Richmond's Enterprises." The stories of these companies and organizations appear in chapters 7 through 13, beginning on page 155.

BIBLIOGRAPHY

"Advertising All-Star Team Picks Five From Richmond." *Richmond News Leader*, February 23, 1989.

Allcott, William. "Greed and Glory on Main Street." *Virginia Business Magazine*, September 1987.

Bacon, James A. "Making Wheat While the Sun Ain't Shining." *Virginia Business Magazine*, December 1988

Bacon, Lisa Antonelli. "Just On Top." *Style Weekly*, February 28, 1989.

Bob, Robert C. "Working Together is the Only Route." *Richmond News Leader*, September 5, 1988.

Bowes, Mark. "Area's Airport Preferred Over D.C. Terminals. *Richmond News Leader*, March 1, 1989.

————. "Cargo Facility Dedicated at Airport." *Richmond News Leader*, May 23, 1989.

"Chairman of Crestar Corp. is Cited for Minority Support." *Richmond News Leader*, May 1989.

Chesterfield County. Budget and Management Office. *Regional Cooperative Agreement*. Chesterfield, Virginia. May 31, 1988.

Churn, Virginia. "Developers Hope to Make the Bottom Tops." *Richmond Times Dispatch*, July 10, 1988.

"Circuit City Sales Rise 27 Percent." *Richmond News Leader*, March 7, 1989.

Clinger, David M. "The Richmond Area Report." *PACE Magazine*. Greensboro, N.C.: 1988.

Commission of the City of Richmond. *Port of Richmond: Annual Report 1987-1988*. Richmond, Va.: 1988.

Crews, Ed. "James River Corp Targets Areas for Growth in Europe," *Richmond News Leader*, March 13, 1989.

————. "Virginia Ranks in a New Report from Fed." *Richmond News Leader*, April 17, 1989.

Crystal, Charlotte. "Who's Building Richmond?" *Virginia Business Magazine*, June 1988.

————. "A Fair Shake and Not a Handout." *Richmond News Leader*, September 5, 1988.

Dabney, Virginius. *Richmond: The Story of a City*. Garden City, N.Y.: Doubleday & Company, Inc., 1976.

Dulce, Maurice, and Daniel P. Jordan, eds. *A Richmond Reader, 1733-1983*. Chapel Hill, N.C.: The University of North Carolina Press, 1983.

Edmunds, Holt. "Developer Henry Raison: Reshaping Richmond's Skyline." *Style Magazine*, January 20, 1987.

"Ethyl Corp. One of Top Exporters." *Richmond News Leader*, June 1989.

"Ethyl Spinoff Receives IRS Approval." *Richmond News Leader*, May 6, 1989.

Hallman, Randy. "Black Business." *Richmond News Leader*, September 5, 1988.

Hingley, Audrey T. "Botton Line Grows When Workers Share Rewards." *Richmond News Leader*, October 3, 1988.

Lohmann, Bill. "UR Examines Separation of Its Colleges." *Richmond News Leader*, May 5, 1989.

Martin, David N. *Romancing the Brand: The Power of Advertising and How to Use It*. New York: American Management Association, 1989.

Menninger, Bonar. "Wheat, First Securities Emerges as Regional Powerhouse in South." *Washington Business Journal*, January 23, 1989.

Metropolitan Economic Development Council. *Richmond From A to Z: A Site Selector's Profile of the Richmond Area*. Richmond, Va.: December 1987.

Moeser, John V. "City Politics Since '48: Three Distinct Eras." *Richmond Times Dispatch*, April 6, 1986.

Murray, Phil. "Tobacco Row Work Under Way," *Richmond News Leader*, March 10, 1989.

Osborn, Maria. "Tobacco Row May Bloom Soon." *Richmond Times Dispatch*, May 11, 1988.

Parthemos, James. *The Federal Reserve Act of 1913 in the Stream of U.S. Monetary History*. Richmond: Fifth Federal Reserve District Bank, 1989.

Robertson, Hugh. "Chesterfield Property Value Up 12.3%" *Richmond News Leader*, February 10, 1989.

Rorrer, Mollie. "Entrepreneur Motivates His Employees." *Richmond Times Dispatch*, March 27, 1989.

Row, Steve. "Mazda has Parts Center Stacked High." *Richmond News Leader*, April 10, 1989.

————. "Local Agency Earns A- From ADWEEK." *Richmond News Leader*, April 10, 1989.

————. "California Ad Agency Opens Richmond Office." *Richmond News Leader*, May 8, 1989.

Sundquist, Eric. "Once-Scorned Suburbs Become 'Outtowns' Rivaling City Centers." *Richmond Times Dispatch*, September 15, 1987.

United States. Small Business Administration. *Handbook of Small Business Data*. Washington, D.C.: U.S. Government Printing Office, 1988.

Ward, Harry M. *Richmond: An Illustrated History*. Northridge, Ca.: Windsor Publications, Inc., 1985.

Wasson, Bill. "Work On Connector Ahead Of Schedule." *Richmond News Leader*, March 11, 1989.

Winthrop, Robert P. "Richmond's Architecture." Reprint from the *Richmond Times Dispatch* Real Estate Section, August 9 through October 11, 1981.

INDEX

This book was set in 10/12 ITC New Baskerville

and composed on a Macintosh II.

Printed on Westvaco 70 lb. Sterling Lithogloss

and bound by Walsworth Publishing Company,

Marceline, Missouri.